EMOTIONAL LABOR

EMOTIONAL LABOR

THE INVISIBLE WORK SHAPING OUR LIVES AND HOW TO CLAIM OUR POWER

Rose Hackman

FLATIRON
BOOKS
NEW YORK

www.flatironbooks.com

Designed by Susan Walsh

Library of Congress Cataloging-in-Publication Data

Names: Hackman, Rose, author.
Title: Emotional labor : the invisible work shaping our lives and how to claim our power / Rose Hackman.
Description: First edition. | New York : Flatiron Books, 2023. | Includes bibliographical references.
Identifiers: LCCN 2022033809 | ISBN 9781250777355 (hardcover) | ISBN 9781250777362 (ebook)
Subjects: LCSH: Women—Psychology. | Women—Mental health. | Emotions.
Classification: LCC HQ1206 .H224 2023 | DDC 155.3/33—dc23/eng/20220728
LC record available at https://lccn.loc.gov/2022033809

Our books may be purchased in bulk for promotional, educational, or business use. Please contact your local bookseller or the Macmillan Corporate and Premium Sales Department at 1-800-221-7945, extension 5442, or by email at MacmillanSpecialMarkets@macmillan.com.

First Edition: 2023

10 9 8 7 6 5 4 3 2 1

To my mother, Judith. Your name was well given after all.

CONTENTS

One of the great problems of history is that the concepts of love and power have usually been contrasted as opposites, polar opposites, so that love is identified with a resignation of power, and power with a denial of love.
    —Martin Luther King Jr.

To begin by always thinking of love as an action rather than a feeling is one way in which anyone using the word in this manner automatically assumes accountability and responsibility.
    —bell hooks

Patriarchy, like any system of domination (for example, racism), relies on socializing everyone to believe that in all human relations there is an inferior and a superior party, one person is strong, the other weak, and that it is therefore natural for the powerful to rule over the powerless. To those who support patriarchal thinking, maintaining power and control is acceptable by whatever means.
    —bell hooks

Complementarity is a common mask for inequality in what is presumed to be owing between people, both in display and in the deep acts that sustain it.
    —Arlie Hochschild

EMOTIONAL LABOR

INTRODUCTION

The summer I turned eighteen, my mother told me something that would take me years to make full sense of.

"Rose," she announced firmly and approvingly from her position in the driving seat of our secondhand car, "you are an excellent man manager." We were driving across Brussels to a neighborhood called Molenbeek, where my then boyfriend lived. I didn't have my license yet and my mother, a single widow and a full-time office administrator, claimed that driving me to engagements when she wasn't working was something she did with pleasure, as a way of getting quality time in. We had grown close over the three years we had become sudden one-on-one roommates—after my father had died and my two older sisters had gone off to college. "To accompany me with the car," as the Belgians would put it, was a tolerant and generous gift on her part. Unfortunately for her, driving me had mostly meant taking me to my basketball games in the most unsuspecting corners of rural, postindustrial Wallonia, the French-speaking half of Belgium, where cows grazed on grass as we entered metal-walled, boxlike gymnasiums, bouncing balls echoing through the fields to the ears of no one in particular.

But today, basketball season was over, and I was off to see Eric, my on-and-off boyfriend of three years. He was having friends 'round to celebrate moving out of his parents' home and into his first apartment. Halfway through our ride there, my Nokia cell phone rang. Eric was on the other end. A string of panicked sentences made their way through the airwaves.

"I don't know how to cook the chicken! I don't know what to do! People are arriving in an hour! It was a stupid idea to have people over! I should never have done this! This was your dumb idea!"

Gray streets of Brussels flashed by. I quietly listened and took in the information. Gradually, a picture started to form in my head. Eric, a man who believed that meals were not real meals if they did not contain protein of a formerly alive kind, had bought chicken to make for dinner but did not know how to cook it. I had been a vegetarian since I was eight. Clearly, I didn't know how to cook chicken, either. I was pretty sure this had been his initiative, not mine. But that's not what I said.

"There is absolutely no need to worry. It's all going to be completely fine. I can make the chicken when I arrive. Couldn't be easier. What else do you have in the fridge? Have you prepared anything?" I asked.

Dessert, the answer came back, a little calmer this time. If I felt exasperation, I didn't let the feeling live for more than a nanosecond. Patience, reassurance, and love were what I knew I should give, and that's what I expressed.

"Amazing," I chirpily said into the phone. "I love it when you make that. Okay. Don't worry about the rest. I will figure something out to go with the chicken and make some sides when I arrive. I have pesto with me. We can do something with that. So delicious."

His mood shifted: I could almost hear it lift. He was totally calm now. The panic had gone. His voice was slower; it had gone back to a cadence that suggested a more relaxed, happy state of mind.

"Are you good? Sorry you had that scare," I continued, bringing my task to a secure conclusion. "I will be there very shortly."

He muttered acquiescence, possibly thanks. "I can't wait to see you," I finished, and pressed the button to end the call.

I put the phone back in my lap, my shoulders dropped, and I breathed out, letting go of some of the anxiety I had been suppressing and feeling relief that I had contained the situation. In my head, I hadn't even arrived at the part of how I was going to cook this dinner.

I had absolutely no idea what to do with raw chicken, the very fleshy peachy vision of which was enough to make my stomach turn. But that wasn't the point. The point was rather getting my boyfriend to feel good, calm, and collected again. What was important—I had known immediately upon picking up the phone—was conveying that the situation was under control to him, even if it wasn't yet. The concrete cooking activity ahead was truly secondary.

I looked at my mother. She smiled. That's when I remember her saying it: "You are an excellent man manager. You handled that brilliantly. I couldn't be more impressed."

Man manager, I repeated back to myself after she said it. I turned my body in the passenger seat toward her. I had never heard the term, and I had no conscious idea it was something I should be striving toward, let alone something I had been performing. But I felt the glow of the compliment, and some kind of a shift in her words, a complicity, perhaps even a new form of respect.

We moved on to discuss ways to cook chicken and what to do with the pesto. She told me about timing and oven temperatures, and even how I should handle the chicken to cut it. My mother incidentally also didn't eat meat, for health reasons, but she had learned how to prepare it and cook it to make the stomachs of the people around her happy.

As unremarkable as it may sound, I never forgot the pesto chicken man manager exchange between my mother and me. Today, it's clear to me that this is the first time I can pinpoint the emotional labor I performed, as a part of my gender and to the benefit of a man, explicitly being acknowledged and elevated.

Of course, I didn't know what to call it at the time. Indeed, it would be another decade before I would read about emotional labor and emotion work in any official context. And even longer before the term would explode into the mainstream as an invisible form of work we desperately needed to reckon with before we collapsed from its effort. But that day, those words, I believe them to be beautifully momentous, because that short comment was in fact one of the most significant mother-daughter conversations my mother and I would ever come to have. With those words, I had passed the final secret test in a rite of passage I had never been told about, and I was welcomed into womanhood.

———————

I may be one of the few to whom the punch line of this lesson was marked explicitly, but women across the world are taught from a very young age to regulate, modulate, and manipulate their feelings in order to have a positive effect on the feelings of others. Women, endlessly told to smile but also tasked with making other people smile, are held accountable not only for the expression of their own feelings but also for the feelings of others.

This happens in families where women are expected to ceaselessly put their energy, effort, and time toward catering to the building of a pleasant emotional world for the group—whether in invisibly forging and reforging a sense of emotional self, belonging, and connection in others, or silently taking on necessary chores and activities everyone benefits from but no one wants to do. It happens in relationships where women are trained to manage volatile moods and tempers and chronically put their significant other's feelings, experiences, and desires before their own. It happens at work where women, in addition to their actual job descriptions, are pushed into performing the roles of mother or sexpot for the enjoyment of others but rarely for any real benefit to them. It happens on our screens where the intellect, morality, and humanity of women are judged based on how these women—their expressions and presentation—make viewers *feel*, not based on what they have to say or what they have done. It even happens on the street where, starting at a young age, girls and women are told to smile by male strangers—and are then taught through traumatizing experience that if they do not, punishment may ensue.

This is emotional labor: the primordial training that, before anything else, women and girls should edit the expression of their emotions to accommodate and elevate the emotions of others. Sociologist Arlie Hochschild first coined the term four decades ago to describe the skill American workers were required to perform in the service sector as it was exploding and slowly replacing the manufacturing one. A pivotal part of jobs was no longer just physical, intellectual, or even creative, she pointed out, but also unambiguously emotive. Employees were now expected to change the outside expression of their emotions in order to provoke an emotion in their clients, customers, passengers, debtors, or patients.[1] Hochschild related this kind of work back to an equivalent and feminized "emotion work" we had long been used to seeing women do in private, without compensation, alongside other forms of unpaid work.[2] "Lacking other resources, women make a resource out of feeling and offer it to men as a gift in return for the more material resources they lack," she wrote at the time.[3]

The study and understanding of emotional labor have remained largely relegated to academia since the terminology was first introduced— a fact that has been immensely detrimental to conversations we urgently need to have across society about continuing harmful inequalities. With these ongoing emotion-geared performances, our position as women in both professional and personal settings is firmly established in the world: the caregiver, the appeaser, the listener, the empath, the subordinate. Is it bad to express empathy? No. Is it bad to use emotions to help others? No. But the expectation that we as women, and we alone, are the main bearer of this burden is no longer sustainable. Our emotional bank accounts are overdrawn, and yet our survival and advancement in this society continue to depend on us doing this invisible work. Such expectations point to an unsettling and enduring distribution of power we have become inured to. These expectations are not only the consequences of living in a male-dominated society. In many ways, as I will explore in this book, they are one of the main reasons we are still in one.

The last one hundred years have seen profound changes in the lives of women in the United States and beyond. American women were granted the right to vote in 1920, in a move that initially mostly benefited white women, but was eventually broadened out to include all women in 1965 with the Voting Rights Act. Women have gone from representing one third of the workforce in 1950 to just under half today.[4] As of 2019, women represented half of the college-educated workforce. Starting in 1974, we no longer needed a husband or a male family member's signature to apply for credit or a credit card.[5] In 1972, birth control was legalized for all, and in 1973 abortion became legal, giving women greater control over their own bodies and the planning and course of their economic, social, and political lives.

But that last right endured for only fifty years. In June 2022, the US Supreme Court shockingly reversed federal abortion rights, suddenly depriving millions of their right to self-determination and bodily autonomy. How could such a snatch back in fundamental rights occur? Hasn't the issue of gender equality been settled?

It has not. We live with the illusion that we have reached gender equity, but so many indicators around us point to the contrary. We are in fact still living in the midst of a thriving patriarchy. That we are is a strange concept to reconcile. Those of us fortunate enough to have been brought up in wealthier economies and democracies have likely also been accustomed to our governments and institutions pointing out how comparatively unequal other societies and cultures are, rarely turning the mirror on themselves. We are also acutely aware of how many more rights and choices we have compared to our mothers and grandmothers. Acknowledging and honoring the sacrifices of parents has especially become a part of the identity of children, including daughters, of first-generation immigrants. Those of us who are white are reminded, quite rightly, that we are accorded more access and opportunities than our sisters of color. Black women are forced to witness a system cracking down on their Black brothers in a way that can corner them into diminishing the urgency of their own struggles.

These comparative advantages are fair and important to point out. But they do not change the fact that women continue to be placed below men, that our experiences are diminished and often expunged

for the sake of men, and that the fundamentals of gender power distribution have remained intact.

Men are still considered heads of households. When men are absent
from households, the household becomes regarded as an incomplete,
defective unit.[6] Women are still expected to take on their male partner's name upon marriage, and even if increasing numbers of women,[7]
albeit a minority,[8] are opting to keep their own last names, men are
still overwhelmingly the ones to pass down their last names to their
offspring—meaning the clan's name is the man's, and women's contributions are, at least nominally, erased generation after generation.

To date, the United States has only ever had male heads of state.
The January 2022 US Congress counted the highest number of women
it had ever seen, with 149 women holding seats, representing 26.9 percent of all members,[9] just over a quarter. As of February 2022, there
were 31 women holding CEO positions at Fortune 500 companies,
representing an abysmally low 6.2 percent total.[10] In 2021, the ten
wealthiest people in America were all men and were all white.[11] On
the flip side, women continue to be more likely to be living in poverty
than men and are more likely than men to be among the working
poor, with the greatest rate among Black and Hispanic women.[12]

Yes, we have made progress, but this is a society that is still plagued
by male domination, and in which it is no coincidence that women are
expected to take on the lion's share of emotional labor.

And frankly, we have reached breaking point.

During the worst years of the COVID-19 epidemic, economists
reported that women were quitting their jobs at twice the rate men
were.[13] By the beginning of 2022, while men had recouped job losses,
there were still one million fewer women in the workforce than there
had been two years prior. In the space of just a couple of years, women's
economic advancement was said to have been set back by a generation.[14] This disparity was due to women being far more concentrated
in the lowest-paying, high-contact service jobs on the front lines of the
epidemic[15] and was also due to women being far more likely to assume
increased childcare and caregiving responsibilities.

These crises only exacerbated what had silently, inequitably long been going on. A 2020 analysis in *The New York Times* found that if women in the United States had been paid minimum wage for the unpaid work they provided at home in 2019, they would have made $1.5 trillion.[16] That same year, an analysis by Oxfam calculated that women's unpaid caregiving work alone was adding value to the global economy to the tune of at least $10.8 trillion a year, a figure three times larger than the money generated from the tech industry and equivalent to the revenue of the fifty largest Fortune 500 companies.[17]

"This figure, while huge, is an underestimate; because of data availability it uses the minimum wage and not a living wage, and it does not take account of the broader value to society of care work and how our economy would grind to a halt without this support," the report stated.

We have fought for gender rights, made key advancements, but the unseen and unequal burden of emotional labor continues to hound us. Women may have entered the formal workplace alongside men, but they are still expected to provide almost all of the either unpaid or underpaid support work that enables economies to function in the first place. This includes child and elderly care, domestic and family work, and community work keeping relationships and societies alive and connected. Humans need to be fed, dressed, housed, educated, tended to, and cared for, and they need to feel meaning, belonging, and connection to be able to function in an economy.

This support work is extraordinarily valuable—vital—even as it is often unseen and unrecognized. But we continue to take work deemed feminine for granted, so that it is ripe for extraction. In the words of radical feminist Heidi Hartmann, "the material base upon which patriarchy rests lies most fundamentally in men's control over women's labor power."[18] One of the cleverest tricks of patriarchy is that it transforms all work deemed feminine into fixed, subliminal expressions of femininity—however much that work involves active time, effort, and skill. The best way to maintain a system in which women work for little to nothing, and for the benefit of others, especially men, is to convince society that they are not working at all.

At the heart of this system, then, lies emotional labor, which is the most invisible and insidious form of shadow work expected of women and extracted for the benefit of men and society at large.

Emotional labor does not encompass all support work that enables society and our formal economy to function, but it is a heavy component of much of it. It is its own stand-alone form of work, as well as the impetus behind much unpaid work continuing to be done. Putting other people's feelings first and crafting meaningful emotional ties between humans is a huge part of care, child-rearing, and connective community work. But putting other people's feelings first is often also why a woman is expected to take on more tasks and responsibilities that are not necessarily strictly emotional. Being the one who drives children to practice on weekends, turning down a promotion and going part-time, showing a relative how to set up their new iPhone, staying up to wash clothes.

Emotional labor relies on the fundamental understanding that women should prioritize other people's experiences before their own. Emotional labor is what is happening when someone first seeks to cater to the emotional experience of someone else and then puts their own emotions to work for that other person. Under the distribution of this form of work, in which women are expected to provide emotional labor and men are not, there is a basic acceptance that a man's existence is to be protected as a priority over a woman's. This system is one in which men's quality of life matters primarily and women are put to work for it. There could not be a starker expression of gender hierarchy than that.

The reality that such a vital form of work is swept under the rug, relegated to women, is one of the roots of gender inequality because at its core emotional labor is not only overlooked, it is also degraded—in turn degrading those who are tasked with performing it.

In this latter manner, emotional labor, when it comes to gender, is describing a state of being that bears many parallels to theoretical frameworks developed by great Black intellectuals and figures of the twentieth century, including W.E.B. Du Bois's idea of double consciousness, Frantz Fanon's description of the white mask, and Ralph Ellison's account of visibility denied. Emotional labor as a more gendered burden has been depicted explicitly many times in fictional works by women—whether in the novel *Sula* by Toni Morrison, or *The Wife* by Meg Wolitzer, which was made into a film starring Glenn Close. But the naming is new. It is also necessary.

This book exposes and challenges these persistent roots of patriarchy—roots that are intertwined with white supremacy and class prejudice. It uncovers the singular form of extractive emotional capitalism propped up by these systems. It points out the unequal—and unfair—distribution of emotional labor, its systemic misvaluing, and the consequences of the chronic protection of men's experiences over women's, and dominant groups' experiences over nondominant groups.

While my reporting has been intersectional, my primary area of concern here is gender as a category. Specifically, I am concerned with the ways in which women continue to patently face extreme forms of life-defining injustices and inequality with only mild concern from broader society. The messaging seems to be that we should accept our gains, and whatever brutality is left is just, somehow, an inherent by-product—or at least something we should put up with out of gratitude that we do not need to put up with more.

Such fatalistic thinking is not only hindering exciting progress, it is false. Understanding how emotional labor operates in homes, in communities, in work environments, on our small screens and our big screens reveals this quite clearly, as this book will explore. This is a form of work that is imposed on those who lack power, obscured, and then used to keep them in place. It is a form of work that has become so equated with femininity that it has almost entirely desensitized us to the ways in which women are perpetually forced into subjugation and then viciously kept there. And yet this is also a form of work that holds deep, far-reaching, unchallengeable worth, that deserves to be seen, that deserves to be valued, even as it needs to be spread out far more evenly. It is, in fact, a form of work that when placed in our pres-

ent context demands nothing short of a total rethinking of our collective moral principles and our attitude toward work itself.

Emotional Labor is the product of seven years of inquiry, five of which
were spent in intense reading, research, reflection, and confrontation,
including through hundreds of interviews in person, over the phone,
and via email. These interviews cut across social, racial, economic, and
age demographics and were mostly performed in the United States,
with a special focus on voices from Michigan, Mississippi, and New
York—where I physically spent most time. Interviewees were typically
anonymized and they chose their own pseudonyms, unless they insisted on having their full name published and were not deemed in
danger.[19] While only a small percentage of people who gave the project
the honor of sharing their stories are featured, those whom I discuss
in these pages reflect the diversity of America as much as possible in a
book that is inevitably—by its very nature—thoroughly incomplete.
If an interviewee's race is not specified, that does not mean they are
white; it simply means that race was not used centrally when they
shared their experience—for instance, in relation to a partner of the
same race.

I hope this book will arm readers with stories and information to
share or reflect on. I hope it encourages readers to reckon with big
questions that will lead them to see the world around them, and inside
them, in a radically different way. I am a journalist, and so here I aim
to share these stories in their truest, most unadulterated form. But I
have also developed strong, informed opinions that I present at times
openly and frankly.

It has been just under two decades since that memorable car ride
conversation with my mother, and much more has continued to shape
me. I went from being a British kid growing up in Belgium to study-
ing in London and then Rome, where I took my first formal steps as
a journalist for the Associated Press. Twelve years ago, I arrived in the
United States, following a man who would briefly be my husband in

a life-defining move that would help solidify my feminism and make America my home. Here, I feel both like an outsider looking in and like I have been brought home to contend with one of the most monumental historical consequences of my own British history. Emotional labor is a global phenomenon, but its iteration in the United States has roots in a brand of patriarchy and white supremacy brought to the country by its former colonizer. This is the voice that informs these pages; this is the voice that has come—through journalistic work and life exposure—to believe in the urgency of the topic addressed in this book.

This book is an exploration of a form of inequality that has persisted untackled for too long. It is a sometimes rageful look at the sacrifices expected of women pushed into falling on their swords time and time again, all too often with the expectation of an apology or a smile as they go. But above all, this book believes in the agency of women and the strength of feminized forms of work and traits, and it maintains hope for the power of care, empathy, and love in action as forces that can lead us forward and call all of us into the best of our humanity.

ONE

What Is Emotional
Labor, Exactly?

POWER

A few days before Mother's Day, a day that ended up being about everything except putting her feet up and being celebrated, Jennifer tells me she reached breaking point. The Rust Belt service sector professional had originally hoped that Mother's Day Sunday would give her something she sorely lacked: quality, restorative time with her young son and husband, maybe even some time for herself. But a few weeks prior to the holiday, members of her wider family started to talk about getting together for another occasion falling this time of year: the one-year anniversary of her father's death. Uncles, aunts, and cousins agreed on the date but couldn't agree on who would organize the minutiae of the event. Quickly, Jennifer, who was still deep in the grieving process, whose schedule was already full, and whose idea this was not, was put in charge of organizing an event she wasn't even sure she had the emotional capacity to attend. Complaining seemed useless. Besides, she was used to biting her lip and taking the higher road for the common good. She placed her feelings into secondary position and focused on the layers of logistics ahead.

The easiest, planning wise, would have been to gather in a restaurant for the occasion, she thought at first, but there were other factors to consider: she couldn't risk being left having to foot the bill, a scenario she thought was plausible. "I love them, but my family is cheap," she jokes when we meet. It wasn't that she wasn't generous herself, but she had her own nuclear family's finances to look out for.

Last year, Jennifer had noticed that her husband of ten years, Shawn, who was generally closed off with his feelings, was acting more distant and down. Jennifer slowly, skillfully convinced him to share what was in his heart. "If you don't open up, you're going to be like a bottle of pop that you shake and shake and shake and eventually you explode," she warned him. "I understand that you are trying to be the man of the house and take care of this stuff. But I can be the person you can unload on, that's why I am here. You're going to give yourself a heart attack if you don't open up about this." Her carefully crafted, therapy-like words paid off. Shawn eventually let his guard down, revealing that they weren't making ends meet and were in such bad debt that they were barreling toward losing their home. A year on from confronting the financial disaster together, and solving it by appealing to one of the very few loved ones they had who could stretch to help them out, the couple had managed to keep the house. But risking being landed with a high-three- to four-figure restaurant bill was totally out of the question, as was trying to fit people inside their already cramped home.

Eventually, she convinced a cousin to host, with promises that she would still assume responsibility for the planning, the catering, the coordinating, the cake, and the ferrying back and forth of those family members who did not have a car on the day. That is to say, she would be in charge of generating a smooth and pleasant experience for everyone attending. And in making sure people's needs were met—that everyone was given a suitable time and place to feel comforted in shared memories, in seamless togetherness, in family bonds and love, without having to worry about outside factors, including money—she would be shouldering the emotional labor necessary to conceive and produce the event.

On the Thursday before the gathering, her ever-accelerating juggling of logistics, accommodating of other people's concerns, expectations, and needs, combined with the unbending nature of time, brought her to an emotional brink. Jennifer's day began with an admonishment by her boss, a male family member who paid her according to how well his company was doing. The reprimand felt unjust and humiliating, but in exchange for inconsistent pay, Jennifer received flexibility of hours that meant she could stay on top of the other moving parts of her life.

That day, she needed this arrangement even more than usual. She had a delicate mission to accomplish, of all places, at the crematorium. A year on from her dad passing, no one had footed the bill for an urn, and his remains were enclosed in a plastic box. To avoid an expense she could not take on, and to avoid bringing her dad's ashes to the gathering, where his presence had been requested, in a Tupperware-like situation, she had called the venue they had used for the funeral. On the phone, she explained the problem and, appealing to the owners' good nature, asked them to loan her an urn for the weekend. They accepted but gave her a narrow window for the urn pickup: Thursday late afternoon, in between one wake and another. So, at work, she sat on her hands, smiled through the unpleasant experience, and focused on the bigger picture. She had a mission to accomplish, and she would not fail at the first hurdle.

First task of leaving work on time accomplished, she headed to school, where she picked up her four-year-old son, Spencer. Second task of speedy pickup done, she whizzed home to drop him off with her mother, Shelley, who lived with them and had agreed to take her grandson on a bicycle ride. It was there, at the third hurdle, that things started to fall apart. Her mother had come to stay four years prior for what Jennifer assumed was a short visit, but she had never left. She had been gravely hospitalized in the past for bipolar disorder and her medication dosage and symptoms needed to be closely monitored. Whether she had forgotten to take her meds, a triggering event had happened, or dosages needed to be tweaked, Jennifer did not know. What she did know was that shortly after the drop-off, her mother started screaming, hurling creative insults at her daughter and grandson—much to the young child's astonishment. She yelled and yelled, and eventually announced resolutely she would no longer take Spencer on his promised bike ride.

Jennifer couldn't believe it. She loved her mother, and she ultimately was pleased she had accommodated her family's home life to welcome her in. Even if she had never asked whether she minded and now Jennifer had an extra person to care for, even if it meant Spencer had to share a room with his grandmother, even if Shelley's late-night television habits had taken a toll on Jennifer's sex life with Shawn as they became reluctant to make any suggestive noises through the paper-thin walls. So little was asked of her in return, and her unwillingness to help Jennifer with this one crucial task felt suddenly infuriating.

For a moment Jennifer let the mask of seamlessness come off. She stopped measuring her tone. Her voice broke, and the toll of the invisible labor she had been doing came rushing out of her mouth. "I am tired of taking on everything for you, taking on everything for him, taking on everything for Shawn," she told her mother. "I am dealing with my own grief. I have been in a mentally very dark place and I was trying, just trying, to get through to Mother's Day. I am sorry, I do not know what is wrong, but I cannot fix it, and I am tired. I don't think you realize everything I do, everything I am responsible for."

Shelley, astonished by the rebuttal, calmed down but was in no state to perform her duty. Once Grandmother was settled in safely at home, Jennifer packed Spencer into the car and headed to the funeral home, late. She ended up doing exactly what she had wanted to avoid: walking through the wake of a stranger not on time with a four-year-old in tow.

The Sunday gathering—featuring ashes in borrowed urn—went well. And in between the driving of uncles back and forth and making sure all were fed with the right foods, she barely caught a breath. By that point, though, she was just relieved she had pulled off the event without any further incident, and it was done.

When I sit with Jennifer, she keeps a pleasant, soft, and sweet demeanor throughout. Over the hours she manages to carve out for us to talk in person, tears intermittently well up in her eyes, but she never lets them pour. Every now and then, as she goes into the layers of uncompensated work she does, her tone starts to sound more pleading and her descriptions sound like questions, like she is clear that what she is doing is there but she needs someone, anyone, to hear her, to see her, to mark what she is doing as real.

"You've been holding shit down," I say to her during one of those moments.

"Yeah. I hold shit down," she answers, her face suddenly lightening up.

––––––––––

Performing emotional labor—identifying or anticipating other people's emotions, adapting yours in consequence, and then managing to positively affect other people's emotions—can often look like someone putting other people's feelings first. This editing work on one's own emotions executed for the benefit of other people's emotions is sometimes easy to identify, sometimes not.

Jennifer intuiting that something was up and then coaching Shawn through his emotions to get him to communicate and find a solution is a straightforward example of emotional labor.

But in other circumstances, emotional labor is hidden just below the surface. Instead of prioritizing her private grieving, Jennifer adapted to broader family members' needs and wishes. She took the high road. She put her own emotions and thoughtfulness to work for the service of others. Her emotional labor was a form of community work that meant her family could come together to mourn and rejoice—experiencing feelings of belonging, connectivity, and meaning.

Producing these kinds of feelings in others often became externalized into actual tasks she identified, performed, or delegated. Carefully anticipating emotions and behaviors, executing a variety of tasks, and managing logistics, including financial restrictions, to create an experience for others, to help maintain peaceful bonds between people—that's a product of emotional labor, too, but it is rarely seen as such. It is mostly not seen as anything, really: not as work, not as an effort or a skill set, not as something time consuming. At best, it is seen as a fixed role. Except, of course, for the person doing it.

But emotional labor—just like physical labor, intellectual labor, and creative labor—is a form of work that does require time, effort, and skill.

Treating it as a form of work that requires time, effort, and skill remains a controversial assertion. In our globalized, capitalistic world, work has remained equated with the production of goods and services for a fee in a public, traditionally seen as male sphere, mostly outside the home. In this market-driven economic system, work becomes real through formal compensation. In other words, if you're not being paid, you're not working.[1]

To many, though, this narrow, neoclassical economic definition of work does not just ring false, it also undermines the vital, often unpaid work that many women do. It helps strip it of its value and hide it in plain sight.[2]

Emotional labor, as a specific form of feminized work, also remains derided and unseen because it is unfathomable to many that tasks and duties tied to love, care, the family, and women could have anything to do with real work. Instead of seeing it as work, we have cast emotional labor as a passive expression of the supposed purest essence of femininity. Insisting it is an effort or anything but a mystical manifestation of woman-at-rest is tarnishing, we are taught, to the point of disempowerment. How dare we touch the figure of the divine, endlessly empathetic feminine?

But is it really disempowering to lift the curtain up and show emotional labor for what it is? And say it is, who stands to gain or lose power from such a revelation? Really. And besides, don't we all know, deep down, that emotional labor is a skill and an effort that holds real value? Because don't we all know someone is doing it? Whether it is us, and we are suppressing our own feelings, justifying it to ourselves with reminders of love and the Big Picture. Or whether it is someone else, and we are proclaiming our own innocence and ignorance, while engaging in subtle arm-twisting to get them to get a task done, followed by restrained gratitude when it is done—not too much gratitude, you see, lest we make the whole charade crumble.

Exhausted, Jennifer tells me she would like more gratitude and acknowledgment but that she loves her family, and she will ultimately keep on doing this emotional labor. "I am a people pleaser," she confesses, "which is clearly my problem."

Is it, though? Is the fact that she self-identifies as a people pleaser her problem, her fault for being someone who understands and cares about other people's feelings? Or is it that she has been trained to do something that she has now internalized as a passive attribute? These questions were at the heart of the reactions I received when I first started looking into emotional labor in 2015. Whether I was met by confusion, shock, or enthusiasm from those to whom I explained what I was working on often depended on their gender.

Women I spoke to tended to ask a few questions and then exclaimed joy in their deep recognition. This was the case with one interviewee, Anita, a woman in her fifties, who had brought up four children with a father who was only intermittently present. She had not only been the main source of financial support for her children well into their adulthood but she had continued to emotionally carry them forward too. She helped them in between jobs with food and shelter, supported one adult child through addiction recovery, and made sure they all stayed connected, came together regularly, and felt grounded and loved. Money had been tight in recent years, but she never failed to find a way. "Emotional . . . labor . . ." she said to me, trying the two words on for fit. "Emotions. As work. But that's what I have been doing for years!" Her life's work having a term was deeply validating, and also relieving. It hadn't all been in her head; her exhaustion did not mean she was morally deficient. Her toil had a name, and a name that included "labor," a value.

Men, on the other hand, had very mixed kinds of reactions. They met me with horrified faces and furrowed brows. "Let me get this straight. You are saying that emotions are *work* women are forced into doing?" one male friend of mine, Tim, asked me, incredulous, over a lunch he was making for us in his Harlem home. Tim was not only baffled by the concept, he was also visibly upset by it. "Why is the fact that women provide emotional support work, though? What if they actually enjoy it? What if women are just better at emotions than men? Why do we have to make that something negative? Why do you feminists have to make normal things into issues to be debated?"

There was, of course, some exasperation coming from Tim, who was a caregiver of sorts himself. He was a constant source of support to his extended family. He loved to fix problems for his loved ones and for his community and had become an informal leader. On the days I popped by when I was in town, I would sometimes watch him out of the corner of my eye, his tall, athletic frame delicately watering and spritzing his plants. As he went by each plant, you could hear him singing and talking under his breath, and it was unclear whether it was to himself or to the greenery.

Didn't Tim perform emotional labor too? Undoubtedly. Men *and* women are perfectly able to perform emotional labor, but the expectations placed on women are far greater than those placed on men, resulting in a notable penalty-versus-credit gulf. Tim would likely get credit where Anita wouldn't. Whatever Tim provided in thoughtfulness and geste was identified and tended to be seen as a plus, as having value, especially because Tim was so stereotypically masculine on so many other fronts. Tim was lauded. But there was an army of emotional laborers who weren't Tim around him, and whose work was expected, rarely highlighted, and mostly discarded to the depths of oblivion. His sisters, his mother, his niece.

And as genuinely caring and progressive on many gender issues as Tim was, that he believed "women were just better at emotions" was a little worrying to me. It was an essentialist view of gender as well as emotional labor that I have bumped into time and time again in the years I have spent researching this. Tim, a scientist, would never have dared say to me that women are better cooks or women are more talented cleaners. And yet Tim did seem to say unapologetically to me that women were just "naturally" more gifted with emotions. Not only that, he also insinuated that if we were "naturally" better at emotions, it was heresy to allow that "natural" exertion to translate into an activity qualified as work. Never mind that men were translating supposedly "natural" male gifts into highly lucrative performances and careers all the time.

This line of argument fails basic logic, but it is so widely propagated; it demands attention. Psychological essentialism still reigns supreme for many people—not just for Tim. Many would posit that Jennifer being a "people pleaser" was just the way she was born, and some might even advance that this is just how women tend to be. These assumptions reflect our persistent cultural stereotypes that maintain that women and men have impeccably opposing personality traits. Under this dogma, women are cast as empathetic, emotional, insightful, warm, expressive, other-directed, interpersonally adept, and more aware of the feelings of others, while men are cast as more dominant, rational, active, decisive, performance- and status-driven, hierarchy-aware, self-directed, selfish, and less aware of the feelings of others.[3]

Despite these commonly held beliefs, research from the fields of psychology and neuroscience shows that fixed gender traits have been exceedingly exaggerated. Cognitive neuroscientist Gina Rippon, author of *The Gendered Brain: The New Neuroscience That Shatters the Myth of the Female Brain*,[4] stresses that today's science shows that brains are prodigiously affected by social cues and stereotypes and react to them, not the opposite. In 2016, in the British Psychological Society's monthly publication *The Psychologist*, she explained: "A key breakthrough in our knowledge of the brain in this century, fueled by the stunning technological advances in research, is that brain structure and function is not fixed and unchangeable, and not the same irrespective of context or culture. It is, in fact, exquisitely plastic, moldable by experience throughout life. It is also 'permeable,' responding to social attitudes and expectations, as is shown by brain-imaging studies of stereotype threat."[5]

Human brains have the ability to constantly evolve and be taught new tricks or skill sets. But their permeability means they are also heavily affected by context and environment. If someone's brain receives positive messages expecting them to perform a task well, they will be more likely to perform that task successfully. The same is true of the opposite: if a brain receives a negative message about performing a task, it will be less likely to be successful at it. Our brains are very aware of gendered stereotypes—and the easiest, least stressful course of action for them is to go along with those stereotypes. Men's and women's brains are not the cause for the status quo then; they are the product of it.

This helps explain why studies that have specifically investigated the performance of emotional labor across gender lines have found that women do more of it than men but that its performance is tied to them performing their gender rather than performing their character traits.[6] But even with this finding, it still remains hard to rigidly separate out a personality trait from the social pressure to develop it.

Jennifer may identify legitimately as a people pleaser, but cultural stereotypes and training have incentivized her brain to focus on this skill set. Bucking expectations is costly. Social scientists and psychologists have found that there is a "backlash" effect toward people who veer from cultural, gendered stereotypes.[7] Openly sensitive men risk being branded as weak, incompetent, suspicious, or even dishonorable, and openly ambitious women risk being branded strident, untrustworthy, malicious, unbalanced, and even dangerous.[8] This backlash mechanism is a powerful tool to keep gender extremes in personality traits intact.

As for the stereotypically feminine trait that is particularly important in the performance of emotional labor—empathy—four decades of research have also shown it to be tied to incentives rather than innate ability.[9] In one influential and rather hilarious paper[10] by Kristi Klein and Sara Hodges at the University of Oregon, researchers found in an initial study that men and women had the same empathic ability (the ability to infer what another person was feeling), except when participants were tipped that the study was about interpersonal skills—traits deemed communal and therefore feminine. In that case, women, incentivized to perform their gender, did better than men on the exact same exercise. This had been true of previous studies that found that women and men exhibited similar degrees of empathic ability, finding a difference favoring women only when participants knew they were being tested on a trait deemed feminine, such as this communal, interpersonal one.[11]

The funny part appears in a subsequent study unpacked in this same paper. Klein and Hodges, acknowledging their finding that women were able to enhance their empathic ability when they were motivated into doing so to perform their gender, decided to try to see if they could enhance men's empathy performance with a form of motivation male participants would respond to. The researchers tipped the participants off that they would be performing an interpersonal task, which would usually only have motivated women into exhibiting higher empathy levels, but this time they added an extra incentive: real cash money. For every answer that was somewhat empathically accurate, participants were given $1, and for every fully empathically accurate answer, they were given $2. The result? Performance shot through the roof for everyone, and men and women scored similarly high. Concluding their paper, the authors wrote: "This is an encouraging finding, suggesting that greater empathic accuracy can be achieved by virtually anyone who is given proper motivation. When all else fails, if you find yourself faced with someone who just cannot seem to understand your point of view, it might be worthwhile to offer him or her a dollar."

Tossing a dollar at someone to get them to put themselves in someone else's shoes seems at once cathartic, absurd, and vaguely demeaning. But it does also drive one undeniable point home. The core skills of emotional labor, including the ability to identify other people's emotions, are skills we all have. Only some of us care to deploy them, though. Some of us—women—have trained to do emotional labor because of a legitimate fear of backlash. This training is often internalized into a personality trait, and our performance is very rarely attached to a dollar bill. Others are not so much devoid of skill as devoid of motivation. They just can't be bothered. The world gets a bit darker when you realize this.

But the $1 study anecdote offers even more insight than its initial conclusion. If all people could tap into their empathizing skills given the right incentive, the fact that some groups—men—are not bothering to is indicative of a general lack of reward system—not only in terms of gender, but in terms of broader value and status associated with the expression of these traits in society. This cracks open the truth hiding just beneath the surface here: emotional labor in our current system is much more about power than gender. We do not currently live in a world where empathy in action translates into high status— quite the opposite. If you think of what emotional labor is—putting other people and their feelings *above* yourself and your own—it is remarkably similar to the idea of serving. In emotional labor, one person serves the emotions of another. With this understanding, the gender divide in personality traits enforces a system where supposedly altruistic women serve supposedly emotionally helpless men.

In a seminal article from 1985, published in the *Journal of Personality and Social Psychology*, psychologist Sara Snodgrass sought to test the validity of the idea of "women's intuition."[12] Snodgrass grouped men and women into pairs and randomly assigned one person the "leader" position and the other the "subordinate" position. The study found that those designated as "subordinate"—whether male or female— were consistently more attentive and perceptive to the feelings of leaders, and that once given either a subordinate or a leader role gender stopped having any effect. The paper concludes that women's intuition might be better described as "subordinates' intuition."

What is fascinating about this dynamic is that it then becomes a self-fulfilling prophecy, or at least a power dynamic that keeps on reinforcing itself. "The prevailing power imbalance between males and females within a culture might actually be sustained and facilitated if the more powerful members of the culture require the less powerful members to 'read their minds,' without feeling any obligation to return the favor," wrote psychologists Tiffany Graham and William Ickes in a paper named "When Women's Intuition Isn't Greater Than Men's."[13]

It makes total sense that the people who have less power in a group end up having to become finely attuned to the emotions, actions, or potential actions of those with more power for fear of violence, punishment, irrelevance, or being cut off from access to resources—and that those with more power need not bother. But the guesswork that positions women and their attention in relation to men inevitably puts women one step behind men. You could think of it as a cruel and deliberately manipulative mind game. Women are told they are equal, but they must also constantly play catch-up.

Understanding emotional labor as being more about power than gender also extends it out as an imposed, devalued performance onto other subjugated populations that also intersect with women: economically disenfranchised people, Black people, Indigenous people, people of color, people with precarious immigration statuses, among other groups.[14]

Contextualizing emotional labor as a performance doesn't just help validate an experience that is real, then—its relation to power offers an extraordinary insight into ongoing forms of inequality, the ways in which they are blindly accepted and, in turn, perpetuated. It offers insight into how much gender and power are still so thoroughly intertwined.

One woman I interviewed, Seema, who works in the same high-stress, male-dominated industry as her husband, Rahul, said the emotional labor disparity at home was galling. Like many others, she talked about assuming sole responsibility for mood boosting. "When he's down, everything is down. It takes a monumental effort to even get him to engage. I say all sorts of positive things, talk about the future, be full of energy, always try to talk about the positive side. Help him plan his day, help him make a to-do list."

Acting in an upbeat way to bring someone else up relies on a commonsense understanding that is so basic, it barely warrants note: that we mirror one another as humans and that emotions are infectious. Yet emotion contagion, which describes the way in which emotions, expressed openly by one person, tend to stimulate a similar set of emotions in people around that person, is an entire field of study in psychology.[15] In particular, it is studied as it affects work performances in for-profit settings. One foundational 2002 study by Sigal Barsade at the Wharton School found, for instance, that positive emotional contagion improved task performances and cooperation and decreased conflict.[16] There is no reason why this kind of emotional labor seen and valued in certain business contexts should not be seen and valued in all spheres. Its private erasure obscures the reality of what is going on.

Seema reasons with herself that her emotional labor is worth it. She loves Rahul, even if she is silently left exhausted. But sometimes, reflecting on other details involving her taking one for the team—like that time she stayed home to wait for the repairman, taking a morning off work and saving Rahul from the inconvenience—she starts to wonder whether she might not be incurring small professional penalties hindering her advancement while Rahul is not. She notes that there is a hierarchy of time that has insidiously instilled itself into their relationship, which, between them, puts a limit on what is demanded of him and no limit on what is demanded of her. Those occasional, quiet thoughts leave her seething.

Seema is far from alone. The subtle coercion involved in the expectation that they should always focus on the interest of the group has left modern women, often also seeking out careers as much as their male counterparts, feeling a deep sense of injustice in their private lives. In heterosexual settings especially, where expectations tied to gender have remained remarkably fixed, emotional labor adds itself to the pile of other domestic chores that are undervalued and unseen and remain overwhelmingly considered women's work.

Worse, while emotional labor is by no means synonymous with all domestic labor, it is often a motivating factor for tasks that go beyond performing strict emotions to affect other people's emotions. Baking brownies for a sweet-toothed family member may be a domestic task, but if it is done to alleviate sadness, its execution is also a form of emotional labor. And because emotional labor is the act of putting other people's feelings before one's own, it can also provoke the taking on of essential tasks other people may be able to do but find undesirable or unrewarding, such as overseeing the kids' remote Zoom school sessions, switching to a part-time job, or taking a morning off work to wait for the repairman. None of these choices necessarily involves active deployment of emotional labor, but if the tasks were undertaken to keep others happy or to avoid outbursts, then they are part of an overall execution of emotional labor.

Being put into this role of the altruistic, thoughtful caregiver, the one who will oversee a family's or community's emotional well-being and take responsibility where no one else will, ends up locking women into a broad, thin layer of experiential inequality that feels as frustratingly unfair as it is, up until now, hard to define. This is the experiential inequality that exists at the heart of the emotional patriarchy we are in—in which men's enjoyment and experience of the world are a priority while women are trained primarily to create and facilitate those experiences.

Here, Seema's insight into a hierarchy of time is particularly profound. Because we each have twenty-four hours to spend in one day but not all work is paid, time is an incredible tool to mark value as well as measure disparities. It is the one common denominator that is everyone's to give, keep, exchange, or hand over forcibly.[17]

For the last couple of decades, time-use surveys capturing the population's paid and unpaid work have been undertaken in the United States following years of campaigning caused by international feminist economics thinking.[18] The surveys reveal that modern men are more involved in domestic work than their fathers were, but time parity has still not been accomplished. Analysis of the American Time Use Survey released by the Institute for Women's Policy Research in January 2020 found that, on an average day, women spent 37 percent more time on unpaid household tasks and caregiving than men.[19]

The disparity held true across all races and ethnicities and all income brackets, as well as in cases where both men and women worked full-time.[20] Straight families that identified as Hispanic registered the most disparity, while straight families that identified as multiracial registered the least disparity, but even those households declared a difference of at least one hour of extra labor for women a day. Asian, Black, and white families all held disparities between one and a half and two and a half extra hours of unpaid and care work for women. Households earning $29,999 and under saw women providing 38 percent more unpaid labor (a little over a third), while households earning six figures—$100,000 or more—saw women providing 33 percent more unpaid labor (exactly a third). These numbers are similar enough that they point to a problem that transcends income bracket and education levels, not the opposite.

It is important to spell this out, because while there are some differences between groups, which warrant investigation,[21] the gender inequalities are stark enough across all categories that there can be no finger-pointing that this is another group's problem, that one can educate oneself out of this, or that this is situation specific. The private time of one group—women—being hijacked for the endless performance of under-recognized and undervalued labor to the benefit and protection of the private time of another group—men—is not situation specific, it is gender specific.

Teasing out emotional labor from the rest of the domestic chores is impossible at a grand scale, of course. There's no telling how much emotional labor is involved in these domestic chores overall, even if it is doubtless present—from childcare to cooking. But there is one way in which emotional labor inequality can be specifically gleaned from these surveys, especially when one thinks of it as the idea of an individual putting someone else's experience and pleasure above their own: by looking at who gets to enjoy the most spare time. More disturbing than simply looking at statistics showing how much extra work women provide at home compared to men is looking at time differences in leisure. In 2018, men averaged forty-nine minutes more leisure time a day than women did. Almost one entire hour a day. To anyone who has come home drained from a day's work and wished they just had time to hit the gym, read a book, catch up with a friend, or unwind with Netflix but couldn't because of having to manage the household, tend to children, or do chores, that number is the difference between getting to do that and not. That number is about living for yourself versus living for others. It is everything.

How are we still here? This system of experiential inequality and unequal emotional labor distribution is propped up in private by absurd double standards we have become all too well acquainted with, even as we let them slide. The idea that men "help out" with duties in the homes they live in, for instance; the idea that men might be seen to "babysit" their own kids; the idea that men would be lauded for being emotionally expressive, thoughtful, and communicative with romantic partners they have themselves sought a committed relationship with and kids they have caused to be born; the idea that men might "sacrifice" some of their "free" time after work to take their own children to the park or put them to bed—these are all ideas that might seem incongruous in a modern world. But these deceitful, falsehearted framings that benefit and protect men's time outside of formal work over women's have remained remarkably common, pointing to ongoing expectations that men should still largely be spared duties tied to the home, to common well-being, to family maintenance, and that women should still take these on.

That the starting point should be that men would provide little to

nothing at home and women should provide most puts men into positions of easy praise when they do more than nothing, and almost immediately positions women in a place of deficiency and easy criticism
if they do less than everything. Beyond this, it also makes women the
default workers *for* men and men the default beneficiaries of women's
work. In this context, saying women are second-class citizens and men
are first-class citizens isn't just a flippant, provocative statement; it is
simply stating that while we may now have the right to vote, women
are still seen to serve at the pleasure of men.

In the context of work, emotional labor occupies a special place behind the scenes. By caring for family members old and young, by creating and maintaining community ties, by performing tangible tasks
for the broader good of the group while keeping communal peace and
individual satisfactions in mind, emotional labor is the form of work
that keeps everyone going and people together. And as emotional labor continues to tirelessly, invisibly be performed in the background,
it is also what enables other, more socially valued—and paid—forms
of work to take place. Emotional labor is the ultimate enabler of
work. A loved, educated, well-fed, healthy, and socialized young adult
goes into the world a capable worker thanks to years of labor put into
their shaping—and years more dedicated to their maintenance and
uplifting.[22]

This emotional labor benefits the whole community well beyond
individual households, and well beyond households headed by two
parents of the opposite sex. Here, too, women carry the majority of the
load, especially in communities neglected by formal infrastructure. In
such cases, women act as buffers for pain inflicted from the outside—
for themselves and for loved ones—but they also act as instigators for
healing, for progress.

In Mississippi, I meet Ashley, who understands emotional labor as
something that touches all aspects of her life—as a single mother, a
Black woman, a health-care industry worker, and a human being who

is barely afforded any space for entitlement or power. She does it ceaselessly, she tells me, for survival, and to breaking point, but also because she insists she and her daughter deserve to thrive.

The health-care industry she works in requires her to be "on" all the time with patients and coworkers, as well as white managers, who often police her tone and appearance—leaving her with no choice but to filter the expression of her emotions to please her surroundings and keep her position. But Ashley has learned her rights, and when she has needed to, she has filed formal complaints against managers and coworkers. "I don't let people stop me from being a good person, regardless of how bad they are treating me," she shares.

For her, this kind of emotional labor starts with refusing to believe negative sexist and racist messages she is repeatedly told. The effects of this draining emotional labor seep into her private life, where she is trying to complete a graduate degree while providing a steady, loving environment for her sixteen-year-old daughter. "People say whatever happens at work stays at work. That doesn't work with me," she says of the supposed clear separation between work life and private life, a complaint that became nearly universal to working women with families during the initial years of the coronavirus pandemic.

At home, as a single mother of a dark-skinned Black female teenager, Bri, Ashley doesn't just juggle all of the domestic duties and bills; she is also sole counselor to and champion for her daughter, whose basic needs she feels the system is failing. After some boys started bullying her for her looks, Ashley noticed her young daughter internalizing more and more negative messages about herself. Her grades started to fall, and Bri began to believe she was dumb. Ashley requested a meeting with school administrators to discuss strategies to get her daughter back on track. After nothing changed, Ashley showed up again and repeated her request for her daughter to receive an adequate degree of attention and support. They owed it to her family to fulfill their public educational responsibilities.

She tells me she is doing this for Bri but also for others like her.

"I have people saying, 'You're doing too much. I wouldn't do all of that.'" To them she responds, "That's you. I am different. I am just doing what's right." High school graduation rates in Mississippi have remained higher for white students than for Black students for years,[23] and the quality of care and teaching given in majority-Black districts is notoriously far worse than in majority-white ones.

In 2017, the Southern Poverty Law Center brought a lawsuit against the governor of Mississippi on behalf of four African American mothers whose children attended public schools lacking experienced teachers, textbooks, basic supplies, and even toilet paper. The suit claimed that the state was failing to abide by a legal obligation to "operate a uniform system of free public schools." At the time of filing, the Mississippi Department of Education cited fourteen school districts as being of the highest quality with "A" ratings—all of them were majority white. Meanwhile, nineteen districts were given the worst "F" rating score, and all of those were majority Black. One mother in the suit, Dorothy Haymer, had spent $100 in the previous year providing her six-year-old's public school with sanitary supplies.[24]

These are acts of defensive, compensatory care for the group, acts of emotional labor that support the needs and survival of immediate family members as well as communities. They, too, are absolutely vital, and yet overlooked, imposed, and unpaid forms of work.[25]

Ashley's extensive emotional labor is hard to quantify. She is not in a romantic relationship where she can point out that her partner watches Netflix for an extra hour of the day while she helps a child with homework. But she is still providing that extra, invisible work. Her abusive, extractive relationship is more directly with a society that has never formally valued her or her work, even as it has relied on both. Meanwhile, she finds herself filling in where she and her daughter have been failed, putting energy into insisting on their being humanized and worthy of equal treatment.

Ashley tells me she believes in generational curses—understanding that the seed of what she is confronting was planted centuries before she was born against her enslaved ancestors. But she is bent on breaking hers. She does it day in and day out "by speaking up, standing for what's right, going above and beyond," she says.

She throws everything at changing the world around her in how it treats her, her daughter, and their wider community. Her battle is different—in its particularities and hardships—from the battles of Jennifer, Anita, or Seema. But at the end of the day, their fights are all tied. They are fights to expose the unfairness that emanates from the devaluing of entire groups of people, the experiential hierarchies that are born from this, and the consequential labor that they are then forced to provide. These are fights to be seen and valued as individuals and, by extension, fights to reclaim the power and worth of their work.

That some take and others are taken from may be what she has always witnessed, but to Ashley this inequality makes no sense. This version of organizing the earth cannot stand. "God says share the wealth," she tells me, sitting on a Mississippi park bench one spring afternoon, lip trembling, defiant.

TWO

Domesticity at Work

COERCION

A couple of weeks after 2020's joyous Mardi Gras celebrations, which saw an influx of over one million revelers to Louisiana's New Orleans streets, local hospitals reported their first COVID-19 cases. A deadly infectious disease that had previously sounded like a faraway problem, continents away, had seeped its way in during one of the most jubilant and lively traditions in America's South.

Lucy, a New Orleans native and patient care technician, remembers hearing about the first cases in the news on a Tuesday, but they weren't at the top of her mind when she headed into work the following Saturday in one of the city's thirty-one hospitals. It wasn't until she got to the doors of her unit and read a sign stating RESTRICTED AREA that she began to understand. "You didn't know?" a colleague asked on their way in, seeing her sudden motionlessness. "This is the quarantine unit. This is where people with coronavirus go."

Lucy's mind raced, overwhelmed. She sat down, focused on breathing, and slowly calmed herself, preparing for what was ahead. That first COVID-19-pandemic shift, there was little reassurance outside of her own to be found. No one had a plan; the nurses around her, her immediate superiors, were scared; and there weren't enough gloves or masks to go around. Midway through her shift, one of the colleagues she had been working alongside went to the emergency room and tested positive.

As a patient care technician, a job also referred to as a nursing assistant, she was expected to take patients' vitals every four hours, but with the new pandemic situation she was tasked with extra duties not usually hers, including meal delivery and general care. Nurses and other hospital workers pulled rank to avoid being too close to the ill. Dazed, and feeling dangerously exposed, she focused on fulfilling the requirements of her job, putting on a strong and reassuring face regardless of the emotions she was feeling inside. Patients needed her. She became a point person for them, and they soon learned her name, crying out, "Lucy, Lucy, Lucy!"

Lucy was used to masking her emotions to get her job done and for the sake of her patients: an explicit form of emotional labor she felt made her a "great worker." But that shift, as she kept a level head and was shouldered with further responsibilities because of being on the lower echelons of the hospital hierarchy, having to bite her lip, the weight of what she was expected to execute, while putting her body on the line, became remarkably clear.

Emotional labor is barely controversial when it is executed within the realm of a hospital. In fact, the performance is core to the "care" part of the colossal health-care industry, which employs an estimated 11 percent of American workers[1] and overtook both manufacturing and retail at the end of 2017.[2] The industry is only set to grow more due to an aging population, large government subsidization, and an inability to either automate or outsource to other countries much of its labor. Registered nurses, nursing assistants like Lucy, personal care aides, and home health aides, each position overwhelmingly occupied by women at rates of eight to nine out of every ten,[3] are all on the list of the Bureau of Labor Statistics top twenty occupations with the most projected job growth over the next decade.[4]

But of those booming jobs, only registered nurses were earning more than America's median annual salary of $40,000[5] in 2019, making $73,300 a year. The rest offered job prospects for sure, but a salary ceiling well below the living wage,[6] all falling between $20,000 and $29,900 a year. As for Lucy? She made $27,000, thanks to ten years in the industry and steady hourly raises. Nor was she complaining. She had come a long way, starting off as a nursing assistant on minimum wage making $14,000 a year—close to half of what she was making now.

She wasn't complaining, that is, until now. In the weeks and then months following the beginning of the outbreak, the necessity for emotional labor, basically the gulf between what emotions she could show and what she was actually feeling, only intensified. "I was nervous and scared just as the patient was nervous and scared," she says. But no one could tell. She held herself to the highest of standards and put the patients' needs before her own. Sick people in her care shared photos of children and loved ones, asked her to make phone calls, asked for updates on spouses who had also come in with the virus but had been separated into different rooms. A "people's person" who says she "doesn't mind getting up and going the extra mile," she tried to be the human face among the horror, even as she felt the need to rush through her duties to minimize her exposure. Shifts were hard. "Lucy's got it," she would hear senior colleagues say. Lower in the hierarchy of the hospital compared to doctors or nurses, she felt thrown in the deep end, expected to be the caregiver in a context that was blatantly not caring for her.

As uncared for, even unprotected, as she felt, people like Lucy became superstars overnight. Around the world, citizens in New York, London, Madrid, and other major cities came to their balconies and front doors every evening, drumming on their pots and pans, cheering and applauding to thank health-care workers whose work had suddenly taken on a new level of heroism. Health-care workers across the board—no longer just doctors but also nurses, nursing assistants, and other hospital workers, cleaners, janitors, and beyond them bus and subway drivers, supermarket and warehouse workers, postal workers, and delivery people—all became known under a new class of "essential worker." As the United States and the world confronted catastrophe, it became abundantly clear to all that the people we relied upon the most were not those in prestigious, celebrated positions—not the bankers, the lawyers, the Hollywood actors, or the CEOs, but those helping us with our most basic needs: health, food, care, access, sanitation.

In July 2020, Edward Enninful, *British Vogue*'s editor in chief, and the first Black person to ever hold the position, chose three essential workers, a train driver, a midwife, and a supermarket assistant, all of them women, and two of them women of color, to grace the cover of the luxury fashion magazine.[7] Temporarily, high-end fashion models and glamorous international movie stars were replaced by heroes of the moment: female workers going above and beyond for duties that superseded the individualistic goals any of the rest of us were pursuing. Here were the faces of sacrifice and reassurance.

Unfortunately, the prestige didn't translate into much beyond pot banging. In the United States, for all the buzz of federal hazard pay that had initially proposed increasing essential workers' salaries by an extra $13 per hour, which would have almost doubled Lucy's income, proposals never concretized.[8] Lucy found little consolation in her job's new level of esteem. Her job had, after all, always been essential. She and her one and a half million colleagues who held the same job title were those who had the most contact with hospital patients during normal times, not just in a pandemic, providing basic care and monitoring, helping with activities of daily living, bathing, feeding, toileting. They were the ones who provided the lion's share of emotional labor, who knew patients' names, who tracked and noticed important differences. They knew who to ask about, which television channel to turn to, how to position a cushion, whether to draw the curtains. They were the most humane representations of health care, the ones providing the most comfort to the ill.

But as much as they were lauded, as much as they were essential in a pandemic and outside of one, as much as they were the backbone of an industry that was a considerable part of the backbone of the American economy, not much came in terms of actual recompense. Little came in real protection.

Why was that? How could it be that we are finally appreciating the value of essential work, much of which is within the caring economy replete with emotional labor, but that it is not translating into cash?

Or into actual status instigating better conditions and regulations within workplaces?

The answer is that this lauding was nothing new at all. Loudly stating the value of feminized work places another veil in front of the fact that we chronically refuse to pay for the work of people meeting our most essential needs. It's a disconnect in geste versus follow-through that continues in spite of magazine covers and in spite of what the science continues to clearly reveal.

Research from the last four decades has consistently found that, as humans, our existence is primarily reliant on our emotional needs being met. Love, a sense of connection, and belonging could not be more valuable to humans thriving—more so than the food that we eat or the roof over our heads.[9] One analysis that looked at results from 148 studies with over 300,000 participants showed that poor social relationships was a more detrimental factor to human survival than physical inactivity or obesity and was at least as impactful on health as smoking or drinking alcohol. People with strong relationships had a 50 percent increased likelihood of survival in a control group than those with weaker social relations.[10] Quite poignantly, and directly, social connection, or being in community, has been found to positively alter and better equip our immune systems.[11]

If the evidence is so clear, why continue the ruse? It doesn't just seem unfair, it seems to not add up in a capitalist economy we have been taught will pay top dollar for what is the most valuable.

The truth is, the rules of our economy are not evenly applied depending on who is doing the work and what kind of work is being done. This is a rigged system that relies on social beliefs that are far more brutal and retrograde than we would care to admit. In a 2010 book on the topic, UC Berkeley professor Evelyn Nakano Glenn spelled out a core dynamic of care as a human activity: coercion.[12] Physical, economic, social, and moral pressures are all used to induce people into performances based on what she called "status obligations," which are often tied to gender and also compounded by race and class. In other words, people who have lower, gendered statuses—mothers, daughters, or wives, for instance—are forced through subtle and not so subtle pressures to perform care based on their status relation to the care receiver, or society at large.

In the marketplace, this coercion holds, which makes care a total anomaly in contemporary times among other forms of work. Starting in the nineteenth century, most forms of work became based in an understanding of exchange rather than an expression of status. Today, we expect a service provided to be exchanged for a fee—hourly pay or a salary. Even when it is not, we will still expect an exchange to take place. A service might sometimes be exchanged with another service or a product in a situation that is more reminiscent of barter. A service might even be performed with an abstract expectation of exchange through future reciprocity (e.g., I will water your plants, but I know you will help me with my cat when I next leave town). Care, however, unlike other kinds of work, has remained what Glenn calls "pre-modern" from a labor perspective. This means that care, including its core performance of emotional labor, has retained the attributes of being a "forced gift," holding barely any requirement or expectation for compensation, recognition, or exchange. While care and emotional labor severely overlap, my theory is that it is the emotional labor component within care, as opposed to the intellectual or physical labor parts of it, that enables it to be so based in status and therefore still coercively extracted—even as a facet of otherwise paid labor.

This comfort we have with emotional labor being mined is perhaps clearest in the tipped service industry, where more than four million American workers, a majority of them women working in bars and restaurants, earn a living.[13] In the restaurant industry, itself the employer of 10 percent of Americans, most establishment owners do not pay servers and bartenders a full wage. They pay them a tipped subminimum wage, which stands at $2.13 an hour federally to this day. Working a ten-hour day shift? Then according to federal law, your earnings for your work could be as low as $21 for the whole day:

an absurdly low amount, which represents a fraction—around one seventh—of the living wage.[14]

Of course, most workers make more than what their employers pay them thanks to tips left by customers, who carry the burden of workers' wages passed on to them by employers. From an emotional labor perspective, this is the ultimate manifestation of the duplicity of a system relying on the emotional labor of employees to turn a profit—but wholly unwilling to pay for it.

What is it that is being measured when patrons decide how much to tip? Quality of service? Sure, but what does that mean exactly? Mostly, this goes far beyond prompt and reliable taking and delivery of orders. It is about the experience provided. Did the servers smile? Were they friendly, agreeable, and professional presenting? Did they create a good experience for you? Really, the core of whether or not servers are seen as doing a good job is the degree to which they are doing the classical emotional labor of adapting the expression of their emotions to transmit a prescribed set of emotions to their customers as part of the brand of the establishment they are working for. Servers are making a living almost entirely off emotional labor. But it is seen as totally acceptable for that emotional labor to not be paid for by employers. In part because of this, tipped workers are twice as likely to be living in poverty as other workers.[15] This schema in turn throws servers into subsistence relationships with customers, setting them up for dangerously unregulated interactions that also become emblems and reinforcers of lower status.

Kelly, a thirty-one-year-old server who works in a hamburger restaurant off a highway in southeast Michigan, confirmed to me that being bubbly for customers is not only the avenue for tips; it is the difference between economic survival and destitution. "You just smile and say cheese, put on a happy face, and do the best you can. At the end of the day, you just pray that you walk away with some money."

A single mother who recently fled a bad relationship, she is staying on her sister's sofa when I speak to her. There is no way she can afford a place of her own. She tells me repeatedly that her job is "hard work," but one of the most important parts of it is not letting customers see what she is really going through—textbook emotional labor. Kelly also makes sure to keep her demeanor upbeat around her manager, who is in charge of shift distribution. Being given weekend and dinner shifts instead of early week and lunch shifts can double, even triple what you take home at the end of the week—less than $200 for a week's work versus upward of $600. Tips are needed to earn a decent wage but also to pay for all the health care, retirement, holidays, and personal days her restaurant employer is legally allowed to withhold from her and her colleagues.

One of Kelly's colleagues, Chasity, tells me she has worked in restaurants for years with excruciatingly painful stress injuries—carpal tunnel in her hands and a weak knee that demanded an operation—caused by the job. But she keeps going, forcing herself to show warmth, deference, and welcome. It is the condition upon which she can make ends meet.

Economists call "feminization of labor"[16] the refusal to recognize and fully compensate feminine fields of work—such as care, service, and attention work—that are becoming the bulk of the economy. Government helps the power holders in private feminized industries, including the service sector, by not requiring employers to provide the same basic labor rights to their workers that have been common in masculine industries, such as manufacturing, since the 1930s. This economic arrangement is heavily reliant on the belief that feminized emotional labor is an expression of diminished status that deserves little in exchange for its performance.

Dianne Avery, a professor emerita at the University of Buffalo School of Law, described tipping practices as gendered, feudal throwbacks. "What tipped workers represent for the moment of that exchange is an intimate master–servant relation," she told me in an interview, remarking on the hypocrisy of the thriving of tipping in the United States, a democracy that prides itself in having left medieval class systems behind in Europe.

The origins of tipping can actually be traced back to Europe, when a servile class of workers hoped benevolent upper-class members would throw them a coin or leave them a note after the execution of deeds. Americans traveling to Europe in the early nineteenth century were reported to be appalled at the undemocratic, class-driven practice,[17] an almost perfect role reversal for what happens today when tourists arriving in the United States are shocked to find that adding 20 percent to the cost of their food outing for the server is not only normal but expected.

This paradox does not just expose the insincerity of America's democratic principles when they are translated into economic practice, it deepens our understanding of the deprivation of liberty embedded in emotional labor. Chasity and Kelly aren't smiling because it's the expression of their natural selves; they are smiling because it's work. But it's their dependency on a customer's uncertain magnanimity—because their emotional labor is not seen as necessarily worthy of exchange—that puts them in a spot that feels compromising to the core.

Diamanté headband sparkling, eyes fixed on me, Chasity confides customers have physically assaulted her, and sexual harassment is so routine she believes customers must think their tipping gives them access to sexual favors entirely outside of her will or job description. It is hard not to see this as a trap. A 2014 study of almost seven hundred tipped workers by the Restaurant Opportunities Centers United found that 80 percent of female servers experienced sexual harassment from customers.[18] Another study from 2020 found that harassment of servers had significantly increased during the COVID-19 pandemic, with the health crisis giving way to a host of new specialized sexual comments. Servers reported patrons making comments like "I can't ever imagine myself social distancing from your sexy ass," and demanding servers take their mask off their face so they could decide how much to tip.[19]

The creative new attacks on bodily integrity, to now include the threat of infection from a deadly disease, only make the power dynamics at play in this scenario more explicit. Avery, the law professor, explained that old-fashioned, classist, and racist views dating back to the nineteenth century still expect respectable women—in other words white middle- or upper-class women—to stay home, and women working in drinking establishments to be sex workers. "There is a long thread that has continued there. Women's place is in the home. Well, if they are leaving the home, then what are they doing it for?" Avery asked, taking on the perspective of a male harasser.

Women may now occupy close to half of the formal workforce, but public spaces are still seen as male, so when women enter them, it is still assumed to be according to men's rules, for the male gaze, or for male entertainment.[20] This leap that associates a status of sex object or sex worker with a woman worker helps entrench a lower status that justifies poor—even punitive—treatment across the board. Emotional labor is joined by perceived sexual labor as feminized forms of work that under patriarchal capitalism belong in the home and are to be shunned if they exit it. Alison, a server I spoke to in Chicago, put the absurdity of the system in the clearest way. "You don't go to a bank and flirt with the teller, and then the teller is relying on you—the customer—for money, for their wage," she implored.

In order to make rent, workers find themselves having to enact a version of a legendary medieval practice according to which feudal lords claimed to have the right to the bodies of their serfs' wives on their wedding nights, referred to as "droit du seigneur."[21] Nor is it in restaurants' or bar franchises' interests to fully protect their workers when they are themselves turning a profit from the very promise of that kind of experience. Positioning a server in a way that is ripe for sexual inuendo allows for the diminishing of their status across the board, which then consolidates the devaluing of emotional labor (that businesses needn't pay for) while requiring it be done (because they rely on it for profit).

Even when it is not an explicit component of a job, such as in the case of care and service industries, women in the workplace find themselves performing emotional labor in ways that are neither fully paid for nor truly optional.

When Devin McNalley, a Michigan native, landed a job in marketing in a large legacy automotive company in her twenties, she couldn't wait to prove her worth and become a valued part of the team. Her university degree in communications and her self-starter attitude that had previously led her to transform a server job into a PR one made her believe she could do good work and get noticed, and even start to meaningfully climb up the corporate ladder.

Devin was entering the corporate side of a male-dominated industry, but she didn't blink at it. Her mother was among the first generation of women who entered previously male-dominated white-collar industries en masse in the second half of the twentieth century.[22] The figure of a corporate woman was normal to her, and she had good reason to believe her qualifications combined with her natural intelligence, charm, and assertiveness would all work in her favor as she sought to get ahead.

Only a few years prior, in 2010, Sheryl Sandberg, Facebook's COO, delivered a viral TED Talk titled "Why We Have Too Few Women Leaders" that was followed by a 2013 bestselling book, *Lean In*.[23] Her insight promised younger women like Devin the tools to not just enter former male-dominated industries but do what few women of older generations had managed once they were there: climb up the corporate ladder and thrive.

In her talk, and more in depth in her book, Sandberg advocated for three broad, individual changes women could make to get ahead. First, she called on women to independently grab a seat at the table, act like they belonged in positions of power, and be as self-assured as the men in the room who didn't hesitate to center themselves and their ideas regardless of whether they had been invited. She posited that women tended to lean out in professional settings, where they needed to *lean in.* Second, she advocated that women understand the importance of picking the right intimate partner: someone who would help share the private load so that women could spend the time they needed at work advancing their careers. Third, she pressed women to be ambitious about their careers—not "clock out," as she put it, years before they needed to. In particular, she warned against defeatist attitudes and worries around motherhood and careers that were expressed years before women were even thinking of starting a family. Focus on pushing for that promotion right now, she invited, and only tackle the barrier you have identified as and when it happens, later. Sandberg's message was clear and empowering: with the right kind of individual attitude, personal life choices, and toning down of apologetic feminine behaviors, women could finally move forward, and up. Her ideas hit a nerve with women in America and beyond. To this day, over forty-four thousand "lean in circles," small groups of women organizing around Sandberg's messaging, have popped up around the world.[24]

Devin, entering the workforce just as this worldwide cultural phenomenon was taking place, knew that if anyone was unafraid of taking a seat at the table, leaning in, and making their voice heard when they knew their stuff, it was her. Soon enough, an opportunity arose.

Invited into an all-male marketing meeting with her team and some higher-ups geared at tactics for "reaching millennials," which was then the largest young generation over eighteen, she remembers listening dumbfounded as the men in the room proposed a strategy centering the use of print magazines for advertising. There was no mention of social media venues like Instagram, Snapchat, or Facebook, let alone any inquiring as to the degree young people actually read physical magazines. It was instantly clear to her that this would not work. Her insight crystallized even further when meeting attendees proposed—to widespread approval—a "sticker" idea, which would involve free stickers in these print magazines that could be peeled out and stuck on objects or cars. The idea could not have seemed more out of touch to a member of a generation that receives most of its information online and is unlikely to subscribe to much at all in print.[25] Devin strongly thought this strategy would not resonate with any of her contemporaries, let alone reach them. As a member of the marketing team as well as one of the youngest attendees sitting at the table, who could actually identify as a member of the millennial group the whole meeting was about, this point seemed pertinent to share.

She recalls plainly enunciating, "This is a really bad idea," before going into a clear explanation of the problems with the proposed ideas. The room froze.

Devin clarifies that this is how she had witnessed the men in the meeting talk to one another, regardless of status or age. She was simply interacting with them the way she had observed them interact with each other. But for a woman, this kind of behavior carried penalties, she learned. Her lean-in moment, alas, did not carry any rewards. Quite the contrary.

A male colleague from another team turned to her and asked whether she shouldn't be quiet and take notes, in spite of her not being a part of any support, administrative, or secretarial staff. After the meeting, well-meaning older women, who had heard of the incident, sought her out. She thought she might receive sympathy or shared shock. Instead, she received reprimand. "They told me the only way you are going to get ahead in the corporate world is to boost the male egos around you"—a form of emotional labor, making male colleagues and superiors feel good, specifically tied to affirming their power. It rang like a metaphorical invitation to constantly be engaging in a ceremony of kissing the ring. The cherry on the cake came when one of her male directors also chimed in in an email, telling her she "came across as really abrasive for a woman."

In particular, the use of the word "abrasive" was a trigger point for Devin. It felt like men around her were allowed to be just as direct, if not more, but she was being penalized with an adjective that was deeply gendered: a double standard in emotion expression requirements that seemed grossly unfair. She never witnessed a man be told off for objecting to an idea, however bluntly, let alone be told they were abrasive or even aggressive. And yet word got around and everyone in the company knew about that one sentence in the meeting and what that meant about Devin.

Devin talked to her mother, who works in human resources. She told her daughter to finesse her tone and learn how to adapt to some of the culture, something that felt hard to swallow. "I entered the workforce sort of naïve. I expected competition. I knew there was a pay inequality issue I needed to be aware of, but I didn't expect this."

The explicit, feminized tone policing and emotional labor expectations that made Devin feel like these new, added rules to the game were going to hinder her from getting noticed, and ultimately figuring out ways of working hard to get ahead, only became worse. Her female boss suggested, among other tips, that she add smileys to emails. Even digitally, she had to present as upbeat and nonthreatening to men. In all communications, she was expected to do the emotional labor of making sure she made people feel good, as a priority over and indeed a prerequisite to the actual requirements of her job.

Devin's lesson was a harsh one, but growing bodies of research show that her experience was somewhat predictable. One paper from 2018 posed the question of why, in spite of shrinking differences in career aspirations between genders over the last decade, women were still a minority in leadership positions and male-dominated professions.[26] Zooming in on 236 engineers at a big multinational company, 23 percent of them women, the study asked the surveyed engineers to answer questions about their own self-perceptions and also had colleagues and superiors assess them. Authors, jumping off evidence showing that men and women have similar self-confidence and understanding that radiating confidence is important to make progress in one's career, sought to measure how confident men and women were perceived by others. The authors found that competent engineers were perceived as equally confident, ambitious, and seeking to get ahead, regardless of gender. The authors then looked at the degree to which "confidence appearance" was indicative of workers' likelihood of getting ahead. This is where they found clear differences based on gender.

For men, being perceived as competent and confident were the two ingredients that led them to gain influence, opening the doors to rise up. Do well and act like you know what you are doing: a simple recipe. For women, simply having these two attributes was insufficient for career advancement. If women wanted to gain influence in the same way as their male counterparts did, they needed to also possess and display what is known in organizational psychology as "prosocial orientation." Prosocial orientation are those communal attributes that are often associated with the female gender: being other-oriented, concerned, and considerate of others' interests, as well as the company's interests, being sweet, caring, nurturing, and expressing thoughtfulness. Performing comforting stereotypes of womanhood was found to be an additional, implicit requirement for women to achieve success. In other words, doing their job was not enough. There was an extra layer of work required for them: they had to perform emotional labor.

For a lot of female workers, this is a catch-22. If you must be seen to be extremely considerate of other people's needs and sensitivities in order to advance, it can be difficult—at the same time—to also present as self-assured, assertive, and confident.

It's easy to observe that, much like the humiliation of sexual harassment acts as a way of making women feel a lack of power and a reminder that public spaces were created for men, forcing women to exhibit supportive, caring, and submissive traits toward others, even as they seek to use their brains on the same level playing field as men, acts as a way of reinforcing women's support-act role, thereby limiting women's ascension. The same applies to men of color, particularly for Black men, expected to engage in constant communication and presentation self-policing and submissive expressions to avoid racist stereotypes and penalties.

Of course, that is part of what Sandberg understood when she told generations of female workers to lean in: to rid themselves of secondary citizen status and behave like a winner. But this cannot be done as long as we haven't identified the selective, uneven emotional labor requirements.

These micro and macro injustices are given life through the deployment of a backlash effect,[27] similar to the one described in the previous chapter, but this time not just threatening individuals straying from gender norms with social penalties but with economic penalties too. This is made possible as people across genders engage in a policing of others and of themselves, conspiring—intentionally or not—to maintain rigid, prefabricated stereotypes. For women, expected constantly to be displaying nurturing, altruistic qualities, taking on what is called "agentic" behavior—dominant, assertive, competitive—seen as male in order to ascend professionally would inevitably cause such a backlash.

In order to modulate the backlash, and not be seen as too hungry for power or too eager to get ahead, women have to play a game of compensation. As they assert themselves as competent and confident, they must also dole out doses of reassuring emotional labor. Because these two sets of character traits are often cast in opposition to each other—as expressions of domination and submission rather than as complementary—conveying both at the same time can feel like an impossible bind. This becomes even more of a burden for anyone who veers from traditional, heteronormative behavioral scripts, particularly for those of us whose brains process social situations differently, whether because of neurodivergence or any other unseen reason. These charades of contradictory communication create roadblocks that compromise productivity rather than promote it, as some would have us believe.

One woman I interviewed, Hailey, who rose up to director in a large, male-dominated West Coast company, identifies and presents as queer, and tells me her instinctive communication style is outgoing, direct, and what might be seen traditionally as alpha. "I always came to meetings with all guns blazing," Hailey says, adding she easily inhabits "a male space in the workplace."

But as she climbed the ladder at her company and became surrounded by only men, she found that her gender expression was increasingly being ignored. Her female identity kept on being forced
down her throat by her male colleagues, and her queer, more masculine-
performing energy was squashed out. "I occupy this middle space. I
am a dyke, of course: I out myself all the time. But I still had to fill
some of those female expectations. I couldn't just live in this male box."

A male colleague sat her down and told her she needed to be more
discreet and couldn't just be her "outgoing self" anymore. She had to
do double the work to ingratiate herself in a way that was more feminine, regardless of whether that felt authentic to her identity. It didn't,
in fact. She started using "soft skills" she had mostly eschewed up until
then in her career and started having water cooler conversations and
coffee meetings on top of formal meetings in order to win people over,
be accepted, and get done the basic things she needed in the department she directed. "I used to think that the higher you get, the
more it's going to be based on accomplishments and skills, but I
don't know anymore."

She couldn't be herself: she was not afforded that space or that
privilege. The emotional labor she was forced into providing wasn't
expected of men, and the expectation, which also violated her gender
expression, felt debasing. By the time she left the company, she says
she is not sure whether she was most discriminated against because of
her perceived gender, her sexual orientation and related identity, or her
ideas, which were pushing for greater sustainability and attention to
underserved communities.

The ability to change, mask, or suppress the expression of our authentic emotions is a uniquely human characteristic. We can laugh to
suit a situation even if we find it supremely unfunny, appear despon-
dent to suit another when inside we are giggling, and appear passively
pleasant in situations in between. We can all do this and, in fact, all
engage in this, to varying degrees, all the time.

At work, the expectation that people should do the emotional labor
to put on a professional face is not something reserved for just women.

Being professional will likely include a basic level of politeness, the exchange of a few formal niceties—greetings, a smile, maybe a question or two about the weekend. There will likely be the expectation of a levelheadedness and an evening or modulating of the temperature of emotional expression in communications—whether in person, over the phone, or over email: not too hot and angry, and not too cold and abrupt.

But because deference and filtering of emotions go with power, in traditional work environments, the higher up you go, the less emotional labor you absolutely have to do. An intern will be expected to be more deferential than a junior associate, who will be expected to be more deferential than a vice president, who will be expected to be more deferential than the founder and CEO. This holds until you introduce elements of gender expression and identity, race and class, as further and less linear expressions of power. A male junior associate might get away with being abrupt with colleagues where a female senior associate will not. A white male associate may feel free to speak loudly and animatedly with colleagues, where a Black male associate may be told to quiet down and be issued a warning.

As it stands, emotional labor proves marginalization from the center—but it needn't.

It has been almost three decades since journalist Daniel Goleman first published his bestselling book *Emotional Intelligence*, which shone a light on the value of nonintellectual, emotional traits in business contexts.[28] The book made a case, which resonated with many and has only continued to be backed by research since, that being self-aware, self-regulated, motivated, empathetic, and having good social skills at work makes for better workers, better work environments, and also, crucially here, better leaders.

The choice to talk about "emotional intelligence" as a set of traits desirable in leadership rather than "emotional labor" as the act of putting emotional intelligence to work was significant. While the cultural moment resulting from the book was pivotal for the valuing of emotional literacy generally, its narrow focus on upward mobility in white-collar industries totally sidestepped what could have been a radically transformative conversation for all workplaces. Such a lapse hindered a deep power analysis of the workplace and obscured the coercive emotional labor already being done by those at the margins. Failing to treat emotional intelligence in action as a form of work that requires time, effort, and skill the same way other forms of work do meant that only some select workers were lauded for its performance. And in not marking its existence in all ranks of all industries, white-collar, service, health care, and beyond, we stopped short of intentionally shifting toward a culture of rewarding emotional labor rather than off-loading it.

———————

As for Devin, she has long since moved on from the marketing job in the automotive industry that silenced her in the meeting. She says she looked around and realized that while there were women working in the departments she was excited about, hardly any of them were trying to climb up the corporate ladder. Their advice was not designed to gain power, influence, or equality. Their advice was survival advice alone. "I never chose that route. I just didn't want to sit and be quiet," she says.

"Women think they have to pick one set of personality traits— that being feminine is incompatible with leading, and that if you want to lead, you cannot be feminine. Let's take dominant and submissive out of the equation. There are moments when I am dominant and moments when I am not. Besides, I am a strong believer that women are strong leaders because of our traits. I believe in leading with intelligence and communicating with empathy."

She found a fit within a firm that didn't feel like it was constantly and unfairly monitoring the expression of her contributions, and she has risen up. But before she left the position, she was thrown a bone she still isn't sure what to make of. A while after her meeting room incident, she was approached by a senior colleague and asked to be the face of the company for an internal communications campaign. She agreed, thinking other opportunities might come with it, but none did.

Instead, a photo of her was blown up to giant proportions, and, for a while, colleagues entering their office were greeted by her smiling face—providing mute emotional labor for all, even as they were largely deprived of her ideas. She was finally given space and representation. But this time, her two-dimensional avatar, fixed in time, displayed and conveyed only the controlled emotions her company wanted out of her.

THREE

The History of Extraction

SUBORDINATION

Anna and I meet one cold December morning in a charming, rickety café nestled among old redbrick homes with fire escapes in her current Brooklyn, New York, neighborhood. The place she has chosen to meet doubles up as a vintage store selling a selection of odd curiosities and furniture pieces. It looks like it was frozen in time in the late 1800s. As I look for her, I am half expecting a man with a pointed gray beard and a monocle to pop out from underneath the counter and ask me what potion I would like today. But before such an apparition is able to offer me snake oil or rhubarb grains from a mahogany chest, I spot Anna in the front room, cat's-eye glasses on her nose, soft-looking black sweater keeping her warm.

Anna is nanny to a five-and-a-half-year-old girl named Mia, the only child of two parents who live around the corner. Mia's mother works in the food industry and her father works in finance. Anna and I have been trying to meet and talk for a few days, but Anna has had to cancel at the last minute a couple of times because little Mia has been sick, and the usual hours she has off work have been compromised as a consequence. Anna is twenty-five and has been a nanny for six years. When I ask her what her job involves exactly, she tells me it "entails everything" tied to Mia: being in charge of her scheduling, clothes, food, schooling, her general well-being, and her emotional, intellectual, and physical development.

Tangibly, Anna's job starts around seven a.m. when she prepares Mia for school. There is a lull in between drop-off and school pickup that Anna either takes for herself or uses to do Mia-related chores, including laundry and scheduling. Active nannying picks back up midafternoon and lasts until seven p.m. or nine p.m., depending on whether Mia's mother is around to put her daughter to sleep. She works at least five days, often six days a week.

Gentle-mannered and warm, Anna describes herself as "the opposite of a type A personality" and is explicit about the emotional labor she performs as part of her duties. "When I am with her you have to be happy and cheery," she tells me, explaining that while Mia is in school or at an activity she has taken her to, she does housework exclusively associated to Mia but also takes the time to unwind and center herself. She knows how important it is that she be "on" for the child in her care. Anna's emotional labor is tied to providing Mia with feelings of love and safety, which involves creating a positive environment and successfully executing the routines of Mia's life, sure. But Anna's emotional labor to the child in her care also involves providing her with an environment for emotional development, emotional exploration, and emotional literacy as she processes the world around her with prodigious sensitivity, ability, and speed. Sensory feelings must be given explanations and translated into emotions that must be given words.

"It's a lot in that she is learning and having all kinds of experiences that need to be synthesized because she is five and a half and everything requires an explanation. Being the adult in the situation, you have to be there for her when she's happy or sad, or [try] to understand where she's coming from. Be very sensitive to her and not lose patience or not get upset at her because she's not being difficult, she's just trying to understand what's going on around her."

Anna's description of the fundamental emotional labor she provides Mia in terms of emotional needs and development is likely recognizable to any adult—parent, nanny, aunt, uncle, or sibling—who has taken care of a child for more than an afternoon. Children do not simply need food, clothing, and rest; they need affection and attention that expands to the expression and containment of moods, the fielding of questions, and the managing of the constant deciphering of internal and external universes. They need the shepherding and secure attachment that will help ground them in those essential human emotions of belonging, connection, and love. Engaging in this kind of emotional labor with children nurtures their emotional literacy—their ability to identify and express emotions—which helps them then create meaning and understanding within themselves and relate it to the outside world.[1]

Anna tells me she has figured out which language of love each child she has cared for needed. Mia's is physical touch. "She loves hugs and cuddles: ninety-nine percent of the time if she is not playing, she will be sitting on my lap or snuggling in my arm. It's how she receives love. Which is really, really sweet. It's a lot, because when she's sick she just wants to curl up, of course, because she's not feeling well."

She smiles describing trying to get various physical tasks done while having a small child in her arms, refusing to leave. She's not resentful though, and besides, Anna says the affection Mia gives her is mutual. "I don't know how I could care for someone else's kid and not grow attached to them. For me the caring for them involves getting emotionally involved in what they're going through and kind of what they need. I don't think that can happen, to me at least, if I do not like them and if I do not end up caring for them." Genuine affection is a part of how she can perform her deep emotional labor duties well, but that doesn't mean it makes the tasks any less wearying.

"It's clearly fun and rewarding but sometimes I am really, really tired at the end of the day. The way I would describe it, if you go on a run, or you go swim for an hour and it feels great, your body feels great, but you get out of the pool and you're just like 'Aaaaah, I have used all my energy now.' Sometimes, it can feel like that a lot."

Anna tells me her exhaustion is tied to her emotional activities far more than her physical ones—like carrying Mia or doing her laundry. It's the always being positive, thoughtful, receptive, and engaging, always being "on": that's what leaves her totally drained at night when she gets home to her boyfriend. There, too, emotional labor awaits. Her boyfriend has his own emotional needs and demands. "I do feel like I do a lot there, too, and then I am left on complete empty," she says of the compounding effects of emotional labor in her work home and her actual home.

Actively loving Mia makes her job feel meaningful, of course, but it also makes it harder. It makes finding slim moments for recovery imperative but stressful, especially as she manages her own romantic and familial relationships. As excellent at emotional labor as Anna is, burnout feels just around the corner.

The mostly female legion of formal caregivers—from nannies to home health-care aids, nursing assistants, and beyond—have so far largely been absent from the debate around emotional labor. This exclusion is curious given that emotions are so clearly at the heart of the activities performed by those propping up our society and economy. This has been done with obliviousness in some cases and with well-meaning but misplaced intentions in others.

Academics[2] tend to talk about the topic of "care" when it comes to these categories of workers, while the term "emotional labor" in private or public is often boxed in to being seen as a problem of the middle and upper classes, to be treated separately. In some circles, popular renderings of emotional labor have become synonymous with whining: entitled white feminism at its worst. One academic I interviewed, a leader in her field, advanced that contemporary emotional labor concerns were totally outside of the everyday concerns of working-class people or people on the losing end of systemic inequality.

Such separations may seem noble, but they enable the overlooking of common origin problems that, if clearly denounced, would help move the entire conversation forward. It is the devaluing of feminized emotional labor that makes care jobs so precarious. It is the propagation of a belief that love and empathy in action are not work that helps hinder labor rights and proper pay. It is the requirement that emotional labor should just emanate, uncomplaining, from feminized and racialized groups of people in exchange for little to nothing that ensures emotional labor go hand in hand with exploitation.

Besides stopping us from seeing the whole picture, the idea that working-class women or women of color are not burdened with heavy, extractive emotional labor expectations at work as well as at home is not only ludicrous, it's offensive. The fact that Anna, a nanny who identifies as Afro-Latina, provides vast amounts of expected emotional labor in her professional life does not, suddenly, somehow invalidate it as a site for scrutiny. And it certainly does not mean that Anna does not have to deal with complaints and pressure from her boyfriend, who wants more time and emotional presence from her in private. These kinds of dismissals deny full emotional landscapes to working-class women and women of color.

One woman employed as a domestic worker in Detroit confided that the extensive emotional labor demands of her ex-husband, who expected to be catered to at all times, had been the most defining aspect of her early adulthood. She left him and was now in therapy. Was her experience with emotional labor not real? Is it really that shocking that she went to therapy? If anything, the additional weight of financial concerns, of insecure wages, and being in an environment with more crime, more historical state violence, or more addiction—these are all factors that make the soothing work of love and the nurturing involved in sustaining communities even more indispensable.

The erasure of emotional labor concerns from the private emotional landscapes of less privileged women doesn't just help further dehumanize them. Treating the topic as exclusively elitist helps ingrain the sexist idea that women's concerns are just *so very silly*, dismissible as irrelevant, trivial. *Complaining about emotions as work? What will these ladies find to complain about next?*

There is, in the short term, undoubtedly a perverse incentive for more privileged women to simply kick the can of devalued labor down the road and pass its responsibility on to a less privileged woman they can underpay. Hanging on to the sense of their own injustice, they fail—or refuse—to see their own complicity in the system toward others. This division that impedes progress is a temporary fix only for some. As long as people performing feminized tasks, including women of different backgrounds, do not see one another as fellow workers, there can be no colossal change.

One woman I interviewed in New York included in her accounts of emotional labor the burden of having to deal with her toddler's nanny, who had a teenage son and an abusive husband and had started confiding in her female employer. The irony in complaining about someone who you arguably depend on for the performance of her own devalued emotional labor left me dumbstruck. How could my interviewee not see the irony, how could she so brazenly heighten her plight above her nanny's? The devaluing and invisibility of emotional labor may have felt real to this interviewee in her blood family dynamic, but it undoubtedly affected her nanny even more—and most certainly to the employer's benefit.

The point with emotional labor is not that it inherently points to an injustice. When seen, when valued or appreciated, or when part of an exchange, a mutuality, an ecosystem where love is power—then it needn't be exploitative. Quite the contrary: doing emotional labor for people who are doing it for you is the goal, not the problem.

We have to connect the dots if we are to expose the problem and heal. The inclination—a sexist, classist, and racist one—with which we jump at the opportunity to commodify-at-a-discount the emotions of working-class people and people of color in public but deny the existence of any full, private emotional landscapes is part of the same sexist inclination that silently extracts women of all classes' labor in private. In very real ways, our oppressions really are bound together.

In a democratic society that would like to claim to have put all instances of status obligations between groups in the past, historical scrutiny that sheds light on the endurance and particularity of emotional labor dynamics across gender, class, and race lines is more needed than ever.

———

In her book *They Were Her Property: White Women as Slave Owners in the American South*, history professor Stephanie Jones-Rogers explains that before the abolition of slavery wealthy white women, who often could not inherit land, were instead left wealth from their fathers through the bequeathal of enslaved people. According to Jones-Rogers's findings, white women accounted for up to 40 percent of owners of enslaved people.[3] Select enslaved Black women who were taken from the field to work in white people's homes were often wet nurses, forced into an intimate form of physical and emotional labor for the benefit of white families.

Among the details bringing home the cruelty of the arrangement between women of different groups is the fact that white women would seek out enslaved Black women who had newly given birth and force them to abandon their own infants for the benefit of the white ones. Worse, historical accounts show that newly pregnant white women would sometimes orchestrate for enslaved Black women to be raped—a sanctioned assault ensuring that white woman and Black woman would give birth within similar periods. One of the reasons white women did this was to avoid the inconvenience of themselves being "slaves" to their biological children, Jones-Rogers writes, citing texts and testimonies from the time.

The violence enslaved Black women faced tied to forced labor was doubled in a way that is hard to grapple with. Through their forced work, they created economic gains for white families. Through pregnancy, childbirth, and child-rearing, they provided the next generation of en-slaved laborers, while sometimes even being forced to care for the next generation of enslavers.

In the United States, to understand the devaluing of emotional labor is to understand some of the foundational principles of an economic system that did not just rely on the free labor of women but on the free labor of people brought from Africa by force, first in-dentured, and then enslaved.[4] The meeting of both gender and race, and how we think of the meeting of the two, exposes some of the contradictions so deep within emotional labor—namely that we see it as so important, so essential, but are also so comfortable with making it invisible and extractive.

One way to understand this, and to understand how unconscionable enslavement mentality endured after abolition when it came to emo-tional labor, is to understand the fictitious figure in the white American popular imagination of the "mammy." The mammy trope, brought to life in every manner of cultural space including books, films, corporate brands, advertisements, and plays, is one of the most enduring racial car-icatures of Black women in America. Under slavery, mammies were por-trayed as large, dark-skinned, smiling, asexual, comforting figures who worked inside white enslavers' homes and took care of the home while playing a nanny-type role with white children. Conjured up as en-tirely, enthusiastically giving and willing, mammies were depicted as having no real connection to other Black people and no emotional life outside the white families they served. Perhaps one of the best-known fictional characters in this role is the one actually named Mammy in white Margaret Mitchell's 1936 *Gone with the Wind*, which depicts the intimate tie between a female Black enslaved woman and a young white woman she has mothered, told from a white enslaver's perspec-tive. This fictional Mammy was depicted in the book's film adaptation by Hattie McDaniel in 1939.

Interestingly, and contrary to popular renderings, scholars have found that only the wealthiest enslavers could afford to have enslaved women inside their homes, and when they did, light-skinned women tended to be invited in, not dark-skinned women.[5] In other words, the figure of the mammy is an ahistorical, fictional white postscript creation that did not represent reality. Why was she created then, and why was she so endemic?

Post emancipation, and during the Jim Crow era, well into the 1960s, the trope was used as a distracting myth to rationalize a newly widespread economic form of extraction: Black women entering domestic servitude en masse under conditions that first-person accounts from the time claim resembled slavery. The willing and comforting mammy narrative served the purpose of preserving white innocence and the social, political, and economic interests of white America as white people entered into a far more common exploitative domestic dynamic than was the case during slavery.[6]

In the first half of the twentieth century, most middle-class white women, adhering to views of white femininity that deemed them too fragile and precious to undertake arduous domestic chores, employed a domestic servant. In the South, middle-class as well as working-class white women employed Black domestic servants. White women were able to perform their brand of delicate femininity only thanks to the underpaid labor of women of color and immigrant women who were judged particularly "naturally" suited for service. Just like when mammies were portrayed as dependent and unintelligent, racist and sexist benevolent justifications included the ideas that Black and Mexican women were unable to look after themselves and that Asian women were inherently quiet, subservient, and used to poor living conditions already.[7]

In one account[8] from 1912, told to a reporter and published in the newspaper *The Independent*, a Black domestic servant in Georgia employed as a "nurse" (what we might call a nanny today) harrowingly described her conditions. Expected to live with her employers, working fourteen- to sixteen-hour days, and allowed home only once a week, she was paid a salary that did not cover basic costs for her and her three children. Her children had to supplement the family income with domestic work of their own, while their mother, in her forties, nursed someone else's eleven-month-old baby on top of being governess and playmate to her employers' other three children.

Speaking of her own experience but also of the experiences of other Black women she knew, two-thirds of whom she estimated worked as domestic servants, she described her intimate labor relations as a mass phenomenon. "A million of us are introduced daily to the privacy of a million chambers throughout the South, and hold in our arms a million white children, thousands of whom, as infants, are suckled at our breasts—during my lifetime I myself have served as 'wet nurse' to more than a dozen white children."

Called "Mammy," she noted how usual it was for Black domestic workers to be called by a reductive diminutive, a first name, or the task they were employed to execute (e.g., Cook, Nurse, Mammy, Mary Lou)—instead of being called with reverence Mr./Mrs./Miss followed by their last name. She was allowed into white public spaces so long as she was with white children, and the master-servant working relationship was made clear, but the absence of white children deprived her of that freedom of movement.

At the end of her testimonial, she wondered whether white women might be possible advocates for better labor conditions. It seemed so logical to her. "What we need is present help, present sympathy, better wages, better hours, more protections, and a chance to breathe for once while alive as free women. If none others will help us, it would seem that the Southern white women themselves might do so in their own defense, because we are rearing their children—we feed them, we bathe them, we teach them to speak the English language, and in numberless instances we sleep with them—and it is inevitable that the lives of their children will in some measure be pure or impure according as they are affected by contact with their colored nurses."

The answer to that call has been a long time coming, but it continues to be dodged. This is true thanks to how blurred labor becomes when it is performed behind closed doors and when the labor is entangled with emotional ties and performances. It is true because of how desensitized we have allowed ourselves to become to the casual labor exploitation of all women, especially women of color. And it is also true because staring at the issue head-on would force us to contend with the fact that believing all humans are equal is fundamentally incompatible with labor exploitation.

The ways in which, inversely, labor exploitation is enabled by subtle forms of dehumanization, including in intimate spheres, was one of the questions that circled through the mind of Kellie Carter Jackson, a historian and professor in the department of Africana studies at Wellesley College, when her grandmother Ethel Phillips died in 2014 at the age of ninety-five. Jackson realized there were many details of her grandmother's life she was lacking, in large part because for fifty-nine years Jackson's grandmother Mrs. Phillips had been a domestic worker. A Black woman who had emigrated from the South to find work, Mrs. Phillips spent most of her six decades of work employed within the home of three generations of a Dearborn, Michigan–based upper-middle-class white family named the Clarks. Jackson reflected that her grandmother's employers had spent more time with her than she had.

The family death coincided with the historian becoming a mother for the first time, and as she prepared herself to go back to work and began a search for a nanny to take care of her toddler, she found herself wondering about her grandmother's time with the Clarks. What had her grandmother's relationship with her employers actually been like? How did they relate to her? And how was the relationship inscribed within larger labor, race, and gender systems? Jackson interviewed members of her own family as well as surviving members of the Clark family and unpacked some of her findings in an academic paper on the subject.[9]

In interviews with Jackson, the Clarks spoke very warmly of Mrs. Phillips, Jackson's grandmother. "She didn't work for us, she was a member of the family," said Diane Clark, who was two years old when

Mrs. Phillips first came to work for her parents as a young woman, and whose own children in turn were sometimes watched by her in her twilight years.

But for all of her familial claims, Diane Clark was confused about what Mrs. Phillips's last name was, never having found out that in her private sphere, outside of her economic home, she had had an abusive and short-lived first marriage to a man named Cleavus Keeten, who abandoned her. After the abandonment, in a much happier circumstance, she went on to meet her second husband and partner of half a century, Edward Phillips. For decades after she remarried and changed her last name to match that of her husband, the Clarks, who had not followed the circumstances of her private life, continued to think Ethel Phillips's last name was Keeten. When her husband would come to pick her up from work, they humiliatingly greeted Edward Phillips by calling him "Mr. Keeten," the name of his wife's abuser. Nobody corrected them, though. The Phillipses could not risk any penalties—job loss among others—that could have come with a correction.

Diane's younger brother Steven Clark also recalled Mrs. Phillips's presence in the home very fondly. Steven was able to recall her work routine and affectionately trace his interactions with her from his own childhood when he would sometimes stay home and "help" Mrs. Phillips work. He also recalled her interactions with him as a young man when he had to get out of bed by midday in time for her to clean his bedroom. Steven, in his fifties at the time of the interview, kept a few pictures of Mrs. Phillips in his home. One small photo of her was in his bedroom and another one of her he kept in his laundry cabinet. He explained to Jackson, Mrs. Phillips's granddaughter, that looking at her photo as he reached for the Tide detergent to do laundry, while he was raising his teenage daughters alone, reminded him of her work ethic and inspired him to know that he, too, could finish chores.

While Steven's placement of Mrs. Phillips's photo close to dirty clothes appeared to tell a tender and inspiring story in his eyes, Jackson has an entirely different interpretation. "The placement of Ethel's picture inside his laundry cabinet relegates his memory of her to another cleaning product, as a proverbial 'Mrs. Clean,' who comes to life and befriends him during childhood. While the image of Ethel posed with his mother, aunt, and uncle may have suggested that 'Ethel was family,' the image kept in the cabinet is perhaps a more accurate summation of her relationship to them, as a laborer," she writes. Jackson compares this act to the use of images of Black people as part of brands to sell products, like Aunt Jemima syrup or Uncle Ben's rice. Such placements and amalgamations do not just reduce Black humanity to something that can be bought and sold, they help disseminate nostalgic, racial stereotypes.

When I spoke to Jackson, the historian, in an interview, she posited that the Clarks would likely be "shocked" if they read her academic paper, which frames the intimacy with which they describe their relationship with Mrs. Phillips firmly within a labor context. "You don't place the photo of someone you love by the laundry. That's not what you do with the photo of someone you love," she states plainly.

In her paper, and to me, Jackson points out that her grandmother did not work until she was seventy-nine out of love for the Clarks, she worked until she was seventy-nine because she could not afford to retire beforehand. She wasn't paid enough by them, and she wasn't eligible for retirement or benefits. Her economic family may have felt genuine affection toward Mrs. Phillips, but that affection was used as a veneer to gloss over the reality of her unprotected employment status they were all implicated in maintaining over decades. Was the affection real, or was it a delusional, sentimental pill they used to help them feel less guilty about that reality?

When Jackson interviewed Diane Clark in 2015, the latter was astonished to learn that Mrs. Phillips's daughter, Jackson's mother, was a professor with a PhD and that three of her daughters, Mrs. Phillips's granddaughters, had PhDs too. Jackson's nephew, who had recently enrolled at MIT in another PhD program at the time of our interview, would represent the third generation of PhDs in the Phillips family—all direct descendants of the woman they knew as Ethel.

"How did that happen?" Diane Clark asked Jackson, incredulous, betraying her own bias buying into a belief system that advances that your circumstances are the reflection of your abilities, and not of a very specific historic and social context that formed them. Indeed, Mrs. Phillips's abilities had nothing to do with her commitment to a lifetime of domestic labor that denied her the dignity of a fair retirement. She was the valedictorian of her eighth-grade class in Mississippi but was unable to continue her education. At the time "there were only four public high schools in the entire South that African American children could attend that would have provided a classical education," Jackson writes. Surely a better question would have been, "What could Ethel, as valedictorian of her eighth grade, have become had racism and sexism not prevented her from achieving her own dreams?" Jackson poses.

The Clarks remained convinced Ethel Phillips had felt part of the family and grateful for her situation, Jackson tells me. But she reflects that the voice missing in her paper was that of her grandmother, who was deceased. While the Clarks seemed convinced of the mutuality of the emotional tie, Jackson pointed out to me that her grandmother likely had no choice in expressing affection. It was an inherent part of the job—a job that, for all its inadequate compensation, she could not afford to lose.

These delusional beliefs of nurturing love as a natural performance deployed by a Black woman for the benefit of white people, as an act of emotional labor they are entitled to be receiving, is one that Jackson can identify with in her own life very clearly. Even with her PhD, her academic accolades, and her appointment as a professor at a prestigious university, Jackson tells me that she is still not exempt from mammy trope–related expectations at the hands of students and people in her surroundings. "People think that just because I have a soft demeanor, because I am a Black woman, they can come to me with their problems, that they will be comforted," she says. These emotional labor expectations in a work context have nothing to do with her actual qualifications but end up taking up time and energy she is not able to put in elsewhere.

There is still an anticipation that white people get to be mothered by Black women, that it is something to be expected, to be taken without question, she says. "America glorifies Black women taking care of white children and white people under conditions of labor exploitation, but then, on the other hand, demonizes Black mothers who dare to have their own Black children," she tells me.[10]

———

Back in the twenty-first century, but in the coffee shop that is reminiscent of the nineteenth, Anna, the nanny, is gushing about Mia, the girl in her care, using words like "spectacular" and "awesome." But as enthusiastic as she is, Anna also understands that there were ways in which she was pushed into this job by her own family dynamics and social expectations outside it.

Aged nineteen, she remembers sitting in an introductory class at New York University, where she got her undergraduate degree, when one of her friends and fellow Afro-Latina students leaned in toward her with a life-changing tip. She confided that she had found a "really cool gig," where the hours gave her the flexibility to be in school full-time but also allowed her to work full-time on the side. The job was nannying. It took her mere days to find her first job working for a white single mother and her newborn. She had experience, even if she had never been paid for it.

If you were looking for Anna during the years she grew up in Queens, New York, where her Puerto Rican family would gather every Sunday, salsa playing in the background, reggaeton down the street, she says you would probably find her with the younger kids, taking care of them. "I was one of the older cousins and I was also one of the only older cousins that was a girl, so my guy cousins were always very sweet but not interested at all in interacting with the kids.

"It was never really said explicitly to me, truthfully. But I always felt like if they [the younger cousins] were in the room, somebody should be paying attention to them. And so I always felt like I had to take on that role."

The situation certainly didn't leave her feeling like she had any choice—however skilled at it she ended up becoming. "It always felt like it was something I was good at. I have always liked kids. Hanging out with them is really rewarding. It's part of who I am. I don't know whether that's something that's innate or just circumstantial because of what was going on."

Other nannies and caregivers I interviewed had similar stories. Large families relied on female family members to help, including young girls, and those girls grew up knowing how to take care of children. One Black woman in Pennsylvania who had never been a formal nanny but had been handed extra children to take care of into middle age, expressed in no uncertain terms that being good at something didn't alleviate the toll and magnitude of the work involved.

Today, women of color continue to make up a majority of domestic workers helping to rear children outside their own communities even as they are now also disproportionately of immigrant origin.[11] Nannying, alongside other professions like nursing and teaching, smoothly fulfills the stereotype of women as nurturers and caregivers and therefore does not rattle the gendered status quo. With nannying and other forms of domestic work involving emotional labor, race stereotypes compound these effects and help justify a situation where pay can be low and labor rights nonexistent. *These women aren't workers; this is just who these women are.* Or so the unspoken understanding goes.

Unlike teachers or nurses, nannies, as domestic workers who perform work tasks in private settings, hold very few formal labor protections. Domestic workers, including home caregivers and house cleaners, are a largely unregulated workforce, where wage theft, exploitation akin to indentured servitude, sexual harassment, and general toxic working conditions are able to flourish with little to no path for intervention.

Domestic workers in the United States do not enjoy anything like the same labor rights as workers in other spheres. In 1935, when the historic National Labor Relations Act was passed, ushering in transformative labor legislation for a majority of the American workforce, two major groups were excluded from the act: farmworkers and domestic workers, the two professions with the highest concentration of Black workers. Only sixty years after slavery was abolished, denying Black workers the same labor rights as other workers was done in large part to appease white Southern lawmakers. But such a decision benefited the pocketbooks of many white and middle-class families beyond the South and set many Black families up with an added generational economic burden.

Congress justified it by explaining that organizing and collective bargaining did not fit the intimate relationship between a householder and a domestic employee. The domestic worker, aided by sexist and racist essentializing stereotypes around women's work, was perceived by Congress as outside the scope of legislation addressing industrial strife.[12] While "Everyone has the right to form and to join trade unions for the protection of his interests" is a basic human right[13] included the next decade in the 1948 Universal Declaration of Human Rights, this basic labor exclusion holds true to this day.[14] In 2018, while white women earned an average of 81.5 percent of what white men earned, Black women earned only 65 percent of it, and Hispanic women 61 percent.[15] Understanding this pay gap doesn't involve just looking at very real discriminations happening within fields where men and women of different races work side by side but also looking at the kinds of fields different groups of women go into and the typical pay and labor conditions within these.

In many ways, Anna is the opposite of exploited—certainly comparatively by New York City or American nannying standards. Her current employers sought her out specifically for her previous nannying experience as well as for her college degree. The resulting $1,000 paycheck each week, or $52,000 a year, as well as benefits, is a far cry from the $12/hour she started on, and at the top of the pay hierarchy for domestic workers, an estimated 23 percent of whom are paid below the minimum wage,[16] which, to be clear, is illegal. And in terms of race relations, Anna doesn't fit into the box perfectly, either. Unlike almost every other nanny in her Brooklyn circle, both Anna and the child she takes care of are Black. "I can count on one hand the number of times I have seen something different than nannies of color taking care of white children. Mia and I are an exception."

"Being Afro-Latina is a big part of my personality. It's nice that we look alike. Being a woman of color for her [Mia] is something she is so proud of," she says. But even with a child who looks like her, racial and ethnic stereotypes loom unmistakably within many of her daily activities. The college graduate who is preparing to apply for graduate school confides that parents and other people she meets outside of New York's schools, in activity centers and playgrounds, are never surprised to find out she is a nanny. But they are often taken aback to hear of her academic accomplishments and goals. "I always thought it was really interesting that they were surprised. I look like I am school age. I thought maybe that was the dynamic just for me. I talked to other nannies who were also in school. And they would say the same."

This is particularly ironic because being college-educated was a requirement for her current job. Her employers wanted to be sure Anna could perform emotional and intellectual labor tasks they felt required higher education. "They made it clear that they were looking for someone who wanted to be emotionally available in terms of supplementing what she was learning in school and helping out in the places where she needed more assistance and being her emotional support.

"Lots of parents in job requirements put that they prefer someone with some kind of higher education. So that's why I am always very surprised when parents are caught off guard by someone either being in school or having gone to school, considering that that is something asked of the nannies."

Anna understands the discombobulation she has faced time and time again in a historical context. "It makes sense, here in the US, because of the history that I have learned. For women of color, it is an industry that we have been in for centuries here. It is probably one that is easiest for us to access—from what I see."

But beyond the stereotyping she sees—that white parents are more comfortable grappling with her as domestic help than as a university graduate—what do these reactions point to? Why is it that employers and parents are so astonished to hear that a nanny has an education from a world-class institution like NYU?

It may be because they fail to see a nanny as a full human being with a brain and ambitions, and as existing outside of the home she works in. It may also be because deep down they do not believe nannying is a worthy job for someone with a college degree—that even as they may require a degree for employment, they still look down on the job they are recruiting for. Or it also may be because learning that Anna has gone to the kind of school they would likely be excited to have their own kid go to one day inextricably puts a nanny into the same social category as an employing family. And that this kind of collision of what was formerly two worlds intimately bound while at the same time rigidly separated is confronting to the extreme. Such a blurring of lines that dismounts a rigid power dynamic in which a worker serves and an employer is served is likely existentially threatening to groups whose identity is far more woven into their unjustified dominance and extraction than they would care to admit. Facing up to a suddenly indefensible assumption of domination—even a quiet notion deep in the background that white people can be served by non-white people, men can be served by women—may put into question the very construction of their worlds and the notion of their own humanity and goodness.

Anna's world remains intact. She is not surprised by her own individual humanity, her accomplishments, or those accomplishments of her colleagues. Just like the women who came before her, that she had the skills to formulate her own multidimensional life was always a given. Whether the opportunities would arise for more accomplishments was the question, not whether she had it in her. In Anna's case, her environmental circumstances and her embracing of those circumstances from a young age have led her to feel like she has developed a strong skill set. The PhD programs she is applying to are in childhood education and teaching, and she feels good about her chances. So much of what she has proven she can do as part of nannying carries over into broader talents.

"Inherent to working with children is endless patience. To lose patience with a kid would be so unfair. They are learning and growing and testing boundaries and figuring things out. I am a pretty passive person to begin with, I am pretty laid-back, but I feel like working with children, it's a skill and a muscle that I have developed over time. It would take quite a bit to make me lose my temper."

To this emotional labor she adds one form that mostly mothers have talked about in interviews—that of keeping endless tabs open in her brain, while staying emotionally present for the people around. "I think that multitasking is something I have got a lot better at over time. You have to when working with kids. There are eighteen million things going on and while they're going on, the kid is trying to have a conversation with you, and you want the kid to feel heard, so you are having that conversation doing a million things. I think that has been helpful."

―――――――――――

I leave wondering whether it is a beautiful thing that Anna transformed a performance she was pushed toward into an expertise—whether this is a goal in some ways—or whether there is still a long way to go before we undo the forces that brought her there.

One way to start doing this would be to formally protect her rights as a worker, and maybe even to double her salary. Six-figure salaries for caregivers would force a better conversation about parenting's value, too, and the value of invisible, necessary domestic support work— including that of rearing the next generation of citizens. Parents in this country are only just starting to be more purposefully supported through official measures like the child tax credit, but still have to do without any kind of formal paid parental leave and any kind of formal universal childcare. With public schools only having to take charge of kids starting at five years old, this leaves a huge burden on parents during early stages of childcare, especially mothers, who are often the ones left to sacrifice for the group.

And while Anna's salary at $52,000 a year is indisputably better than many other nannies' salaries, is it the right pay for a graduate of an excellent university, with six years' skilled experience living in New York City, one of the world's most expensive cities? Anna is arguably being paid less than she should because of how bad her colleagues' pay and benefits are, which is not the only hidden financial penalty of the job. After her employers requested that she live close to them in their hip neighborhood in Brooklyn, she and her boyfriend moved into an apartment that was far more expensive than what they were used to in Queens. It made appearing to take care of Mia at a moment's notice easier and continued to blur the hours she would be available to her employers' around-the-clock whims.

I wonder whether the call the nanny put out in her 1912 testimonial for white women, which today would go to all privileged women, to understand that this was their own battle, too, will ever be answered. What would such a reckoning look like? Would it involve putting a price on love and expert emotional labor as a part of care? What would a society—and an economy—that doesn't off-load childcare, family work, and love look like?

As I do, I also start to connect, viscerally, to what love is masking, systemically, and what the semblance of love has justified in our vision of reality as we have built our own version of democracy steeped in extractive racial and gendered capitalism. It is obvious that we cannot conceive of building a society that is anti-racist and anti-sexist without transforming it into one that truly values and sees the work of love and the work of care as paramount, central to its existence. For now, a world that hides and marginalizes its most essential work makes it a complicated load to take on.

Toward the end of our interview, Anna tells me more about her boyfriend, a man she describes as a wonderful partner. They have known each other since they were thirteen. He is someone who can hug her in her real, emotional home, not just someone who demands to be hugged in her economic one. But on the topic of a future family, Anna is unyielding. Having children is totally off the table. "I really know how much work it is. I am not sure I would want to take that on."

FOUR

Disciplined into Obedience

HUMILIATION

When young women come to work for her as swim instructors, Joann, a recreation and parks manager in California, has to sit them down and have a very particular kind of conversation with them she does not have with her male recruits. While new coaches' induction might include conversations around safety protocols, kids' ages, and progress reports, the conversation Joann finds herself having with young women is around word delivery. Joann says instructors, male or female, will shout "KICK! KICK! KICK!" in the same way to the children perfecting their swim strokes, but to very different reception from closely monitoring parents.

"Female swim coaches who don't add enough upspeak in their voice when they are yelling 'kick' across the pool deck are often seen as mean, while their male coworkers can yell all they want," Joann explains, referring to the practice of rising intonation at the end of a sentence so that it sounds like a question. She also suggests they add positive, encouraging phrases like "You got it!," something men do not need to do.

If women do not sweetly modulate their voices as they question mark their way through "Kick? Kick? Kick?" leg movement directions, Joann says she has learned the hard way it will only be a matter of days before parents will come forward to complain.

Joann does not need a sociology textbook to teach her about counter-stereotypic backlash—that punishing effect that happens to women refusing to adhere to the kind, sweet, and demure trope mentioned in earlier chapters. She has seen it summer after summer, with every new cohort of swim instructors coming in. "That is the only way that people can take women's voices," she states bluntly.

Tweaking and altering your authentic self to adhere to what is expected of you as a woman, either to please others or for fear of serious repercussion—in the form of social penalties like angry parents, economic penalties like job loss, or physical penalties like violence—is emotional labor. It is not only emotional labor; it is emotional labor with the threat of a slap on the wrist or more if you don't do it.

When performed in public, before an audience, emotional labor imposed on subjugated groups serves to infantilize and delegitimize those doing it. As an active expression of a submissive, nonconfrontational status, it also presents the power status quo as inevitable, paralyzing those doing emotional labor in place.

Detecting how thoroughly and actively enforced these processes are helps lift the curtain on the ways in which persistent forms of inequality are maintained. Even emotions as they are felt and displayed are far more intertwined with cultural context than most realize.

Over the last ten years, the field of neuroscience has moved away from understanding emotions as innate and universal—stamped on the brain from birth. Instead, it now sees emotions as creations of the brain, influenced by the constant, active absorption of the world around us through our five senses, mixed with predictions based on experience.[1]

If emotions do not just happen *POOF*—like a sneeze or a knee jerk—but are instead constructed by our brain, itself reflecting information it has collected from the broader environment, emotional labor describes the part of the process through which emotions are not just produced but managed. As our brain manages the production of emotions, it pays attention to context, understanding nuances of appropriateness or the weight of expectations. It is aware of conventions of feelings that dictate that we should feel happy at a party and sad during a wake. Even when our internal emotions do not match the occasion, we are aware of cultural display rules, which will guide us to appear somber, as a form of respect, even if we are not internally feeling desolate at that wake.[2]

When you assess your surroundings and modulate your emotional display, or even your actual emotions, to suit and interact with the context, you are performing emotional labor. In sociology, tweaking your internal feelings to match the situation is referred to as deep acting, and tweaking the display of them is surface acting. Both are emotional labor.[3]

These feeling rules, which take into account the situation and conventions, can be totally different for two separate people in the exact same social context.[4] Feeling rules women are expected to abide by, for example, are often vastly different from those required of men. This is why Joann has to advise the young women swim coaches to channel Marilyn Monroe in *Some Like It Hot* when they are giving basic swim instructions, and needn't bother with the young men.

While men are limited from childhood in the range of emotion they are expected to have the capacity of feeling, they are paradoxically given more space to be unfiltered in public. Women, treated like emotional thermostats whether they like it or not, not only must constantly manage their own feelings but they are also held responsible for the feelings of others. When women are told to "smile" by a stranger on the street, they are being reminded of this through harassment. When women going about their business are accused of having a "resting bitch face," they are being reminded of their expected constant enthusiastic performance for the benefit of the world. A man not smiling while going about a task is never told he has a "resting dick face." He's likely treated as busy and important, if his expression is noted at all.

In recent popular memory, nowhere was this kind of feeling rule double standard more evident than during the September 2018 public confirmation hearings of now Supreme Court Justice Brett Kavanaugh, and his sexual assault accuser Dr. Christine Blasey Ford, watched by an estimated twenty million people across America.

On the morning of September 27, 2018, an emotionally affected but never overridden-by-emotions Dr. Ford gave a contained, clear testimony of her alleged assault at the hands of then Judge Kavanaugh and a friend of his while they were all teenagers. Not once did she raise her voice, and every detail of her interaction with the Senate Judicial Committee was polite, deferential, and sweet, from asking for a Coke—"I think after I read my opening statement, I anticipate needing some caffeine—if that is available"—to putting her questioners' needs before her own when they proposed a break—"Does that work for you? Does that work for you, as well?" Peppered throughout the heart-wrenching testimony was a constant lowering of the gaze.

In the afternoon, an angry and at times tearful Kavanaugh gave his own roaring, combative testimony. He raised his voice constantly. When it came to questioning, Kavanaugh was elusive, unaccommodating, interrupting, rude, and at times bullying. Kavanaugh's gaze remained undaunted, his eyes looking straight ahead.

When Senator Amy Klobuchar probed him on whether there was any time drinking had caused him to forget what had happened or part of what had happened the night before, he answered provocatively, "You're talking about blackout. I don't know, have you?" After she insisted he answer her question, his interjection doubled down on insolence. "Yeah, and I am curious if you have?"

Kavanaugh was not only being the opposite of deferential, he was flauntingly disrespectful and belittling of the senator. In fact, Kavanaugh refused to answer dozens of questions put to him, whereas Ford dodged none.[5]

The juxtaposition of the two testimonies makes for a perfect example of how two members with the same background are often encouraged to adhere to entirely opposing feeling rules. Both Ford and Kavanaugh are of a similar origin class: white, privately educated, both enjoying privileged socioeconomic status, which they have maintained in part by reaching the highest levels in their respective professional fields of psychology and law. The contrast in their starkly disparate emotion display can be boiled down to one key difference: gender.

Ford, a well-respected professor of psychology at Palo Alto

University and researcher at Stanford University, could never have behaved the way Kavanaugh did and remain credible.[6] Everything about her demeanor and expression was the emblem of what is not only expected but *allowed* of a woman in public. To be not only likable but amenable, too, always putting others' needs before her own. Emotional labor, taking cues from cultural display rules, becomes the way in which women are forced to express their place in the hierarchy: serving others as a priority. That is the only way women will be given space. As perfect as her gendered performance was, Ford's testimony was ultimately disregarded, even if her courage in testifying and taking space undoubtedly moved the cultural conversation forward.[7]

To gain access to a public arena only with the precondition of performing the opposite of defiance—affability, compliance, submission—may prevent women from being booted out or discredited entirely, but it also minimizes any challenging of existing structures of power, which is undoubtedly the point.[8]

When, almost four years after Kavanaugh's confirmation, the nation watched Senate confirmation hearings for then Judge Ketanji Brown Jackson, the first Black female nominee to the United States Supreme Court, the gendered double standards on display were compounded with the double standards of race. Jackson's countenance as she faced at times mocking and aggressive questions from male members of the committee was a discouraging reminder that while this was a historic moment, Black women still faced perpetual, public indignities, however polished or impressive their track records were.[9] The now justice's composure and endurance, as she maintained an emotional evenness over days, were rightfully lauded, but it was hard not to also see the moment as a public exhibition in racial and sexist abuse, performed with impunity. Nor would a woman in her position have had much of a choice.

For women who are not white and people from minority groups, prioritizing the feelings of people from more socially dominant groups—whether white people, men, or both—can present itself as a precondition for taking up any kind of public space. But the act of adapting to living in a white male supremacy can quickly deviate into sacrificing parts of oneself in order to exist.

One woman I spoke to, Danielle, recalls learning to "code switch" as a Black kid in white spaces, developing a strategy of "killing them with kindness." When a white girl at school took to calling her "Danny," she didn't fight it, even if she loathed the nickname and felt robbed of the ability to define herself on her own terms. "I remember that was the first experience accepting a thing I hated in order for me to be accepted. I was just like, *Fine. In order to manage this space, being accepted in this white space, I have to accept this nickname*," she recounts.

She carried this emotional labor lesson—"that to be kind and to be loving somehow diminished the walls of difference"—through to her work as a professor in public health at an elite, majority-white institution. There, she chose early on to connect with her students on an emotional level, on top of an intellectual one. As an openly queer Black woman and working mother in a long-term same-sex relationship, she found that using her experiences helped students fully grasp the gravity and complexity of issues discussed. Listening to her, their professor, they couldn't look the other way, they had to face realities they were unfamiliar with, they had to empathize. "I am not only teaching through the texts; I am talking through my life. I have used my body, my identity, myself as a teaching tool by my own volition, but still appreciating that that requires emotional labor and work."

But this emotional labor deployed for the benefit of others, for the benefit of pushing culture forward, building empathy, and enacting progress, as needed as it is, has started to be weaponized against her—almost as if the act of performing this emotional labor has given students carte blanche to treat her as a mere tool to make them feel better.

Increasingly, Danielle has found that the limits of consensual emotional labor are being pushed, often violated, by the same students whose compassion she is trying to build. She shares one story about a young white male student who recently asked to meet with her after a class she taught on the negative impact of racism on health outcomes. She sat with him and expected questions about the course material—but he had none. Instead, he recounted a racist incident he had participated in, and that he now felt bad about. It quickly became apparent that he had no intellectual question to put to her. Rather, he wanted to feel better about himself, without doing any work, and he thought she could—or should—give that to him. He wanted absolution.

The worst part, she tells me, is that this is hardly the first time she has been in a situation like this: obliged to not only bear witness to the recounting of violence but also carry the burden of that violence and in turn perform some kind of added ceremony of emotional labor, waving an imaginary wand and reverting the person's conscience back to innocence. This is emotional labor that frays at her sense of full personhood: the one that is claimed from her by people who believe it is *her* job as a mammy-meets-genie-meets-Jesus-Christ figure, not theirs, to cleanse them of their own wrongdoing. It is a strange, degrading mechanism where she is reduced to being the object through which other people expect to have their emotions validated.

For women generally, being treated as the vehicle for other people's feelings is an exercise in objectification that often merges both emotional and physical presentation requirements. Being held accountable for the entire emotional experience of the people around them means women are often forced to present—as a perceived part of emotive expression—in very narrow ways.

This checks out for Joann, the recreation manager, as the emotional labor performance she feels forced to introduce to her young female recruits extends to physical appearance. "I tell them, I know other men dress like that, like in cargo shorts or whatever they want, but people will expect you to dress better."

Is it fair? No. Is it practical to tell them? To Joann, yes, it is. "It is all part of the female experience," she tells me.

Even in arenas where pleasant behaviors and appearance seem totally secondary, like politics, how people *feel* when they look at women is a subject of scrutiny first, serving as a disqualifying factor. In the run-up to the 2016 presidential elections, presidential candidate Hillary Clinton was continuously slammed for not smiling enough, not being likable enough, and her appearance examined ad nauseam. In a 2020 Hulu documentary named *Hillary*, Clinton explains how, unlike her male opponents, she felt she had no choice but to spend one hour a day on hair and makeup. Over the six hundred days of her presidential campaign, she calculated that that amounted to twenty-five days around the clock of time she lost to hair and makeup alone.[10]

Spending twenty-five days around the clock in hair and makeup when all you want is for your brain to be listened to sounds like the plot of a horror movie: like a feminist version of Jordan Peele's 2017 movie *Get Out*, a nightmare you are stuck in and can't figure your way out of.

These forced gender practices, a balancing act full of land mines that could lead to failure at any time, are an entry fee into public life for women and are a price men do not have to pay. This gives women a very real handicap, in Clinton's example time equivalent to almost one entire month.

But the handicap extends itself out beyond being a simple drain on energy and time. As opportunities to be in the public eye have hugely expanded for women over the last decades—as previous formal barriers to public life have lifted—so, too, has the volume and level of feedback audiences inflict on them. This is true whether audiences are parents at a swim lesson, friends and acquaintances on social media, or television viewers of a political debate. These audiences' belief that they have blanket entitlement to women's emotional labor creates a feedback loop that transforms any moment a woman is watched into an opportunity for disciplining. Watching and commenting as a woman tiptoes her way along, awaiting a fall or a stumble, has become a public spectacle in which humiliation is both a tool and an objective. Because the performances women are pushed into doing—from tweaking attractiveness up or down to voice sweetening and grinning—are easily seen as superficial, slutty, or silly, pointing the finger and laughing condescendingly is all too easy.[11] This reality, instead of receding with women's legal progress, has only intensified.[12] Today, women are more scrutinized, and more set up for humiliation, than ever.

Younger generations of women, well acquainted with punishing double standards they have seen their mothers cope with, are bravely and explicitly confronting rigid gender rules and seeking to define themselves on their own terms. They face a choice of rejecting limiting rules altogether and risking navigating a hostile world, embracing them while trying to make these rituals their own, or forging their own path somewhere in between. For them, automatic scrutiny means that public-facing emotional labor—even in the rejection of rules—is an active negotiation regardless.

Some have made the aesthetics and emotional labor of femininity, displayed in public, a form of high art in itself, insisting that feminine displays and power need not be separated out. This is the kind of engagement the public loves: a woman willing to play the game. She may be lauded for it, temporarily rewarded, and given more space, but she will often also be subjected to more vitriol and mockery than others. In this scenario, the possibility of social disciplining is seen as fair game against a woman who *chose* to step out in the first place.

One woman who stepped into performing femininity in public as a form of affirmation and empowerment is Arianna Quan, who goes by Ari. In 2016, Ari was elected Miss Michigan, becoming the first Asian American ever to earn the title. Breaking barriers had been part of her motivation in taking part. As a Chinese American woman who had grown up in a majority-white suburb in Michigan, Ari always felt on the margins: like she didn't fit in and she wasn't pretty. In competing in pageants, the design student was drawn to the potential of earning scholarship money that would help pay for school, as well as the hope of finally feeling beautiful and accepted.

To win the state title, going from small, local competitions to Miss America in just a couple of years, she concentrated on perfecting an array of desirable traits. She worked on her breathtaking piano skills, many years in the making, honed a slender physique over hours in the gym and at the beauty table, and practiced presenting her sharp brain in answers to questions in the most convincing and digestible ways possible.

To these skills, she also added the emotional labor of evoking an overall demeanor of grace and poise, which she learned was a core part of how an ideal woman should present. This made sense to her, even if, gradually, in the months leading up to the Miss Michigan final contest, the scope of what was understood by "gracious" started to expand. Members of the judging committee repeatedly described former winners to future hopefuls as being "ungrateful," having "a horrible attitude," and lacking in grace. As the negative feedback was hammered in, the message became clear to a competitive Ari: winning would involve an added layer of emotional labor specifically tied to compliance. She found herself professing preemptive vows of amenability to her directors. "Oh, if I were to win, I would have a great attitude. I would be grateful. I would be able to do a good job," she remembers effusively telling them. Looking back, it is hard not to think that this was a grim grooming ritual for acceptance of the layers of trials and tribulations that were to come next.

The first form of backlash she faced after victory seems as peculiar as it was pure bad luck, even if the level of cruelty involved was entirely predictable.

A few weeks after her state title victory in 2016, the news of her victory reached China, where she was born, and the media there went wild. Photos of her were blasted all over Chinese news for the opposite reasons you might expect. "It became a national sensation in China that the first Asian American woman to win for Michigan, going to Miss America, was ugly," she explains. "I didn't fulfill their standards of beauty."

The story went viral. Reporters found out where her grandparents lived in China and camped outside their home. Back in America, media hounded her and called her school, colleagues, and friends. She received death threats. Well beyond China, Ari's story was featured on CNN, in the *Daily Mail*, and even in *People* magazine, where readers in the comment section eagerly joined in on the debate: beautiful or ugly? "I couldn't really get away from it," she says of the time.

At home and during this period, her minder, the Michigan pageant director, questioned her American citizenship. She had been crowned to represent her home state, but her Asian-presenting body was still causing her to be treated as suspicious on a whim. "It was this strange paradox of them [people in China] not accepting me, and then the pageant community here not accepting me because I am not white. Bizarre."

This part of Ari's story not only reflects the subjective, culture-specific nature of beauty ideals that reinforce local racial and class hierarchies[13] but also speaks to the ways in which women are encouraged into a posture of display that then marks them as an admissible target for public humiliation. The whole mechanism is a setup that enables us to blame and dehumanize women for the very exhibition we are so hungry to consume.

A woman's pageant journey may seem like an old-school matter to some, but far from being passé it is exceptionally pertinent to the mutations of modern life. Taking the stage before spectators primed to judge emotional display, looks, and less a brain than how a brain is *presented* is the norm now for most women existing online as well as off—especially professionally. Even for those avoiding any public limelight, tales like Ari's serve only as further discouragement from stepping out or seeking ways up.

It can be hard to fathom that requiring women to be nice-looking, sweet, supportive, and focused on others as a priority can also be a damaging force that keeps women down. After all, what is so wrong with smiling at all times, tending to others, and making people feel good? Don't we need more kindness in the world, not less? Isn't it human to enjoy pretty things, pretty people?

Social psychologists Peter Glick and Susan Fiske[14] in the late 1990s offered a great answer by differentiating between two forms of sexism—hostile and benevolent—that, respectively, threaten women with the stick of hatred and lure them into submission with the carrot of adoration.

Hostile sexism is sexism we tend to be familiar with; it is overt, tied to prejudice, negative stereotyping, and discrimination. This includes saying women are manipulative, conniving, stupid, claiming women are bad leaders, calling women who veer from conservative sexual norms bitches and whores, and claiming women are unethical and untrustworthy. Hostile sexism is not on the margins; it is present all around us, and it sells.

A good example of the pervasiveness of this form can be found in Chris Brown's 2014 song misleadingly called "Loyal" in which the chorus affirms "THESE HOES AIN'T LOYAL!" about women, dubbed "hoes," eleven times total. The video to this extraordinarily catchy song has been viewed more than one billion times on YouTube.[15]

Benevolent sexism, the less well-known of the sexisms, relates to actions and words directed at women that seek to compliment, infantilize, and cajole them into accepting a subjugated position with gender-stereotypical roles and attributes. It is more covert. This includes describing women as pure, caring, and virtuous beings in need of gallant protection. It includes calling adult women "baby" or "girl." They are the selfless mothers, the innocent daughters, the sex to be venerated, cherished—in a way that might initially seem doting to women rather than restricting. Benevolent sexism showers women who behave correctly with the momentary gratification of validation and acceptance, but sanctions are only ever one misstep away.

A perfect example of benevolent sexism as a sprinkling of sugar disguising a gendered threat in pop culture is the 1965 song "Run for Your Life" by the Beatles. In it, the male narrator addresses his female partner as "little girl" sixteen times as he simultaneously informs her that if she were to leave or cheat, he would kill her. The ominous refrain set to a counterintuitively upbeat melody goes: "You better run for your life if you can, little girl / Hide your head in the sand, little girl / Catch you with another man / That's the end . . . little girl."[16] Yes, that's right: the song, said to have been written mainly by the legendary John Lennon (although Paul McCartney is also credited), is a proud anthem to femicide.

While the two records cited use drastically different terminologies to describe women—"hoes" versus "little girl"—it is notable that both feature a panic over the possibility of women exercising agency and leaving the men they are with. The hostile sexist one is perhaps unexpectedly considerably kinder toward women. It is primarily a dis toward broke men who are warned they could lose their women to more promising male prospects. Women are thrown under the bus insofar as their being self-interested romantically justifies them being called hoes. But the benevolent sexist one is the truly atrocious one. It is a mark of the culture we live in, and the blanket acceptance and embracing of female hatred—of misogyny—that this song has not discredited the Beatles altogether. I cannot think of another category of people—aside from women—that a band could sing about explicitly menacing to kill without it entirely muddying the way they are collectively remembered.

Ultimately, both starkly contradictory sexisms that rely on nonsensical essentialized beliefs result in women being controlled, their actions, emotions, and life options limited. But benevolent sexism gives women some choice—a little carrot incentive. They can be good girls and accept their inferior position, performing all the sweet, smiley, demure, and compliant traits that might get them protection from society and a man. They can do that emotional labor. They can accept this limit on their freedom of expression and freedom of speech. Or they can refuse to, in which case they will become bad girls and be outcasts. It is a false choice, of course. Good girls are only ever one step away from being branded bad.

Feminist Andrea Dworkin, in her provocative and still remarkably contemporary 1987 book *Intercourse*,[17] points out that women being forced into the two vastly oversimplified categories of virgins or whores face an impossible choice. Virgins, or good girls, are considered full humans but lack power, while sex objects gain some power but face a reduction in their full humanity—with their full humanity never again recoverable. "Damaged goods," bafflingly, is not just an expression deployed by a fictional 1920s *Downton Abbey* England, it is still an expression deployed toward women whose supposed market value has gone down due to perceived sexual activity.

The obsession with differentiating good girls from bad girls extends to all quarters. I have long noticed, with dismay, that hating women in this way is one of the last totally socially acceptable forms of sexism. Progressive circles, still deep in the mud of unquestioned misogyny, seem to have come up with their own virgin-whore complex that casts good women as using their brains for money and influence and bad women as using their bodies, especially sexually, for money and influence.

When I had a peroxide buzz haircut, men would sometimes compare me to writer, businesswoman, and organizer of "LA SlutWalks" Amber Rose, who carries her sexuality on her sleeve and came to prominence as a model when she appeared in a music video and dated rapper Kanye West. "Don't worry, though," a couple of well-meaning men said. "We don't think you're the same kind of woman." Another remarked that it must be hard for me to take the comparison, especially as an engaged feminist.

It wasn't hard at all. I took this as a massive compliment: she was a badass and hot as hell. What those men presumably meant was that the use of my brain as a source of income—instead of, say, my body and my brain—marked me as different from Amber Rose, in some kind of positive way. It didn't, and it still does not.[18]

I was taken aback a few years later when a journalist and male colleague dismissed a cheerleading labor dispute as unworthy of note or concern. Reports revealed that professional NFL cheerleaders entertaining audiences during football games, in which players were frequently in multimillion-dollar contracts, were often paid below the minimum wage when you added up the hours of their training, preparation, and performance.[19]

"If they don't like it, they can go and get a real job," the pro-union, pro–worker rights colleague told me to my absolute shock. Even when women are in formal jobs at a national level, like cheerleading in the NFL, which involves high degrees of athleticism, training, skill, and aesthetics labor, to say nothing of the massive amount of emotional labor, they are still being told their feminized jobs are not real jobs. They are still being told to go and get a real job. They are still treated as undeserving of basic labor standards. Progressives may be eager to fight for nurses' and teachers' rights ("good girls"), but not for the rights of women using their bodies for professional advancement ("bad girls").

The prolonged moment of triage between good and bad and the endless discussions around it are a total distraction from what is actually going on. These scrutinizing and ridiculing moments of triage have one main end goal: to deny ascendance or power by denying women full self-determination, specifically here economic self-determination. These moments of rewarding versus shaming penalize all women as we get swept up into a mirage of fake morals and ignore the bottom line.

For Ari, the beauty queen, distraction over performing model femininity, overcoming media-fueled trolling, and enduring the highs and lows of wins and losses lasted only so long. Eventually, her reality collided with debilitating, nonexistent labor standards.

The day she was crowned Miss Michigan—aside from feeling a deep sense of accomplishment—she remembers feeling excited about her prize scholarship money too. She received $12,000 for the title plus $500 for winning talent. Immediately after winning, she was sent to stay with a volunteer host family and was expected to dedicate the following three months exclusively to prepping for Miss America, which her state title had qualified her for. At Miss America, where she received $6,000 "just for showing up," Ari didn't place among the finalists, but she still won three talent awards again, amounting to $2,000 combined. Added up, that was $20,500 earned in scholarship money over the course of a few months, to be applied exclusively toward education or tuition fees. It seemed far from bad.

Upon her return to her home state, she was excited to focus on providing a "year of service," an expectation that came with the Miss Michigan title. There were to be school events, charity events, speaking engagements, and opportunities to travel. It seemed thrilling. But in practice, under the guise of what was officially a "volunteer position," she was entering into an opaque, unregulated work arrangement, which required her—if she wanted to keep her title—to put studies and formal jobs on hold for a year. For having such strict rules, it was a distinctly unreliable gig. Ari estimates she ended up averaging four bookings a month, where people were supposed to pay her $250 for speaking and $300 for performing her talent, the piano. As low as that was in monthly income, she estimates only a quarter of the people asking her for an appearance ended up ever paying her. She was also expected to keep up a high appearance standard, spending her own time and money on clothes, skin care, makeup, nails, and hair.

She pleaded for help from the Miss Michigan organization to collect her debts, but this only made matters worse. Ari had already been reprimanded by her minders for posting one of her classical drawings of a nude woman on Instagram and for being honest to "local girls" about what Miss America was really like. She had likened the experience to "watching a sausage being made," sharing stories with future hopefuls about being stuck inside for days, exhausted and hungry from dieting, with some contestants stopping eating altogether.

Complaining about her lack of funds was the final nail in the coffin. Her pageant minders ceased to even pretend to help. She had become the ungrateful, problem Miss, just like the Misses who had come before her: the very role she had been warned against—and sworn with all her heart she would never be. "Once you're in that position, you're like, *Oh my God, I have no money for gas, and I am supposed to be driving up north and I am so hungry, I have been living out of my car. I am not allowed to work, I can't go to school, but I don't have any events to go to because no one is marketing this.*"

That year, as her face graced newspaper articles, as she clipped through ribbons and wore a glitzy crown that young girls dreamed of, she estimates making no more than $25,000—most of which was locked in as school fees and could not be put toward her living costs. The period ended up being one of the hardest of her life to date, she shares over the course of multiple interviews. She ended up feeling like she had no choice but to secretly reenroll in school so that at least she could get ahead in her studies. She also moved in with her boyfriend, something that was yet again against the rules, to save money.

She didn't want to be the bad Miss, the ungrateful Miss, the make-trouble Miss, she hated it, but being the good Miss seemed impossible. She felt caught in a bind there was no good way out of. "I am struggling. It's really difficult for me to put on a brave face and lie to everyone when this is my reality," she tells me of that time, and of the extreme emotional labor of total obedience she felt she just couldn't bring herself to perform.

To be a good girl, or a good Miss, she was given little space to complain about what effectively was a total lack of labor rights. Her position was further weakened by the fact that beauty is still seen as a private project, not work in our society. This functions in a similar way to other forms of devalued feminized labor that hit the marketplace—like care, service, sex, or domestic work. But because aesthetics work as a way to seek income is seen at best as trivial, and at worst as illegitimate—because of its proximity to sex work—onlookers continue to focus on the virtue of workers rather than reckon with a system of labor exploitation. This, in spite of the fact that the cosmetics industry alone—just one part of the beauty industry—was worth an estimated $60 billion in 2020 in the United States.[20] There is no verifiable number for the net worth of the beauty pageant industry, but one number that is widely thrown around just for the children's part is that it is worth $5 billion a year in the United States.[21]

Our economic system is all about making money from feminized forms of work, but it isn't sharing much, if any, of that money with the workers. It does this by managing to con us—once more—into believing that women fueling these multibillion-dollar industries aren't workers at all. Because who is driving these types of industries but women like Ari: women putting themselves in the public eye, for other people's pleasure, consumption, and viewership, either on physical stages or on virtual ones like Instagram, YouTube, and TikTok. Instead of understanding the role they are playing in an economy, we continue to be sidetracked into absurd conversations that viciously police the perceived exchange of money for sex, money for femininity.

We are led to believe that these conversations are about the deservedness of a few women at the top, the celebrities who have made it, in part through their bodies: the reality TV stars, the influencers, the singers, the actresses. Even as we put them on pedestals, we are taught to hate those women who have made real money from feminine work. But such women are the exception, not the rule. Their gleeful demonization and belittling only help diminish the plight of the majority of those performing feminine work, who are neither privileged nor wealthy.

Women are pushed into performing this embodied emotional labor of creating experiences for others, pushed to package themselves as products to be enjoyed and consumed—and profited off of. Good girls, it is understood, should generously exist for others and would never dare sully themselves with vulgar claims for money. As soon as they dare ask for a paycheck, for a share in the money and value they are creating, they become bad.

Requiring this false high road of women, at the same time as we require them to perform constant rituals of femininity, is hypocritical beyond belief and the opposite of progress. It also justifies and takes the side of patriarchal capitalism that pretends that withholding money from women using their bodies for profit is a moral act, not an act of market exploitation. After all, someone is going to be taking home that money—the value the women are creating.

We can fight for a world where women can step into their power in ways that are not just through the use of their body—but as we do that, we cannot deny the value of women who want to step into their power with the instrumental use of their body. The point is to destroy the virgin-whore binary, not to pick one side of it. The point is to denounce the disciplining of women's behavior—and see it for what it is: a way to disincentivize women from stepping out and finding power.

But for now, most of us are still stuck in the in-between phase, during which women work to push to take up space, to be heard, to be accepted; during which women seek a place at the leadership table; during which women try to fight for the world they believe can exist, for progress. As they do this, they use emotional labor as a defensive shield, even as it is used as a weapon against them to measure whether they are good or bad. During this time, they are shoved into an ordeal of perpetual hazing, and they are taunted into daring to keep the mask on, daring to keep striving for something more, something better.

Months after we meet, I watch a couple of videos of Ari being interviewed by the media in 2016 just after her Miss Michigan victory and the stories started circulating over her looks. Her emotional labor performance is immaculate. She appears serene, collected, graceful, eloquent, and sincere—the opposite of what she tells me was really going on inside.

Ari tells me she strategized and decided to suppress her initial feelings of hurt and humiliation, put on a brave face, and redirect the inordinate amount of attention she was getting in the best way she thought she could. "I tried to use that attention as leverage in order to talk about something I cared about, which was my platform," she says, using the term to designate the kinds of issues a beauty queen will seek to highlight during her year of rule. The platform she chose was "immigration and citizenship education," a particularly sensitive and important topic at the time. This was just months before the US presidential elections, during which time soon-to-be-elected Donald Trump, a former pageant mogul himself, reiterated plans for the building of a physical wall on the country's southern border with Mexico and laid out more explicit plans for a so-called Muslim ban. Ari led voter registration drives and advocated for immigration reform, but people seemed more interested in the spectacle of her theoretical downfall. "Looking back at it now, I was very naïve, but I thought, *I am going to make a difference, I am going to be heard. It's going to be great.*"

In one video clip,[22] she tells her male interviewer that knowing she is the cause for people engaging in discussions about pageantry, beauty standards, and immigration has made her "quite thankful."

"Really?" he retorts incredulously.

"Yeah," she responds, nodding her head, appearing totally calm and happy, and not letting any negative feeling of anger, rage, pain, or humiliation transpire.

"I think a lot of people would be surprised to hear that," the male interviewer pushes back.

"A lot of people ask me, 'How do you feel about these comments about you being ugly?' And I think it's cool that so many people are coming together and talking about things that haven't been brought up in the past," she concludes in the clip.

To me, a couple of years on, she tells her truth. "It was an act. I knew. What could I do? There was nothing I could do. At that point

I was being dragged. I was getting torn apart. If I were to show anger, people would rip that apart."

Her grooming to be grateful and the cold reality of the circumstances made her swallow her authentic voice and emotions, and any burning feeling to defend herself. Such a realization, for me, was shattering. She was humiliated, and felt like her only option was to swallow. As women, we are taught to swallow. We are put up on a pedestal so that we can be torn down, and as we are, we swallow and smile graciously, expressing, of all things, gratitude.

Seeking a silver lining, I ask her whether, in spite of it all, there was one moment during which she felt she had achieved an ultimate moment of femininity or womanhood to hold on to. The crowning maybe, I suggest.

"I always refer to it as my disguise. I am putting on my pretty girl disguise. I felt more beautiful because I got the attention. But right now, I feel more beautiful because I have learned how to accept things with grace. And rest in feminine traits of surrendering myself to a process that I might not agree with. And to have to accept things where normally I would have spoken out and expressed my masculine traits. I think learning to appreciate that role makes me feel more feminine and beautiful.

"I don't mean surrendering as quitting," she continues. "I mean I found that surrendering was very empowering."

I am quite floored by her answer. She is telling me that stopping the resisting, suppressing the frustration and anger, has been the most feminine part of the process? This forced emotional labor that disciplined her into silence, acceptance, and ultimate obedience? I try to keep an even tone when I ask her to confirm what I think I have heard.

"As in accepting what was going on and not fighting, not speaking out? Learning that acceptance to go along with it. And you found that very empowering?" I ask.

She acquiesces. "Yeah, because I think everyone's first instinct in uncomfortable situations is to fight back. But I think I learned a lot in just resting and observing. And feeling those feelings."

FIVE

The Constant
Threat of Violence

PUNISHMENT

In the fall of 2017, just a few weeks after the #MeToo movement went viral, I published a callout in *The Guardian* asking people to share their emotional labor stories with me. Women and a small handful of men wrote to me from all corners of America and beyond describing their experiences. Often, people told me they were sharing details of their life for the first time.

Many responders included tales of a particular kind of emotional labor imposed on them as a result of being the target of sexual assaults and harassment, an emotional labor that in turn left them living life in fear and on the defensive. It wasn't just the incidents themselves, they wrote to me; it was the pervading effect these incidents had on the rest of their lives.

A few days into 2018, as I was sifting through some of the hundreds of emails and messages I had received, I stopped on a short note written to me by a woman in her fifties. "I married my husband in 1979," she wrote. "He was 24, I was 20. Three times in the first five years of marriage he demanded sex and when I adamantly said no, he basically raped me."

As I read, my adrenaline levels shot up. A deafening, sharp buzz started humming in my ear. I was suddenly hyperaware of my environment: the varying browns of the sofa I was sitting on, the shape of the television producing flickering images ahead of me to the right.

"That created a negative environment of hatred from me," she continued. "I ended up dreading sex and being repulsed by men. We stopped having sex when I had early menopause (thank goodness)."

I went through the note again, trying to wrap my brain around what I had just read. I tried to imagine what her emotional labor must have felt like: the disconnect between feeling violated and not having anywhere to turn, of sometimes putting on a strong face, sometimes letting the rage seep out. I pictured the load of having to live with your violator, and for years not even having a right to call him that. Marital rape became illegal across all American states only in 1993. In the late seventies and early eighties, the majority of the United States did not believe a spouse could be raped by a spouse, making it easy to uphold the longer-standing credence that a woman was there to serve her man, which included her serving his feelings, his desires, and the particularity of his sexual rhythms.

I pictured the silent trauma, the humiliation, the utter and complete pain, the betrayal, the years of suppressed emotion, and the weight of a lifetime. I closed my laptop and waited for my senses to come back. There would be no more reading that day.

The worst of it was that this was not even the most alarming of the emails I had received. The stories of assault, harassment, abuse, and rape women entrusted me with were each uniquely harrowing. Alarming tales that make the heart pound and the face flood with helpless fury were the rule, not the exception.

There were several women who wrote in about romantic partners who had drugged them and then pimped them out to friends, either for a fee or for what the men must have felt was just a good time. There were women whose male professors or teachers had demanded sex in exchange for decent grades or a pass, women who were chronically harassed at work, women who were raped by their dates, women who were told of their mothers' and grandmothers' assaults and then faced their own preemptive, generational trauma.

There was the woman who left her abusive husband after being a supporting wife for decades and who found herself shamed for "abandoning" him by her lifetime community. She was now surviving in isolation and on food stamps in her seventies. Should she have continued the charade? The socially expected emotional labor of not just catering to her man's needs and feelings but also feigning happiness—contentment even—through abuse?

There were the women who turned for help after assaults but were met with silence or indifference; the women who knew not to "overshare," who knew to use euphemisms and codes rather than speak the truth; women who knew they shouldn't be the "problem girls" so they suppressed, compartmentalized. The women who knew that reporting anything would be fruitless, but then were left on guard for the rest of their lives. Women who acquired dogs, tasers, pepper spray, crowbars, baseball bats, guns. But these didn't always help with the emotional and mental wounds, and the objects became physical representations of the emotional burden they had to carry, silently.

Women filtered their real emotions because they were shown they wouldn't be believed, because they were taught to adhere to appearances *or else*, because they were expected to prioritize other people's comfort levels, because they wanted to get on with their lives and had little trust in a system not built for them. This emotional labor imposed on them was as much about maintaining the power status quo and protecting men's position and interests as it was about a blanket social refusal to face up to the real, deeply disturbing effects of what is hiding behind the thin veils of civilized pretense: a gendered hierarchy that violates with sadism and impunity.

Even women who spoke up, even women who pursued justice through the criminal system, reported that the emotional toll was mostly unaddressed. And the added layers of emotional labor performance remained. There was little onus on healing, little prioritization or concern for their internal lives. Except that was what these women were left with: the negotiation of their internal selves with the outside, the modulation of their real emotional landscapes, repackaged to hide their wounds. One woman wrote a note as devastating as it was brief. "I'm still crying. And I'm 66 years old. 55 years later." That was it. A dozen words to describe the emotional burden of a lifetime.

What I realized as I sifted through messages was that the hundreds of women who honored me with their stories were not so much just sharing details of their assaults, they were sharing the impacts of them with me. They were sharing the emotional labor they did as a part of living in a rape culture.

That I was sent a deluge of testimonials related to sexual assault especially was most likely because my callout for emotional labor stories coincided with the work of community organizer Tarana Burke gaining traction in 2017 with the #MeToo movement. During this time, women across the country, and the world, of all ages and backgrounds were moved to share their stories of assault publicly. The moment had the effect of bringing home how widespread sexual assault and harassment were. Men may not all be perpetrators, but there were enough perpetrators out there that most women had their own examples to share.

Substantial attention to this issue has been a long time coming. In America, one out every five women will be raped in her lifetime (one out of every seventy-one men will be). Often, the men women have to be most afraid of are not strangers but the very men they are sharing their lives with. Women still face distressing levels of domestic violence (one in four) in countries with advanced economies as well as those in developing economies. Chillingly, of all the homicides of women in the United States reported to the FBI in 2019 where the perpetrators could be identified, nine out of every ten killers of women were men the women knew. Worse still, of those men, two-thirds were men who were either current boyfriends and husbands or ex-husbands of the murdered women.[1]

These statistics reveal the absolute ubiquity of the threat of violence for women from men. Beyond pointing to singular instances, they reveal a culture in which women have to watch their backs at all times—having to both bow down to the dominance of men and revere them, and also be on the lookout for ones who might turn bad. This demands from them a very special and constant form of emotional labor in bracing for potential violence, and in coping with it in its aftermath.

The stories that started coming up from all corners as 2017 came to a close were horrifying, but to many of us they also seemed all too familiar. Not to everyone, though. And therein lay the tension. The horror coupled with surprise and shock from many of my male acquaintances was in direct opposition to the knowing familiarity displayed by women across the globe.

For many women, this wasn't news; it was the way our world worked, the way our sisters' worlds worked, the way our mothers' worlds worked. Preparing for this world had been years in the making for me as a woman. How could these men not have noticed something that colored every single day of our lives, so many of our small choices, and so many of our big ones?

And for goodness' sake, *come on*. These men, who were feigning shock and indignation, they *knew*. Why else would my male friend stop me from taking the bus at midnight when I was a student, and insist I take a cab, even if that would make a massive hole in my monthly budget? What about the basketball community I grew up with, which looked the other way when the elderly club owner kissed the children in the girls' teams a little too close? Why would the young coaches make sure nobody ever had to ride with the club owner in his car alone on the way to games? Why did the bouncer and owner at the bar and restaurant I worked at make sure the female staff left quietly through the side door on nights the male clientele was getting too rowdy?

Because they *knew*, that's why. Because the threat of rape and assault, especially on girls and women and perpetrated by men, is not only everywhere, we all shift to accommodate it. People know. Women and men know. We warn women, we shield girls, sometimes boys. The whole way we operate makes space for it.

If we had previously insisted on treating tales of harassment and assault as exceptions, surely now we could see them as prevalent enough that women lived with them as a rule. The constant threat of assault happening meant women were forced into a survival form of emotional labor that had a chilling effect on the ways in which they could live their lives.

One woman, Kim, started her email describing herself growing up as a farm girl whose upbringing was steeped in "common sense" and "freedom." As an adult, she was raped by an acquaintance who put a knife to her throat. "I survived," she writes. "I told him to just remove the knife and I'd do what he wanted."

She was one of the few who did report her rape, and the report resulted in a conviction. But the conviction didn't take away from the pain of her radically altered reality. "He got 3–7 in prison. I got life," she wrote. "From that point on I have lived in awareness of my vulnerability."

Decades on, she described the many considerations she had to manage from morning to night. She was constantly checking in with herself and her surroundings, assessing whether she had measured her exposure to the right degree and applying the correct degree of precaution.

Once, when she was walking in town alone, a man asked her where her dogs were. She answered they were home, but later she fretted about the exchange. A neighbor shared with her that someone had mentioned while drunk that he was looking for a woman and she might do. Romantically she might do? Forcefully she might do?

The freedom she recalled running with as a girl was long in the rearview mirror now. Together with her sense of safety, she was having to mourn her sense of freedom. The emotional labor she used to negotiate this lack of freedom, she wished she didn't need to deploy.

The threat of rape and assault has a paralyzing effect on our ability to live life to its fullest, our willingness to jump on a bike, take a walk, use public transportation, explore the world. It has a paralyzing effect on our freedom. Worse, those trips we do take outside, and even—as it turns out—when we stay inside, all of these situations still require us to be on the lookout: assessing situations and people, scrutinizing the possibility of danger, the proximity of a man, the friendliness level of a new acquaintance, of an uncle, of a family friend. The anger of a husband.

This constant lookout is a form of emotional labor that conditions us to double, triple think, to be hesitant and impose limits on ourselves and on our lives. To be a strong, empowered woman does not mean no longer taking precautions; it means making painstaking decisions about freedom versus safety, saving versus safety, economic opportunity versus safety.

We are squarely placed with the responsibility, with this burden years before—lo and behold—we are assaulted, and then so often *blamed* for it. But haven't we always been blamed for it? Haven't we been placed with its emotional labor years before anything happened, just in case it ever did, in preparation and as a part of the blaming framework?

Adding insult to injury, because we do not yet live in a society that will take our side, when sexist incidents just short of full-blown assault happen, we must participate in a damaging, wearying process of de-escalation: downplaying incidents to protect our physical safety, downplaying incidents to protect our income, downplaying incidents not to upset those that we love, downplaying incidents to simply get through another day.

This pushes us into an unwanted complicity with the system: by not naming incidents, we do not sound the alarm, we keep others protected from the knowledge that casual humiliations, harassment, assaults, and rape are everywhere and constant. This kind of emotional labor ends up enabling an obliviousness that men can keep on professing that we are all living in an innocent reality surrounded by good people who only do good deeds. This emotional labor protects brazen humiliators, harassers, rapists, and assaulters and stops significant scrutiny to this form of suppressive power.

At least half of the population lives in constant expectation of this threat and carries its burden, emotionally, very often silently. From a young age, either through conversations with older women or through experiences of our own, women are taught what might expose them to more sexual violence and what is likely to expose them to less. I remember being eleven and wearing a short skirt, when an older female family member advised me to change. "You're sending the wrong message" was the euphemism she used.

There is no way I would have understood the full meaning and weight of that phrase at such a young age. In fact, I would go on to hear it time and time again well into my teen years, when I still was not fully cognizant of what was being insinuated. What was being said? That my skirt was a form of communication signaling my sexual availability and willingness? Who wrote the rule that one inch below the knee meant no sex, and one inch above the knee meant more sex? When it came to an eleven-year-old? Not an eleven-year-old, that's who.

It is incomprehensible to hold a child responsible for other people's sexual thoughts to the point that she is expected to manage them. Sex-related emotional labor started for me, as for many others, years before I had even formulated the existence, let alone the boundaries, of my own sexuality and sexual agency. Carrying the effects of other people's sexual desires on our bodies is taught to us before we get to define our sexuality for ourselves. Sexual emotional labor performed for others predates much of our own sexuality—to the extent that our sexuality is often shaped by it.

Living with the knowledge that there is a significant possibility we will be sexually assaulted leaves women living on the defensive. It forces us into behaving like prey, even if that is not a willing choice. And even if, for women and men, including when we participate in rituals leading to consensual sex, to cast one of us as prey and the other as predator is intensely reductive and debilitating for everyone involved.

In science, the term "ecology of fear" describes the behavioral, physiological, and neurobiological costs borne by animals avoiding predation. This framework takes into account the dissuading effects of predators on prey's lives and livelihoods—beyond a simple death toll when they are hunted as food. Active threat of being hunted may prompt prey to avoid areas where they would otherwise thrive, for instance, pushing them to seek less bountiful territory with extended debilitating ecological effects on their survival.[2]

Fear ecology begs us to include the costs of avoidance strategies beyond being eaten when looking at predator-prey impacts. I came across the term while reading about the reemergence of shivers of white sharks on the New England coast of the United States in the 2010s. Sharks were mostly stalking seals, but instances of targeted humans were growing.[3] Fear ecology logic can easily be applied in purely human contexts too.

The worst of emotional labor in a white male supremacist rape culture is that, as it is used by the less powerful to cope with and de-escalate an unjust and violent system, it often perpetuates it. Emotional labor as survival—in its limiting of women's speech, lives, and freedoms—becomes its own violent way of upkeeping the system.

This is particularly burdensome to some. Prejudice against women is compounded by other forms of dehumanizing stigmas like racism and transphobia. This leads women from minority groups to not only be more exposed to the threat of violence, and to the generational impacts of its trauma, but also less likely to be met with helpful resources, let alone justice.[4] For women who are Black, for women of color, for Indigenous women, for trans women, and especially for trans women of color, the use of emotional labor as survival is even more stifling to everyday existence, and even more starkly the difference between life and death.[5]

But as I contended with the impact of this collective horror and grappled with the stories that were shared with me, I realized that the ties between emotional labor and rape culture were deeper than even I had first realized. In a system that props up—punitively—the idea that women exist for the sake of others, and largely relieves men from mutual empathy, it is not only easier to disregard women's self-governance; harassment and assault become a way of violently enforcing the gendered experiential hierarchy. Assault and harassment weren't just extensions of living in a world men believed was built for their enjoyment and experience; assault and harassment were the punishments deployed on those women who veered. Entitlement to emotional labor was the reason for rape culture, not just its result.

In the fall of 2021, I had an unexpectedly illuminating conversation around the deadly aspects of the current unequal distribution of emotional labor that brought this last point home—particularly around gender. At the time, I was writing a story highlighting the vast number of women killed by mostly male current or former intimate partners in the United States, making a case for us to call it a specific American "femicide" problem.[6] The story was prompted by the disappearance of a young white American woman, Gabby Petito, whose body was recovered in Wyoming after she'd spent months living on the road visiting national parks with her fiancé, Brian Laundrie, with whom she had a history of domestic violence. Her death was ruled a homicide by strangulation, one of the more common ways in which women are killed in intimate partner settings.

To me, aside from being uniquely devastating, this tragedy also highlighted a larger problem America had almost entirely chosen to ignore, in spite of statistics being hard to dismiss. Among them: Ongoing female homicide numbers show three women are killed every day in the United States by boyfriends, husbands, or ex-husbands, and five every day by men they know.[7] Homicide stands as the fourth leading cause of death for girls and women one to nineteen years old, and the fifth leading cause of death for women twenty to forty-four.[8] Unlike male victims of homicide, who are mostly killed by members of the same sex, 98 percent of killers of women are men.[9]

Nor was the femicide problem getting any better. Although gender-specific homicide data hadn't yet been released by that point for the time in question, people were reporting from all parts of the country that COVID-19-induced lockdowns had caused women to be stranded in domestic situations without escape, and to desperate effect.

The links between this femicide crisis and emotional labor became clear to me on two fronts: first, in revealing just quite how dangerous women being trained into being mood managers and the passive bearers of men's pain in romantic relationships can become, and, second, beyond grappling with the disquieting reality that the man a woman has intimately laid next to is statistically the most likely person to be her killer, emotional labor presented itself at the root of the motivation behind these gendered killings.

This latter point became apparent when, to get a picture of what the femicide problem looked like on the ground, I talked to a small handful of prosecutors who were each dealing with this reality directly. One of those I spoke to was Scott Colom, a close acquaintance as well as a district attorney, who was elected on a progressive platform to an area in northeast Mississippi of around 140,000 people. He explained to me that domestic violence was one of the most common calls his police department received on a daily basis. Colom was barely astonished to hear the high rate of femicides nationwide. Just over the course of the few months of that 2021 summer, there had been three new cases of women killed by current or former male romantic partners in his district. Their names were Lisa Brooks, Whitney Taylor, and Kaliyah Brooks—and they were all three Black women, a group that is far more likely to die in this way, and far less likely to have their cases highlighted or reported on.

Colom explained that the judicial system was ill-equipped to deal with the broad problem of domestic abuse before it turned deadly. This was in large part because of a punitive focus on convicting abusers that rarely bore results, and a lack of meaningful attention and resources afforded to victims—like access to housing, money, jobs, and solutions-oriented counseling. When I spoke to Colom, he gave the example of a middle-aged woman that very week who had been beaten by her husband with a crowbar in one of his counties. She ended up in the emergency room, needing surgery. But when pressed by investigators, the woman said that while she was scared of her husband, she was also financially dependent on him to pay rent and get by, and she could not afford to divorce him. While there was federal funding for prosecutions, there was barely any funding to help women like this simply figure out the logistics of leaving. The system was myopic to the practical needs of a woman wondering whether to denounce, leave, or accommodate an abuser, and the result was an inability to curb domestic violence as it escalated.

As Colom reflected on a problem that felt overwhelmingly alarming and yet quite coolly ignored, he pointed to another root cause he had noticed in these killings, which were the attitudes and expectations of the male killers as they framed what they believed was owed to them by women. The vicious acts were caught up in power and control and a notion of ownership of women, but also in an ingrained view that women were responsible—liable even—for men's well-being.

"What I see is that they are treating women like their property. Like—*this person belongs to me. If I can't have her, nobody can have her. If I am not happy, it's her fault.* It's a frame of mind of toxic masculinity that I see all the time."

In particular, one case Colom prosecuted that resulted in a life sentence during that same summer of 2021 sprang to his mind. The case in question involved a middle-class white man, William Chisholm, who in early 2018, one month after his white optometrist ex-girlfriend, Shauna Witt, had broken up with him, stormed her eye clinic inside a Walmart with a gun and shot her dead as she attempted to flee.[10]

Colom explained that communication Chisholm, the killer, had with acquaintances in the run-up to the shooting revealed a deep sense of entitlement over Witt, his ex-girlfriend. He not only appeared to believe she was his property, he also believed she owed him his happiness. In other words, Chisholm had such a deep sense that Witt owed him perpetual emotional labor that when she chose to stop their relationship, and stop the emotional labor she performed for him, he ended her life.

This kind of view that downgrades women to mere mood enhancers and belongings of men is a constant, common theme, not an exception, Colom told me. "Historically there's been a problem with how men have been taught to view women. And some of that manifests itself in what we see with these murders," he said, adding adamantly that this was about gender, and gender education, rather than generalized mental health or isolated personality traits. "People say that a lot of this is anger management. But that doesn't make sense. A lot of these people do not have anger management issues with anyone other than women."

What is it that we are teaching men that allows them to think killing women in these contexts is okay, Colom asks rhetorically, where it would be unfathomable for them to resort to fatal violence with anyone else? "They get into an argument with somebody at work, if they get into a fight with somebody at a bar, it doesn't escalate to murder.

"Chisholm: he wasn't a threat to anybody else. Why is that?"

This is the dark side of a system that throws women to the wolves for men's enjoyment. This is the dark side of a system that teaches people not only that women owe men emotional labor but also that men's existences and emotional experiences stand above those of women. Such an unequal gendered distribution of emotional labor consolidates women as creatures worthy of life only to the extent that they hold an ability to enhance the lives of men. Cut off from men, their humanity wanes. Taken to an extreme, this humanity downgrade results in a casual taking of life rooted in delusional disconnection and superiority.

These femicides are not exceptions. This is the system expressing itself at its clearest. We are so immune to it, we are barely paying attention. But Scott Colom, with caseloads mounting, couldn't look the other way. And prosecutions and convictions seemed far from the long-term fix the world needed. To him, the solution was as pressing as it was simple. "In my mind, you are not going to be able to prevent a lot of that without a significant reeducation of men."

Figuring out ways forward has been the emotional labor taken on by some, yearning for ways that allow for progress, hope, and even forms of amends. To some, the reeducation of men Colom called for is an act that we cannot afford to put off.

In 2015, at sex and technology conference Arse Elektronika, Mattie Brice, a game designer and cultural critic, explained the precarious educator role she was forced into taking on after sex.[11] As a trans woman who had sex with cis men, she said she had little choice but to find prospective romantic partners in niche corners of the internet, marginalized from most other spaces. But as she engaged with men she met in this way, she found that lovers often cried and expressed intense emotions like shame after intimacy, expecting her to step in as a de facto therapist. She did not seek out this emotional labor, but containing the men in these moments was necessary. If the men spiraled, she knew it could be dangerous to her personal safety. "I had to learn how to navigate these waters in fear that he could turn violent if handled improperly," she said.

She did this even when her male partners were emotionally divested from her, which meant the emotional labor felt distinctly unequal. In those moments, Brice found herself explaining concepts like sex, gender, and sexuality to men who would not seek out the information elsewhere. With her, men learned about safer sex practices and informed consent. The true silver lining to providing a critical theory 101 class to people after they undermined her personhood was the knowledge that they would be more decent to the next trans woman they encountered.

Three years later, at Theorizing the Web,[12] Brice expanded on her analysis, reflecting that she saw her personal experiences as tied to a momentous arc. "I start to realize that in this very strange way, when I encounter men in this way, the next trans woman who encounters them will have a better experience. There is this very interesting movement where people think we are just becoming progressive because of time, however we are becoming progressive because of labor. Through a whole bunch of sexual labor, we are having movements go forward."

Just like Danielle, the professor in the previous chapter, Brice found herself putting herself on the line as she did emotional labor in a way that frayed at her sense of self, for a larger goal of progress. In her case, as taxing as this emotional labor was, understanding the impact and momentousness of what she was taking part in was also affirming. She also felt that in order to be sexually active, she barely had a choice.

By the time I interviewed Mattie Brice in 2021, by then a professor at New York University, she had begun to think about addressing the inequities in emotional labor exchanges through a gamer and social arts practice lens. She had experimented with monthly gatherings during which attendees explicitly announced to the group what their need was, and what they were willing to offer—in a kind of emotional labor trade gathering. Her efforts had proven hard, in part because people who were willing to show up to be a part of an arts experiment were not necessarily "committing to being a part of an emotional network," which was required for a reckoning with emotional labor.

"Communities are way more foundational, way more structured, way more deep than what we see as community: as people who mutually affect each other," Brice said of people reluctant to fully engage with their interconnectedness. As she moved on to thinking about accountability, and how to get people to commit to it, she had turned her mind to models of transformative and restorative justice.

For true change, the teacher cannot bear all of the emotional labor for the sake of her students. For true change, an emotional laborer cannot take on the emotion work for the whole group. The group needs to see, understand, and even name emotional labor first, and each individual must bear emotional responsibility not only for themselves but for the wider group. That is the paradox Brice had connected to changing, and that is the paradox she met some resistance with.

Teaching others about realities outside their own in such an embodied way that it becomes emotional labor may have the ability to move minds and hearts in a more justice-oriented direction, but so long as members of more powerful groups refuse to shoulder their own responsibility within an emotional network, nothing radical can happen. Nonconsensual emotional labor emanating from entitlements based on power hierarchies is not the root of change; reversing the trend and shifting the emotional labor onus is.

For one Detroit-based organizer, therapist, and clinical social worker, Kalimah Johnson, part of the solution is freeing harmed parties from the burden of emotional labor and shifting the burden of emotional responsibility onto those who did the harm. Johnson is the founder of Detroit's SASHA Center, which caters to Black women, mostly under the form of support groups, acknowledging, honoring, and incorporating into its programs the specificity of the Black female experience and history in relation to sexual assault.

"Black women have never had dominion over their bodies; our bodies were never ours. When we were brought here, no was not an option for us anywhere. Not with other Black men in the field, not with white masters, not with white women partners of white masters.

"We've never been allowed to say no. It's not an option. It's never been an option. SASHA Center spends a lot of time trying to teach women that it is an option, that you can say no, that you can break your silence, and that your silence breaking is not going to break you or others. Silence breaking is about your own liberation."

Black women are used to having to do a very specific form of emotional labor, which Johnson calls donning a "cape": acting as a bulletproof superhero who as a priority holds together the community. Because of the specificity of this experience, her center is only open to Black women who, in a group of peers, can feel comfortable lowering their emotional shield. "In our community, if you ask Black women if they want to come to a group for rape, they will say no, no—the hell fuck no. Because now you're fucking with my cape—my superwoman shit. Or now you're asking me to disclose about my family. Now you're asking me to be weak and talk about something and I am sure that if I talk about it, I will lose the breath out of my body and die."

Her center fosters the exchange of a classic form of emotional labor, provided in a group setting, in a way that uplifts and pays attention to broader community. As a practice, it is close to the one form of emotional labor we are comfortable paying for well: psychotherapy. The value here in the emotional labor, though, is in its mutuality and in its act as a form of community healer beyond just individuals.

But Johnson doesn't stop there. She believes that healing can be found among peers, but also sometimes by requiring perpetrators to take part in the process. In her personal life, Johnson explains she was able to experience restorative justice through conversations with her first abuser, a female cousin. She was also able to experience restorative justice in her direct reckoning with another, generational trauma.

Seeking a better sense of self, a couple of decades ago, the clinical social worker researched her genealogy and traced her family back to a plantation in Kentucky, identifying the descendants of the family who enslaved her ancestors. She recalls with great precision when she first contacted one of them, a woman named Betty. Johnson called and left her a voice mail. "I said, 'Hi my name is Kalimah Johnson. I am from Detroit. I am doing a little bit of research on my family, our migration patterns. And I learned that your family was the family that owned my family when we were enslaved; and if we could talk, I would appreciate it.'

"She called me back straightaway. She said, 'Wow-wow-wow-wow.' She said, 'I knew I had this in my family, but I never knew it would meet me in person.' Then she cried. I let her cry for about five minutes.

Then I said, 'Betty.' She said, 'Yeah?' And I said, 'These tears are okay, but we have work to do.'"

For Johnson, that moment in the conversation was the first step in the journey toward repair, in which Betty was required to play an active role well beyond tears and into reckoning.

In 2004, Johnson and her sister made a trip to Kentucky, visited four plantations, and met with some of the descendants of the white family who had profited from the enslavement of her ancestors. Betty, a retired white teacher, had them for dinner in the town house she inherited, serving asparagus and chicken on old, fancy plates. Johnson's sister lost little time in asking their host whether she felt she owed them an apology.

"She said, 'I absolutely do think that we owe you an apology. Not only do I think we owe you an apology, I think we owe you much more. I don't think that we can ever repay you. And I am so sorry. So sorry. I know we benefit from free slave labor. I wouldn't have this house if it wasn't for our old money, and our old money is tied to your family being sold.' She said, 'I am very clear about that.'

"My sister gets up so casually and walks up to this woman and they embrace and cry. I think this is what has not happened in this country, and that needs to."

Restorative justice requires all parties involved in wrongdoing to heal, "holding people accountable and making people pay in ways that are less traditional and less criminalized," in Johnson's words. Emotional labor deployed in this way is no longer part of a stifling defense mechanism for already stifled groups but instead becomes a powerful force for transformation.

Part of the solution to the emotional labor drain on women and minorities is to demand its execution from the top. Under the current system of experiential hierarchy, beneficiaries of privilege and power are able to endlessly demand emotional labor from those at the margins. Not only does reversing this demand for emotional labor create a path for accountability and redress, it also stops one of the causes for violence—which is the demand, sometimes deadly, of emotional labor itself.

"Sometimes blindly and sometimes not so blindly at all, I believe people can get better. I really believe that healing is possible, and forgiveness is very possible. Some people don't ever want to forgive, and they don't have to, but forgiveness is really within yourself," Johnson shares of her own experiences.

When she works with male perpetrators, she tells me, she has an acronym, ARRA, which stands for accountability, remorse, root cause, and action. "You have to take accountability for what you did, express some kind of remorse, you can't express remorse without addressing root cause—What was the root cause? What fueled [the] behavior?— and then: What action are you going to do after this? How are you going to get better? How are you going to get back? That's all restorative justice for me. I really believe that's how we get better. You've got to be present for that. In order to be present for that, you've got to be able to see the humanity in people."

It's a tough order, and as she points out, not everyone wants to forgive, not to mention that some perpetrators may certainly not be willing to do the work. But spreading the load and shifting the work onto the harming party, requiring a reckoning that results in real introspection, dialogue, growth, and connectivity, is a solution when willing parties are involved—the kind of work of deep love that can affect systemic change.

For Kalimah Johnson, these instances of restorative justice can be planned, but they can be deployed spontaneously. During our interview, she recalls a recent visit to the Detroit Institute of Arts, a world-class museum, containing masterpieces by Louise Bourgeois, Kehinde Wiley, Vincent van Gogh, Mickalene Thomas, and Diego Rivera, among many others.

"I had this beautiful scarf. I was in the souvenir shop. Two white women just came up to me and grabbed my scarf. They walked up to me and started touching my clothing! I felt like an exhibit." Johnson laughs, describing something that is in fact tragically unfunny: her bodily integrity unceremoniously being disregarded and disrespected.

"I am not part of the museum, ma'am," was her immediate retort. "I said, 'You all have to get consent to touch people. What are you doing?' They weren't even conscious of it. They said: 'Oh, oh, I am sorry.' Then I said: 'No, no, no, stay right here, now it's your turn. Now I am going to touch you.' They were uncomfortable. I said, 'It's uncomfortable, isn't it?' They said, 'Yeah, yeah, you made your point.'"

The story is a good reminder for white women, and other women who find themselves in positions of privilege, that they are not absolved from becoming emotional or physical violators. But it is also a reminder for everyone to take responsibility in complicated emotional networks, where being prey in one situation does not mean you are not predator in another.

With this important reminder and consequential nuance, I am still left wondering how women across all intersections of identities even function, let alone function with joy, optimism, and defiance. How are women able to feel pleasure when it comes to their bodies and sex, when those very things are used as tools to dismantle their power, to dominate and silence them? How can women become emotional agents for themselves, before being committed to the emotional service of others? How do they live in this world accommodating for very possible future trauma, trying to prevent it in the present, while dealing with trauma from their own past, as well as from generations that came before? How do they not become the traumatizers themselves?

The morning of my sexual assault I was wearing jeans, a T-shirt, and no makeup. It wasn't dark out; I wasn't drunk. I was on the way to the airport, suitcase rolling on my cement street in Rome. When a man approached me offering help with my bag down the stairs to the tunnel that would take me to the train that would take me to the airport, I did think, *Does he really want to help me with my suitcase or am I in danger?*

I told him no. He took it anyway. My buzzing mind, my lesson to doubt the chivalry of a stranger: they didn't change a thing. My emotional labor would not stop the knife he put to my neck or his pressing hands. What did change the outcome of that morning were the people whose voices I heard at the other end of the tunnel that later caused him to flee.

I don't want to have to warn my niece. I would like to think I would not make my niece ever feel like her appearance is responsible for the thoughts and actions of others. I would like to teach her she is free to wear what she wants, to paint her lips or not, just as she wants. I would like to tell her that if she wants to save her pennies, she should feel free to take the bus. I would like to teach her that the street belongs to her as much as it belongs to others.

I would like to free her of that emotional labor and have her put that energy, that constant buzzing in the back of her mind—*Am I safe? What does he mean? Was that a sound? Is he following me? Does he seem upset?*—to better use.

I want the buzzing in the back of her mind to be something more like: *The water is glistening. What did I think of that film? It was funny when she said that. How might I reform the electoral system? Maybe tomorrow I will wear my happy shoes.*

I want to fight for a world where mutuality and consent rule, and people are brave enough to free her of that kind of survival emotional labor. I want her to think of emotional labor not as something she deploys out of desperation to conserve herself at a low, almost undetectable frequency, but instead as a valuable tool that all should be performing to improve and protect the community.

I want her to demand growth and reckoning from people who have done her wrong. I want them to give it to her willingly, and for her to give it in turn to those who have earned it. I want her to operate at her highest possible frequency, in symphony with those around her, receiving and giving the most radical kind of love—the kind of love bell hooks refers to as an action, not a feeling that just sits; the kind of love that demands responsibility and accountability—and is always accompanied by growth.[13]

Above everything else, I want her to think about happiness not just as an experience that she is on earth to facilitate in others, and I want her to think of her body not just as a canvas for the actions and feelings of others. And I want others, especially boys and men, to understand that she is everything except the simple vehicle of their own emotions and experiences when they relate to her. That is the key to restituting freedom to women and girls, and it is also not so incidentally the key to resolving the worst kind of gendered violence. That is the key, also, for freedom in men.

SIX

What About the Men?

CONFINEMENT

Comedian Hari Kondabolu, known for his 2017 documentary *The Problem with Apu*, which critiqued *The Simpsons'* reductive portrayal of Indian immigrants in America and launched many an internet troll, has a stand-up piece about our culture's way of deploying the expression "Boys will be boys."[1] "Nothing good has ever come before that phrase! It's always the worst thing ever," he exclaims in the piece.

"It's never like: 'Hey, did you hear Obama signed a nuclear deal with Iran? *Boys will be boys!* Using nonviolent means to end conflict!' It's never that.

"It's never: 'Hey, did you see Channing Tatum dance at a gay pride parade? Yeah! *Boys will be boys!* Being so comfortable with your sexuality that you support the sexuality of others!'

"It's never, 'Hey, Hari, did I see you under a tree with your headphones on, crying? *Boys will be boys!*' I was listening to the Cure and their hit song 'Boys Sometimes Cry.'"

They all sound delightfully absurd, of course, which is the point the comedian is making: we never use men's gender to accentuate positive behaviors of emotional intelligence, empathy, or emotional literacy. Instead, we brutally box them out of these by highlighting some of the worst conduct individuals might display. This doesn't just have the effect of giving these behaviors a free pass based on a cultural understanding of what is "normal"; it also has the effect of directing boys and men toward what performing their gender should look like.

Kondabolu ends his skit pointing out that "boys will be boys" is mostly preceded by words describing male violence, sexual harassment, or "your roommate sticking his balls in your peanut butter." None of the actions are laudable, but all of the ways in which the comedian deploys the justification are painfully realistic.

In recent memory, this kind of excuse was even deployed to brush off the responsibility of a soon-to-be-elected United States president. In October 2016, *The Washington Post* released a tape of then presidential candidate Donald Trump back in 2005 talking to an entertainment host, bragging about his ability to sexually thrust himself on women without their consent, which is sexual assault. On the recording, he can be heard saying: "I just start kissing them. It's like a magnet. Just kiss. I don't even wait. And when you're a star, they let you do it. You can do anything. Grab 'em by the pussy. You can do anything."

When he issued his apology, Trump dismissed accusations, stating he had been engaging in "locker-room banter."[2] This was simply how men spoke to each other when they were around one another—casually bragging about how good they were at rape, he implied.

But such statements that excuse behaviors and push men into thinking that if they are to be seen as men, as *men's men*, they should be aggressive and insensitive to the point of becoming violators don't just put women at risk, they fail men too. They dehumanize them, cast a dark shadow over their entire gender, and put them in harm's way.

Such an example may seem like the simple, foolish iterations of a public figure known to be crass, but locker-room excuses for boys and men continue downstream, away from celebrities and formal halls of power. In 2013, two teenage boys and star members of the high school football team in Steubenville, Ohio, were found guilty of the rape of a teenage girl the year before. The assaults took place over the course of an evening during which the victim was transported between party locations, unresponsive. Footage of the incident was unashamedly shared across social media. The events drew national coverage as an interesting rape case in the internet age, but as they did, they also drew attention to the level of empathy expressed in town—and beyond—toward the boys performing the crime rather than toward the girl.[3] Parents, coaches, and school officials looked the other way to protect their beloved local football team, shrugging their shoulders at boys being boys. Months after the initial convictions, four more charges were brought against two coaches, a principal, and a school superintendent who were accused of helping brush the crimes underneath the table.[4] In a 2018 documentary on the subject called *Roll Red Roll*, director Nancy Schwartzman drew attention to the culture in this football town that was putting its daughters at risk to protect its sons—caring first and foremost about the futures and well-being of their boys over those of their girls.[5]

Men objecting to feminism online and off-line often push back with questions that can be summed up in the following five words—but what about the men? Men struggle with depression and are dying at greater rates of suicide, they protest. Men are sent to war and to prison. It is hard for men, too, they plead.[6] These men have a valid concern, but they are mis-framing themselves as standing in opposition to women. Complaining about greater suicide rates and trauma related to war or incarceration doesn't put men and women on opposite sides; it very simply points out that men stand to lose from this patriarchal, white supremacist, capitalist system too. Patriarchy insinuates men are in power, not that all men are in power over others, and certainly not that all men stand to win.

The system operates under rigid rules, with harsh costs as well as the promise of great gains. Patriarchy cedes control to men by requiring domination. But this domination is paradoxically an extraordinarily destructive force—for the people around them as well as for the men themselves.

Emotional labor occupies a very special position here. When interpreted as the act of caring for others, of being emotionally expressive and communicative, of putting others' interests before your own and having a communal mindset, emotional labor is seen as women's work. Not only is it mostly seen as women's work, it is simply perceived as the act of women being women. Emotional labor, for all the effort, time, and skill it takes, is often just taken in as women in their natural state.

But by isolating emotional labor to women, we invalidate men as caring, compassionate, gentle, nurturing, or any other attribute stereotyped as feminine. For men in this world, the most dangerous thing they can do status-wise, still, is be seen as feminine. As long as emotional labor remains seen as an essential part of being a woman, it can be dangerous for men to even try to partake in it. But if you understand emotional labor as not simply a burden but a healing tool, an essential way of connecting and thriving as a human, you see how men being cut off from this kind of performance stands to make them losers on a deeper level. Through being told they can show only a minute set of emotions around dominance, aggression, competitiveness, and risk-taking, they are also robbed of an essential part of what it means to live a full, healthy, and connected life.

While emotional labor may be the tool that has enabled women to survive and adapt to oppression, it is also a transformative, restorative force when distributed across power differentials. Deny that to men by threatening their masculinity if they even dare to hint at compassion or sensitivity, and you deny them the possibility for communal and sovereign healing.

Of all the men I spoke to on these themes, race and gender advocate and award-winning author Jimmie Briggs's story stands out the most for the lessons learned and for the hope. Jimmie grew up in Ferguson, Missouri, four decades before the small suburb of St. Louis made international headlines after white police officer Darren Wilson shot and killed unarmed Black teenager Michael Brown in 2014, sparking nationwide protests and contributing to the modern-day beginning of the Black Lives Matter movement. Jimmie's father was emotionally and physically abusive toward him, behavior Jimmie specifically pins as a reaction to his not fulfilling traditional ideals of masculinity from an early age. He was the sensitive, short, chubby kid with glasses, he tells me, and his father loved to ridicule him for it in front of others.

"My father mocked me for my physical awkwardness, not being able to succeed in sports, not really thriving in any one sport, and being seen as the soft kid. The kid who cried, the kid who was awkward around girls, who couldn't ask a girl out, much less sleep with a woman in high school or college."

By the time he graduated from Morehouse, the prestigious historically Black men's college in Atlanta, Georgia, famously attended by Martin Luther King Jr., he was ready to forge ahead and reconcile his father's engraved expectations with his skill set. His plan was to be a journalist and cover war.

When Jimmie first opened up to me in a coffee shop off Lenox Avenue in Harlem, I remember him falling silent, staring down at his plate. He had ordered a sandwich that came with potato chips. His food remained untouched until, searching for words, he started picking up one potato chip at a time and putting it back down. His head bowed down to the table, he repeated the gesture until he eventually shared.

"Covering conflict as a journalist was a benchmark for me. For me, that was a way I could prove my ultimate manhood. If I cover a war or cover wars no one can refute. Like—'What have you done?' I was in Colombia, I was in Afghanistan, I was in the Gaza Strip. Like, 'Okay, top that. You can't challenge my manhood. No one can challenge my manhood.'"

Jimmie told me he also had a "fear of invisibility," of forever being the boy at the party standing all by himself against the wall, too shy to ask a girl to dance. Cultural messaging was cruel to those boys and those men, especially Black men, he knew. It wasn't just a question of conforming, it was fear of being overlooked. "I felt like if I didn't make myself fit into the man box, then I would never be seen."

"Man box," a term increasingly used by psychologists and advocates, refers to a very rigid set of behavior and personality rules men are expected to adhere to if they are to be safe from being challenged on their status as "real men." While women have spent the last few decades challenging traditional notions of femininity and breaking down barriers for increased rights, the same change has not happened for men.

In a 2017 study that surveyed more than one thousand young men in the United States, the United Kingdom, and Mexico, respectively, led by the organization Promundo, the man box is defined as the combination of seven pillars.[7] The first pillar is self-sufficiency, or the idea that men should be self-reliant emotionally and physically. The second pillar is toughness, understood as the ability to display physical and emotional strength in all circumstances. The third pillar is physical attractiveness, achieved without signaling too much effort. The fourth pillar is fulfilling traditional gender roles, financially providing for a household, and avoiding tasks deemed feminine. The fifth pillar is being both straight and homophobic. The sixth pillar is being hypersexual with no ability to say no. The seventh pillar is having the final say at home, having control over women's movements, and the belief that violence and aggression are sometimes necessary tools to gain respect.

To be clear, these pillars, which are sometimes also referred to in the context of what is called "toxic masculinity," are not a positive list or a how-to for men; rather, they are a condensation of the restrictions imposed on men. Harsh emotional rules are not just for women but apply to men, too—with very different requirements and consequences. Gender performance and oppression, at its most harmful, is a tight, two-way street. Penalties for those who deviate are severe, and in some ways harsher for men than for women. Calling a girl a tomboy is mostly an affectionate description, but calling a boy a sissy is an insult. In a misogynistic world, anything at all feminine is tarnishing.

In the Promundo study, which interviewed 1,318 men in the United States aged eighteen to thirty across all backgrounds and demographics, representative of the overall populations, three quarters of the men agreed with the statement that "society as a whole tells me that guys should act strong even if they feel scared or nervous inside." The one form of emotional labor men are actively socially trained to perform is emotion suppression, followed by displays of strength or aggression. Anything beyond is transgressive.

This kind of restricted emotion expression stands in huge contrast to what emotional labor usually refers to—as a form of work that prioritizes other people feeling good. In fact, many of the pillars are the perfect opposite of emotional labor, not only requiring men to cut themselves off from truly understanding and managing their own emotions but also, through the imperative of aggression and dominance, priming them to disregard the emotions of others, thereby centering their own.

In my interviews with men, this often made it feel like the topic of emotional labor was a complete dead end. This was not only because the concept of emotions requiring time, effort, and skill astonished them to the point of deep confusion but also because so many professed themselves to be nonemotional.

One of the men I interviewed, Jeff, a straight white man in his late thirties in a long-term relationship, was dumbfounded by the concept. After I repeatedly explained what emotional labor referred to, Jeff finally announced he had understood what I was talking about. He then proudly made another firm assertion. "I am not an emotional person, so I do not need emotional labor!"

As Jeff expressed the thought that emotional labor was irrelevant to him, I realized our interview would not last very long. I initially thought the interview would go into the unusable pile, but it soon dawned on me that Jeff was actually expressing the crux of the problem. "I am not a particularly emotive person," he continued, "which I am sure is somewhat familiar for men. I am generally considered pretty flat."

If the first man box pillar is in part the idea that men should be self-reliant emotionally and the second pillar is in part emotional toughness, it didn't take me long to understand that getting men to open up would also be asking them to violate core guidelines of gendered behavior. To an extent, all Jeff was really doing was refusing to play with those very rigid boundaries. But to another, Jeff was engaging in a bad-faith power play. By refusing to acknowledge the existence of his own emotions, Jeff was relinquishing the need for any emotional effort or the belonging to any emotional network, further rendering the work of others around him, absorbing and caring for his emotions, invisible.

Unlike what Jeff may like to believe, men do, in fact, possess emotions—just as much as all other humans. The work of psychologist and neuroscientist Lisa Feldman Barrett, referred to briefly in chapter 4, has shed light on the ways in which emotions entirely inform our understanding of the world.[8] Importantly for debates around gender, her work confirms that the separation between what we have thought of as rational and emotional is totally fake.

As humans with brains, we receive all the information from the world through our five senses—sight, sound, smell, taste, and touch. Based on how our body is reacting to these five senses, our brain processes the answer to simple questions: Am I feeling good or bad? Am I feeling stimulated or unstimulated? Neuroscience calls the answer to these simple questions "affect," or base feelings. Erik Nook, a professor of psychology at Princeton University, described affect to me as the "undifferentiated, unconceptualized tone of how you're feeling." Combining affect with past experiences and environment, the brain then forms what is referred to as "emotion concepts," more complex emotions like guilt, joy, embarrassment, apprehension, and sadness.[9] The brain processes the entire world through this mechanism. It operates like a scientific experiment that constantly makes predictions and corrections, using affect transformed into emotions to produce conscious thoughts on the world. Thus, for humans with functional brains, including Jeff, there is simply no such thing as being "unemotional." Even the most intellectual-seeming thought originates in a base set of feelings.

Understanding this is momentous. It exposes simplistic theories of the brain we have long relied on in pop psychology as beyond questionable. In particular, a theory of a "triune brain" wrongly differentiates among three types of brain: the reptilian brain (the most basic or primitive), the mammal brain (the emotional one), and a rational human cortex (signaling a supposedly evolved brain).

Neuroscientist Barrett painstakingly points out in her book *How Emotions Are Made* that our brains' mechanics do not separate us from the rest of the animal kingdom. "The human brain is anatomically structured so that no decision or action can be free of interoception or affect, no matter what fiction people tell themselves," she writes.[10] "Your bodily feeling right now will project forward to influence what you feel and do in the future. It is an elegantly orchestrated, self-fulfilling prophecy, embodied within the architecture of your brain."

Far from being unevolved, the emotional nature of our brains makes them brilliant. One thing all humans are born with, Barrett writes, is "a fundamental ability to learn from regularities and probabilities around you."[11]

But most people—when it comes to making sense of the world with science and the brain—do not think of Lisa Feldman Barrett. Instead, they rely on outdated, largely discredited ideas from the nineteenth century.

Charles Darwin, the British Victorian biologist who is often described as the father of evolutionary science and is known for coining the theory of natural selection, undoubtedly revolutionized our understanding of the natural world. But his theories on race and sex do not stand the test of time. In his book *The Descent of Man*, he claimed:

> Woman seems to differ from man in mental disposition, chiefly in her greater tenderness and less selfishness; and this holds good even with savages, as shewn by a well-known passage in Mungo Park's Travels, and by statements made by many other travelers. Woman, owing to her maternal instincts, displays these qualities towards her infants in an eminent degree; therefore it is likely that she should often extend them towards her fellow-creatures. Man is the rival of other men; he delights in competition, and this leads to ambition which passes too easily into selfishness. These latter qualities seem to be his natural and unfortunate birthright. It is generally admitted that with woman the powers of intuition, of rapid perception, and perhaps of imitation, are more strongly marked than in man; but some, at least, of these faculties are characteristic of the lower races, and therefore of a past and lower state of civilization.

The chief distinction in the intellectual powers of the two sexes is shewn by man attaining to a higher eminence, in whatever he takes up, than woman can attain—whether requiring deep thought, reason, or imagination, or merely the use of the senses and hands.[12]

Darwin's observations seek to justify the white supremacist, patriarchal state of the world as inherently natural with no proof except the arrogance of his own belief systems. He uses the fact that female bodies bear children to cast women as more tender and selfless, a set of attributes we can today understand as casting women into emotional labor–heavy roles. In a classic benevolent sexist way, he lauds women for positive attributes like being "intuitive" but in the same breath infantilizes them and marks them as inferior.[13] Propping up his argument are racist beliefs about "lower state[s] of civilization" and "savages."

This obsession with marking a "natural" inferiority in women rages on to this day. Clinical psychologist Jordan Peterson, branded the "custodian of the patriarchy" by *The New York Times*,[14] insists that domination, selfishness, self-sufficiency, and competitiveness are all superiority signs of evolved masculinity. To back up his claim, in his bestselling book, *12 Rules for Life*,[15] he famously describes the highly hierarchical social functioning of lobsters. The crustaceans' nervous systems reward aggressive lobsters with the release of serotonin into their bodies, reinforcing their future willingness to fight and win. Peterson insinuates that this finding shows that hierarchies are hardwired. We are therefore presumably to believe, based on lobsters, that striving for equality, or disrupting systems of domination, goes against nature.

This selective kind of thinking has made Peterson extremely popular, especially among groups desperate to justify long-standing systems of oppression that are starting to unravel. But for all the lobsters, Peterson does not mention the plethora of counterexamples, such as elephants, who live in matriarchal societies, where the oldest female elephant leads, using her long experience to remember the location of far-flung resources like water. She makes decisions for the benefit and survival of the herd based on wisdom, not aggression.[16] Collaborative societies that share rather than compete for resources—like trees in plant communities that operate through complex subterranean networks to heal one another—thrive rather than self-destruct.[17]

Peterson loves to quote the aggressive patriarchal social structures of chimpanzees,[18] which are evolutionarily close to us, as elucidating the validity of our human, male-dominant status quo, but omits to mention an equally close ape cousin we have that suggests the total opposite. Science journalist Angela Saini, in her book *Inferior*,[19] writes that bonobos, unlike chimpanzees, live in communal, matriarchal structures, where cooperation is key and aggressive male bonobos are often shunned from the group. Meanwhile, more collaborative male bonobos who are able to live side by side with female bonobos with little conflict and under the matriarchal order end up fathering the most children.

These examples that focus on the greater world—from oceans and deserts to forests and beyond—may seem compelling and even mystically revealing (which is likely what authors seeking to normalize violent hierarchies are going for), but we needn't go that far. There is simple evidence in the boring human world that exposes the premise of this kind of thinking—that current social orders are natural and should be accepted—as totally off the mark.

As discussed in the first chapters of this book, our human brains do receive neurological feedback from perceived status, but because brains are so impressionable, because they are so plastic, they tend to just go along with expected stereotypes—to avoid backlash. But when stereotypes or expectations change, human brains change along with them.

Once more, the world around us isn't shaped by fixed attributes of the brain; our brain reacts to the cues it receives from the world around us. Thus, changing expectations and stereotypes in the outside world can have formidable impacts on individual brains.

In 1990, analyzing millions of test results from that time period, Janet Hyde, a psychology professor, together with colleagues, found slight gender differences in math performance in high school students favoring boys. This confirmed a stereotype that boys were, on average, better at math. But at the time, more boys than girls were taking advanced mathematics in high school, and more boys than girls took chemistry and physics, where math-adjacent problem-solving skills were also taught. In other words, girls weren't training to the same degree. The reason for a slight difference could be difference in abilities, or it could be difference in interest and training. Over the following couple of decades, sociocultural stereotypes changed, and programs started encouraging girls to take STEM subjects where they had not previously. By 2008, looking at millions of test results again two decades after the initial inquiry, Hyde and Janet Mertz, a biochemist and molecular biologist, found that that difference had disappeared.[20] Boys and girls were now equally talented at math.

This strongly suggested, they found, that gender difference in mathematics performance was not tied to natural ability or factors that were "innate" and "immutable" but rather to changeable sociocultural factors. Basically, once messaging changed, and high schools and their staff stopped passing on messages that girls were less good at math than boys, girls stopped being less good at math than boys.

Thinking that accepts the status quo and justifies it as evidence of its own validity risks limiting this kind of exciting catch-up. Why would we want to stand in the way of such progress?

My own mother's two older brothers went to the University of Cambridge and studied law. By the time she graduated the equivalent of high school, my mother wanted to follow in the family tradition, but she was told by her parents that women did not go to college or university. She traveled, married, had three daughters, and led a happy life. But when my father died unexpectedly early, her lack of a university degree significantly affected her economic ability to support herself and us as children still of school age. She did support us all, though, but on a fraction of the salary she could have earned had she been afforded the same chances as her brothers earlier in life. She never remarried, is the most positive person I know, and continued working until she turned seventy. She could not afford to retire before.

Does this family story mean women are inherently less talented at law, inherently less rational, or inherently less good at making ends meet? No. This story reflects belief systems that radically altered many women's socioeconomic conditions and outcomes. We cannot have an honest, good-faith conversation about inherent differences between groups until these kinds of obstacles have truly been lifted.

Beyond individual examples, the truth is there is a fundamental, logical flaw in much of the patriarchal upholders' reasoning. If, as Darwin believed, species evolved to survive longer, men would be evolving to community settings because that is what allows longer life. If humans were to adapt and evolve to live longer, better lives, then men would not be forced into aggressive performances that harm them and shorten their lives. From an evolution standpoint, thriving men would be those who were able to practice self-care, live connected, empathetic lives, be in happy relationships, and center and understand their emotions as well as the emotions of others.

A change like this would make so much more sense on many levels. Life expectancy has been declining in the United States since 2014,[21] especially for men,[22] in large part because of an increase of deaths of despair tied to alcohol, drug use, and suicide.[23] Other developed countries are not facing the same decline. It is hard to pinpoint an exact reason for this increase in national mortality rate, but lack of social support at systemic and communal levels contributes to the problem, as do macho beliefs tying emotionality and connectivity to weakness. A male refusal to acknowledge, let alone deal with, emotions is a drain of epic proportions on our society—not only in terms of the work it creates for others but, critically, in the threat it poses to the survival of the men themselves.

Unlike Jeff, Jimmie, the former war reporter, did not feel like gendered standards led to men not having emotions but rather required men to edit their emotions to be in line with specific masculine ideals. The acceptable ones he identified were "anger, impatience, frustration, arrogance, dominance, overpowering, recklessness, boldness, assertiveness." None of these proved useful in understanding and addressing his own turmoil.

"The real me [was] so torn up emotionally about what I was seeing, what I was experiencing, and not being able to talk about it. Covering wars is probably the worst thing I could have done in my life, but that's a choice I made because it reaffirmed what I thought was missing. You know, my sense of manhood."

As Jimmie was going back and forth to conflict zones, it might seem to outsiders like Jimmie had achieved peak masculinity. Here was a man who was using great courage through emotional and physical strength to bring to light global atrocities and combat. But Jimmie wouldn't even entertain the idea of peak masculinity when he talked to me. All this time period reminded him of was an inability to connect with what he was going through internally. "My male programming wouldn't allow me to look in the mirror and see I was in distress: I was in emotional and psychic distress."

Where they caused Jeff to entirely suppress his emotional range or at least his professed awareness of it, these gendered expectations stopped Jimmie from doing any emotional labor on himself. "I wasn't doing the physical self-care and I damn sure wasn't doing the emotional self-care. I wasn't actively processing what I was experiencing or seeing, I wasn't talking to friends or colleagues, I wasn't talking to my wife at the time, I wasn't going to see a therapist, I wasn't doing spiritual work. Because I felt like to do that in the face of what I was facing would be an admission that I couldn't hack it, that I couldn't cope, that I wasn't strong enough or good enough to do that kind of reportage."

Jimmie connects this self-censoring to a broader problem all men face, even when they do not go to war. "I think the crisis in manhood comes from the limited expression of emotional range. I think for all men, myself included. I think we are punished for expressing a fuller emotional range, which all humans possess [. . .] I think the crisis comes in not being supported or encouraged or being recognized as men when that fuller range of emotions is expressed."

Psychologist Michael Reichert, the founding director of the Center for the Study of Boys' and Girls' Lives at the University of Pennsylvania, told me that men stopping themselves from identifying, expressing, or sharing feelings beyond anger came as no surprise in our current climate. "Too many men are punished and brutalized if they show vulnerable feelings," Reichert said. This culturally enforced rule was the equivalent of men and boys becoming "cut off from their hearts," a mechanism that starts at a young age.

"Stereotypes and myths prey on parents, teachers, and coaches, causing us to forget that boys are relational," Reichert said. He pointedly explained that boys are just as relational as girls, meaning their brains need just as much connection and community to develop and thrive. But rather than giving boys what they actually need, we live in a world that still believes close relationships are bad for boys, especially when it comes to their mothers. This is in part because of disproven, homophobic convictions that a boy who is close to his mother and is emotionally literate is not performing straightness (which violates the fifth pillar of the man box).

The mama's boy myth is heartbreaking, Reichert said. "Given the division of emotional labor in most households, it is most likely the mother who will provide the emotional container for the boys." If she is taught to distance herself for what she thinks is the boy's best interest, her son might be left with no one to speak to. We not only need to be encouraging dads to be doing more emotional labor in the family, including with their kids, we have got to stop denying young boys their full humanity.

"I think that the dimension of being human is so fundamentally important that when we restrict it and deny it all together, we are cutting boys off from so much of life. We are emotional creatures. We experience our emotions and express them in relationships. If we do not provide relationships where they can be true in their hearts, the upset tensions and stresses are going to leak into and impact their behavior."

For Jimmie, devastations came in many forms. One of them was a failed marriage he directly pins on his adherence at the time to a lack of emotional labor with himself and others. At the same time, what he was witnessing on the job—sexual enslavement of girls, rape as a weapon of war—had the unintended effect of helping Jimmie identify and then question gender norms. Subtly, he felt himself hurtling toward a breaking point, which eventually came in eastern Congo in the fall of 2008. Fatefully, the story he was covering for ABC News was about the lack of mental health and psychosocial resources available to people in areas that had gone through mass, collective conflict-related trauma. There was one psychologist for the whole country.

One interview became the turning point to connecting back to the emotions he had refused to deal with within. "I met a woman who was living at a women's shelter, a twenty-year-old woman who had been gang-raped, her kids had been killed in front of her, their father killed, and she had been gang-raped multiple times. Interacting with her, interviewing her, having talks with her, kind of broke open—cracked that thick shell that I was keeping up in terms of inuring myself to what I was seeing, experiencing, in terms of what I was dealing with. I was carrying so much trauma and pain, and interacting with her, the shell cracked."

Jimmie returned home and turned a new page. He quit journalism for eight years and founded a nonprofit named Man Up, centering the role men can play toward a more gender-equitable world. But he also got seriously physically sick: he had a heart attack, his kidneys failed, and he spent four years on dialysis waiting for a transplant. If ever there had been a clear sign to slow down, be more caring of himself, and heal, this was it.

Years later, Jimmie is a tireless writer and lecturer, advocating for race and gender rights, and particularly for boys and men to break with gender norms for the sake of their own health and the health of others around them. At the time of his interviews and this book's writing, he was the only male member of New York City's Commission on Gender Equity. He is also a father, and a mentor to young boys and men, who speaks widely and unflinchingly about his emotions, way beyond the masculine ones he listed off.

During one of our three interviews, he told me he didn't reject the idea of manhood, he just felt like it was important for men to define what that meant, individually, for themselves. "I wish for us that this thing we call manhood, there's no one archetype, there's no one definition. That as an individual you create your manhood for you. You can be gay, you can be tall, short, fat, asexual, whatever, and still be a man. It's how you define it."

Why is it so hard for men to feel like they can decide for themselves what their identity looks like? Why is it that we deny them vulnerability? The truth is that challenging masculinity norms and getting men to define themselves on their own terms is even more threatening to the system than women gaining their rights and challenging norms around femininity in society. The system relies on the inherent myth of male aggression and dominance to maintain its legitimacy.

Reichert spoke plainly on this. "We are more rigidly wedded to masculine norms, norms for male development. This is for a variety of reasons. There hasn't been a movement comparable to the women's movement advocating for freer expression of male emotions and challenging stereotypes. Also, I think it's important to say that reproducing a prototypical male identity is more at the core of our social organization."

Female identities, because they are not cast as the leading forces but rather as the following forces of our society, are treated as secondary. "The idea that a boy may be empowered to define himself as a man on his own terms is too threatening to the predictable reproductive process," Reichert said, referring to reproduction in an academic sense—as the social organization that reproduces itself from generation to generation.

All of this has culminated in a notable absence of a gender revolution for men. While the idea that women are naturally communal and emotional and men are naturally self-interested and rational has stuck over time, women have been narrowing the gap when it comes to embracing more masculine-type behaviors including being competitive and individualistic. But there has been very little narrowing on the other end.[24]

This can be partially explained by a lack of cultural or institutional change in the ways in which we devalue female-type characteristics, activities, and jobs. Where "women's work" is seen as less prestigious, less skilled, more menial or petty, the incentive for men to leave their traditional spaces and take on such work is very weak. On the other end, many women seeking upward mobility are incentivized by the high value—culturally and institutionally—of men's work.

To put it bluntly, our gender revolution may have succeeded in helping some groups of women access opportunities their mothers couldn't, but it has failed abysmally in changing cultural norms around what is valued. This has not been just a gross oversight of the movement; it has so far been a fatal one.

In this case, telling women to hoard male-type opportunities, and not insisting on a full revaluing of gendered roles and work, still leaves large groups of women forced into performing essential and invisible emotional labor at a discount—or worse. And denying men basic human features like emotions and connected relationships is a short end of the straw for them too. Forcing men to be hypermasculine pushes them into destructive behaviors that threaten us all.

In the Promundo study, men in the United States and the United Kingdom who identified more strongly with the seven pillars of the man box were six to seven times more likely to report perpetrating physical in-person or online bullying compared to men who did not strongly identify with the pillars. They were six times more likely to report perpetrating sexual harassment and were more at risk of violence from others. They were also likely to engage in destructive behaviors like binge drinking and less likely to have close personal relationships.[25]

Most pressingly, in the United States, 40 percent of the men who identified with the seven pillars of the man box reported having had recent thoughts of suicide, while only 17 percent of men who did not identify with the man box pillars did. This is a troubling statistic. Suicide killed 3.5 times more men than women in 2018, according to the American Foundation for Suicide Prevention. The group most at risk of suicide are middle-aged white men. Cutting boys and men off from the expectation of emoting is damaging, sometimes fatally so.

The opposite is conversely true too. Studies are increasingly finding that men who are strongly connected to family, friends, and community are happier and physically healthier, and they live longer than men who are not. In two landmark studies, Harvard researchers followed hundreds of privileged and non-privileged boys and men from their teen years to the end of their lives and found a strong association between connected, high-quality, positive relationships and life longevity for men.

"The people who were the most satisfied in their relationships at age fifty were the healthiest at age eighty," Dr. Robert Waldinger, a professor of psychiatry at Harvard Medical School and one of the leaders of the research, said in a TED Talk on the subject.[26] Good relationships were shown to protect not only men's physical health but their mental and emotional health too. "How happy we are in our relationships has a powerful influence on our health," Waldinger said in an interview with *The Harvard Gazette* titled "Good Genes Are Nice, but Joy Is Better."[27]

Treating men as entirely rational and never emotional cuts them off from positive, connected relationships and time spent alive on Earth. As things stand, women are responsible for keeping men alive.

Many of the women I interviewed talked of worrying about their male partners' physical health on top of their mental health, with partners who had family medical issues, especially heart disease, but refused to adapt their lifestyle toward preventative care. The preventative care was then left to women to try to implement in subtle and explicit ways.

One woman, Crystal, talked of her partner who had type 1 diabetes, which required daily shots of insulin and close monitoring of blood sugar levels. Crystal's partner often "forgot" to refill his prescriptions in time, causing her to go on desperate last-minute trips to the pharmacy. Untreated type 1 diabetes can lead to loss of eyesight and kidney and nerve damage, among many other grave, even life-threatening consequences. After a scary trip to the hospital, Crystal ended up taking charge of her partner's medication and health monitoring altogether. Being perceived as a nag seemed like a small price to pay to keep her partner alive.

This is a kind of man's man behavior, all too known to women, that pushes women's emotional labor to the extreme, compensating for the lack of emotional exuberance, holistic self-care, and communication on the other end.

Women are doing this, not only because they feel they are trained to but because they realize, just as the Harvard study shows, that men's health and often survival depend on it. We do this kind of work, having been trained to understand the value of community and the health of those around us, to compensate for those who won't do it for themselves.

The literature on widowhood mortality is compelling here. Studies over the last few decades in heterosexual settings have found that men losing their spouses suffer greater risk of mortality than women losing theirs. These kinds of findings reveal that in a society where men still tend to support their partners more financially and women tend to support their partners more emotionally, the more important of the exchanges for survival is emotional labor, not money.[28]

One 2014 study found that men whose wives died unexpectedly were at a 70 percent higher risk of dying than men whose wives died with warning.[29] There was no equivalent impact on the opposite scenario: whether or not a husband was expected to die had no differentiating effect on women's survival. "This finding may reflect the fact that men receive a greater social support benefit from marriage than do women and may thus have more difficulty adapting to new conditions," its authors, Allison Sullivan and Andrew Fenelon, wrote.

While we now tell girls that they can be anything they want to be—from astronauts to deep-sea divers—boys have not seen their options expanded. Masculine traits are still seen as immutable and superior in men. "We say biology is destiny when it comes to male attributes. That hormones and testosterone rule. That is the cultural message they receive. That we are hardwired. That we are sexual predators. Despite the fact that research shows the incorrectness of those myths," the psychologist Michael Reichert told me.

Emotional labor should be viewed as highly valuable, which is what evidence continues to suggest, and afford high community status to those doing it—whether inside or outside of the marketplace. Instead, its manifestations remain overlooked and undervalued, upheld by belief systems that are antiquated and fail to pass basic logic tests.

If emotional and social support is the kind of activity that helps people not only survive but thrive and live longer, healthier years, far more than money does, then should that not be seen as the ultimate creator of value—or even the ultimate value itself?

Should value really be seen as simply measured in dollars, or should we not now insist that value also be seen as time, not only hours of the day spent on specific activities but years of one's life, lived fully, happily, free of unnecessary burdens of mental and physical ailments? Should that not be the measure of true value?

For journalist Jimmie Briggs, the only solution for a transformative future lies in championing a form of emotional labor as empathy. "All of us have a need to release our emotions," he stated. Jimmie told me his heart broke, especially within his own Black community, where men were rarely able to fully process emotions, even in the darkest of times. "I have been to so many funerals of people who have died from violence or natural diseases. I have watched boys and men being discouraged from crying or grieving, where their female counterparts are [encouraged to do so].

"Those of us who are more likely to experience disenfranchisement and oppression, we especially should understand the necessity of helping create gender equity—for everyone," Jimmie said.

"If we don't reckon with this toxic masculinity—this octave of masculinity—that is not allowing us to express our full emotional selves, I think it is going to get worse. We are going to see more restrictive behavior, in ourselves but also externally."

Do we really want to see where a world that continues to prize aggression, disconnection, and dominance above collaboration, connection, and love takes us next? Even if it is nonsensical, even if it has started to cannibalize not only the system's losers, but its supposed winners too?

Jimmie confided that he believed white male supremacy, by its very nature, was anti-empathy. This was a truth that posed a threat to everyone.

"Without empathy, it is extraordinarily difficult to see the inherent dignity and value and power in others. And so, the less empathetic you are, the less willing you are to recognize [that] particularly women are deserving of demanding of whatever privilege or equity that you possess."

A world that forcefully imposes a lack of empathy, especially from those at the top, justifies the brutal enforcement of its own existence. In this system, the less empathy you express, the more perceived power you retain. But look closer, to the details, and all anti-empathy does is reveal that the promise of power is empty and destructive. Look closer at the details, and you start to reevaluate how you thought of power and value in the first place.

SEVEN

The Reality of Emotional Capitalism

VALUE

One January afternoon, a professional acquaintance sent me a friendly text message: "Just heard a story on the radio about a woman who earned $80 an hour performing cuddling—can you say emotional labor?" she asked.

"I should think so," I replied. I thought about it some more. Hugging as an expression of affection performed regardless of it genuinely feeling good for the hugger and for the benefit of a huggee—and all of that for a fee? It's pretty textbook, actually. I then added, "Now there's emotional labor valued at a decent hourly rate."

"Ha, for real," the answer came back, betraying a hint of frustration. However much interviewees and acquaintances sometimes professed they took pride in emotional labor once they understood what it was, there almost always was the parallel exasperation at how invisible, devalued, or dismissed it remained. Hugs for a fee? You might squirm—*How could you sell something as sacred as a hug?*—or maybe even scoff—*How lonely or pathetic is the person buying that hug?*—but at least a hug entering the marketplace in this way was finally showing that giving and receiving a hug held, well, value.

But why was something as innocuous as hugging for a fee newsworthy anyway? For all of our advancement on gender norms, including in progressive circles, we remain uncomfortable with anything resembling love and care, represented here in the form of a hug, being exchanged for money. We often take a moral stance, saying that love is so vital, so irreplaceable, so *in*valuable that it is impossible to put a dollar number to it. Love is priceless.

That line of argument often goes one step further and holds that putting a dollar number on anything approaching love and care would tarnish the act—rendering it fake, or even dirty. But fees are everywhere. As we started to see in chapters 1, 2, and 4, one of the lies of this version of capitalism is that women's work is either worth little to nothing or so valuable that it is incalculable, making it sacrilegious for it to be paid.

Not for nothing, the debate over whether or not—and how much—emotional labor should be remunerated has been at the center of popular discussions since the topic was brought into the mainstream in the mid-2010s. Many of the people forcing the conversation were advocates from the sex work industry, who, freed of the cover of performed respectability, offered a unique, unhypocritical perspective.

One sex worker I talked to, Lilith, explained that emotional labor was not an add-on for her work on top of physical acts, it was the crux of it. Lilith worked as a self-employed dominatrix for years before she was forced to quit. Based in Texas, where sex work remains illegal, security concerns tied to the profession's lack of legal status eventually became overwhelming. While she did have niche skills such as practicing shibari, an ancient Japanese art of rope bonding, from the get-go, Lilith's work was majority psychology and emotional labor, and minority sexual act, she said. These main requirements came easy to her thanks to her upbringing. "I am a Southern woman," Lilith, who is white, explained. "I know how to put on a face."

Lilith's work followed a simple pattern. She advertised her services online (on Craigslist or Backpage, which has since been taken down), then arranged meetings with potential clients in a public place for one hour. If the meeting went okay, she wasn't spooked, and the client was able to prove that he could pay her fee, she would move ahead with scheduling a one-hour domme session. The interview component was free, but the follow-up one-hour session cost a nonnegotiable $1,300—including for repeat clients.

The initial meeting, to which she always turned up dressed "vanilla" to avoid raising eyebrows, took the form of an interview, serving as a way for her to scope out the men, do a detailed background session on their medical and personal history, and draw what she calls a "map of their desire landscape." Her practical, preemptive inquiry was a classic form of emotional labor, making sure to take care of the male client fully. "Literally, I need to know every cardiac problem you have ever had. I ask specific questions about joints, asthma, allergies, blood pressure. I have to be very grueling because I need to know where I have range. I need to know if something might be dangerous. I also think it sets them at ease."

Having ascertained their physical health and boundaries to the best of her ability, she would move on to their private lives, focusing more explicitly around the emotional and the erotic. "Are you in a relationship? Do you prefer leather or lace? Do you want a role-play scenario? Do you want pain, roping, sensation play, humiliation, or is there a specific story you have in mind? How do you deal with your fetish? What is your desire?"

This involved adopting a neutral, nonjudgmental tone. "Some want to wear a diaper and for me to treat them like a baby, some want specific humiliation, some want to get flogged." The briefing background interview occasionally bordered on a therapy session. This was fine, she reassured me: she was getting paid. "These men, they can't be open with others, they don't feel like they can. What I am doing is listening and practicing compassion, understanding, identification, and recognition. My role is to address the symptoms of what very often is their shame."

Lilith understood well the value of her emotional labor, and the way in which, in those moments, her clients were reckoning with their place and positioning in society—turning to her for visibility, acceptance, and unmasked truth. "They struggled with being able to face themselves. Some of them went into very confessional modes and asked me why I thought they were that way."

Once she had figured out "what their fetish zones" were, they made a date and scheduled their one-hour appointment, which would take place in an apartment in a residential neighborhood. That hour was meticulously prepared for with makeup, clothes, tools, and accessories to give clients the best and fullest experience. On the day of and from the beginning to the end of the appointment, Lilith was in role and her mission was to enact the dedicated experience that would fulfill the man's fantasy. "I would bring them in, establish a strong power dynamic. A huge part of domming is prohibition. They're not good enough for you."

Performance was everything, and Lilith found she could provoke the best emotional reactions in her clients—reactions her clients were paying for—by being as quiet and suggestive as possible. "I believe the best power involves doing things rather than saying things. I am not a screamer. Few people want to be screamed at, I have found."

Emotional labor was also performed on the fly as she kept close tabs on how her clients were coping. "Some clients get roping anxiety. It truly restrains men. Sometimes you need to get them out very fast to avoid them having a panic attack."

Putting on a face may have come easy to Lilith, but she was under no illusion that this was all an act. There were other moments when rather than saving her clients, she felt she might not be able to suppress bursting into fits of laughter. During those, ever present to their experiences, and molding the situation for them, she resorted to blindfolding her clients, so that if her mouth broke her emotional labor and displayed giggling authenticity, they wouldn't notice.

She found the sessions interesting intellectually, she told me—"a window on humanity I couldn't see any other way"—and she noticed the requirements of the job had the effect of increasing her ability for compassion. But she was also clear that the sessions gave her no real pleasure. At the end of the day, she was doing them to get paid.

Demanding money for emotional labor in ways that grated at polite society is part of how it became known by name outside of academia. Emotional labor as a forceful yet erased form of work was a core part of an impromptu online campaign that started in the spring of 2015, with the hashtag #GiveYourMoneyToWomen. The hashtag was similar in geste to a parallel hashtag—#PayPalMe—that also emerged around that time. With #PayPalMe, women, initially Black women, tasked to explain their oppression to fellow users on venues like Twitter, would only be drawn into debates if their intellectual labor was first compensated for through their PayPal accounts.

Taking it one step further, the #GiveYourMoneyToWomen (or #GYMTW) hashtag, created by Yeoshin Lourdes, Bardot Smith, and Lauren Chief Elk, invited women to share their PayPal account details with men online who demanded even the slightest amount of their attention or energy.

Lourdes and Smith came from a niche part of the sex work industry, called financial domination, itself derived from BDSM. This fetish involved the exchange of money from male clients—sometimes referred to as "cash slaves" or "pay pigs"—to women working as dommes in interactions that resembled financial extortion for play.

Under this fetish, men could hand over cash or make bank transfers to women with the expectation of little more than basic acknowledgment. Sometimes, they even gave women they barely knew full access to their bank accounts as a first step of engagement.[1]

Instead of Lilith's male rope tying, here men's relinquishing of power, or their desired humiliation, was achieved through cash forfeiture at the beginning of any contact. Handing over money was a condition for entry for men into an interaction rather than something that marked the end of one or the receipt of a service. This effective lack of guarantee as to what the money would get them constituted a radical reversal in traditional power dynamics.

As customers in the marketplace, we are used to paying for a service at the end of it: we throw bills on the table for the server as we leave, and nurses will usually get paid at the end of the pay period for work they have already done. But giving women financial power at the beginning of an interaction is a deliberate shift of power from the person requesting the service to the person providing it—in a way that reverses what women have had to grow used to.

The emergence of #GYMTW was an invitation for all women to reevaluate their true worth in interactions—casual or close. Instead of having their attention, emotional labor, and support work taken for granted or exchanged precariously, women were seeing that there was a way of bringing the true value of what they were performing into the broad, bright daylight by asking for the money up front.

This reversal in the rules for engagement revealed that women operating on their own terms did not owe men their attention, their politeness, or their emotional labor. They could withhold it until its true value was acknowledged—here, through money. Forcing the value of emotional labor and attention work usually expected and extracted for free into the open in this flipping of the script is as radical as it is unsettling.

"This isn't about us needing to be paid more in the patriarchal-dominated wage system, or 'wanting cash for nothing,' it's about *not* being paid for what *is* wanted and desired from us, and now monetizing that," explained hashtag creator Lauren Chief Elk in an interview published in *Model View Culture* in 2015.[2]

"If you look across the spectrum, things women do for society are valued little or not at all in terms of money," said cocreator Bardot Smith, pointing to the vast array of female labor from sex work to emotional labor that was derided and all too often provided in coercive situations, at a discount, or for free.

The three women's framework refused to take on male-type attributes and see the white-collar workplace as a potential place for liberation—something "lean in" feminism famously did. Instead, it demanded women and people in feminine roles turn a mirror on themselves and recognize the power they already held. If they framed it right, and stepped into that power, the rest of society that needed it would have to follow suit.

The #GYMTW movement wasn't just meaningful for women in the sex industry; it was relevant to all women and groups whose attention and emotional labor were expected, or even demanded, from men. Writer Jess Zimmerman humorously expressed her satisfaction with it a couple of months after it started in online publication *The Toast*.[3] "It was beautiful to watch #GiveYourMoneyToWomen unfold. Men got angry, and then women explained to them that to have their anger acknowledged, they would have to pay," she wrote.

Zimmerman, whose article prompted a viral MetaFilter with thousands of contributions,[4] suggested, tongue in cheek, that we might think of an emotional labor menu, with price tags attached. "Acknowledge your thirsty posturing, $50. Pretend to find you fascinating, $100. Soothe your ego so you don't get angry, $150. Smile hollowly while you make a worse version of their joke, $200. Explain 101-level feminism to you like you're five years old, $300. Listen to your rant about 'bitches,' $infinity."

The framing of the sex worker–led movement ended up provocatively shattering the boundary of public and private—by demanding we acknowledge the existence and vitality of emotional labor and insisting that we see its nonpaid iteration not only as work but as something worthy of pay. In so doing, it also broke down the boundary between sex workers and non-sex-worker-identifying citizens. After all, weren't so many of us engaged in this kind of work? Wasn't it only fair that we should all be compensated? How different were so many of us, really, as we monitored the well-being of lovers, partners, and friends, from Lilith—except in our lack of compensation of $1,300 an hour?

Unexpectedly perhaps, the three women founders of #GYMTW, who identified as women of color from non-privileged backgrounds, gained inspiration for the movement after they read an article detailing the lives of very wealthy, overwhelmingly white housewives living in New York City's Upper East Side.

The piece in question, called "Poor Little Rich Women,"[5] published in spring 2015 in *The New York Times* and written by anthropologist Wednesday Martin, depicted the gender-retrograde arrangements of Manhattan's elite. Martin, who wrote a book on this topic after living among this population, described the zealousness with which women reared their children, applying their world-class graduate-level education to a host of exclusively unpaid activities—from sitting on boards and staying perfectly in shape, to running their homes like CEOs and practicing competitive mothering. She wrote that women she interacted with could work thanks to their extensive qualifications but told her they choose not to, causing them to be tightly bound into financial dependence with their working husbands.

No one would have likely batted an eyelid after closing their Sunday paper had it not been for one detail. Privileged women she interviewed, and who did not hold formal employment, expected end-of-year wife bonuses. Martin wrote:

> A wife bonus, I was told, might be hammered out in a pre-nup or post-nup, and distributed on the basis of not only how well her husband's fund had done but her own performance—how well she managed the home budget, whether the kids got into a "good" school—the same way their husbands were rewarded at investment banks. In turn these bonuses were a ticket to a modicum of financial independence and participation in a social sphere where you don't just go to lunch, you buy a $10,000 table at the benefit luncheon a friend is hosting.
>
> Women who didn't get them joked about possible sexual performance metrics. Women who received them usually retreated, demurring when pressed to discuss it further, proof to an anthropologist that a topic is taboo, culturally loaded and dense with meaning.

The detail caused a media whirlwind, shock, and mockery—and, of course, a backlash. The wife-bonus women became a trope of elitist female depravity.

But to me, the criticism missed the mark. The wealthy housewives seemed onto something—remuneration for work even in private. As high society as their arrangements were, they recalled a mostly forgotten cry from feminists over the last fifty years for feminized work to be recognized as the pillar upon which the rest of wealth creation depends.[6]

What was wrong with the bonus system was not that it existed but that it depended on unregulated metrics, including for sex, that took advantage of the taboo aspect of these exchanges to remain opaque. If anything, this revealed these women's relative disempowerment. Really, they needed a union. What was worrying was not the pay but the power imbalance that still set women at the mercy of their wage-earning husbands.

Beyond this, what could be improved on in this bonus system was that its existence was among only the elite. This made it all too easy to sneer at, when actually this kind of valuing of private, feminine work was needed across all classes and demographics. We need the bonus housewife mentality to spread and even out—even if it takes on different formats—not for fake outrage to make it go back underground.

These kinds of exchanges, and the reactions to them when they are brought into broad daylight, highlight the moral, social, and economic contours of emotional labor—and why it is so hard to shift the ways in which it is negotiated between people. The social and economic contracts around it cannot be changed until we fully see it. As long as we keep seeing exchanges for feminine labor as distasteful or even outlawed and buried below the surface, the line between consent and coercion will remain blurred, and the atmosphere prone to abuse.

One Upper East Side woman I interviewed, Clare, told me that financial dependency on her lawyer husband had initially made her feel "icky" and "weird" even if they had agreed on this arrangement as she finished school. Performing much of the emotional labor and homemaking, she explained that she was reluctant to engage in any conflicting dialogue with her husband, raise any issues, or push back on his behavior patterns because of his financial support. "He's giving me this gift of freedom, so I don't want to rock the boat." That changed once she had her first child and stepped into the lauded feminine role of being a mother. She had brought a whole human being into the world and was the primary parent; now the fruits of her literal labor were visible. "I felt a little bit more power back to me."

The financial "freedom" she identified her husband "giving" her went hand in hand with a loss of power within her relationship. The hush-hush nature of the exchange enabled money to buy subjugation, whereas true appreciation of feminine labor would have empowered her.

Another person I interviewed, a man named Lou, who was in a same-sex relationship with an older man who earned considerably more than he did and covered their joint rent, recalled a crude exchange between the partners that left him incensed. While Lou assumed much of the housework and saw himself as a caregiver, which matched the dynamic of their relationship, he maintained a sense of integrity that at times was pushed to its limits.

One day his partner, Steve, initiated a conversation about their waning intimate life. "He said: 'I don't see how you see this working out. The rent is not going to pay itself by itself. Like, I need something in return.'

"It was weirdly explained," Lou told me, remembering the incident. "But I knew what he was talking about." Steve wanted sex, more sex, and thought being the one paying rent should have the consequence of him accessing that. Lou refused, and the relationship suffered, Lou's dignity and sense of bodily autonomy stricken.

In a system where dollars and feminine labor remain in opposition, it is easy for the person bringing in more money to claim infinite, unregulated access to feminine labor, including coercive or near-coercive sex. Unstated boundaries around feminine labor, and the emotional labor expectation that one party should put the experiences of the other party first, can make it seem bottomless and beyond consent.

In a new social and economic contract that valued emotional labor, among other forms of feminine labor, the work of women and other performers of feminine tasks would be legal, open, and acknowledged. It would also be far more clearly defined and far fairer to its workers. This would enable the possibility of profit generation when desired or appropriate, or alternatively require another form of exchange like mutuality. Such a system would provide fair negotiating terms and conditions, making sure that the work performed or commissioned was clear, defined, and therefore finite.

Such worker rights would make sure nobody was subjected to the arbitrary whims of a partner, the impulses of a client, or the fear of crackdown and arrest from a criminalizing system. Emotional laborers would no longer be exposed to the moods of those who benefit from the fruits of their labor to get paid or to gain status. They would no longer be punished violently and seemingly at random if they decided to withhold their labor.

Such a new order still seems far-fetched, even if the advent of the internet has laid some of the inequality in gendered labor extraction bare. Unlike what many a Silicon Valley entrepreneur would like us to believe, the proliferation of new technologies does not magically propel us into a utopian problem-free future where exotic feminine robots deliver us from systemic inequality. Instead, our online avatars continue to be subjected to the same exploitative dynamics. But watching the same old dynamics unfold online makes it easier to observe what, and who, is actually creating value. Yeoshin Lourdes, one of the #GiveYourMoneyToWomen cocreators, explained it as follows:

> Mainstream social media platforms like Facebook, Twitter, Snapchat, Instagram, and others capitalize on female participation. On Facebook, people who click on profiles are mostly men, and people whose profiles are clicked on are mostly women. So my having a personal account on Facebook makes me a product for Facebook to sell to men. And now that site is worth $250 billion. Likewise, nightlife venues thrive by getting women to participate in their business operations, and they do so by waiving or discounting cover charges or otherwise marketing to women specifically.
>
> Women are the product these establishments are selling to men, who then arrive and spend heavily just to be in the same room as women. But I've never received a check from Facebook or any club for

my business development services. So, instead of wasting my time generating revenue for corporate entities that aren't paying me, I'd rather make my social interactions profitable to me.

Money for attention, for kindness, or even for care, love, and a sexual experience might seem cynical to some. Back to that original question at the beginning of the book: How could we treat emotions as work? Some might even see this as the symptom of the out-of-control nature of our current capitalistic system that has increasingly sought to profit off of and monetize everything it can, at an ever-accelerating pace over the last fifty years. This state of economic affairs that elevates profit-making as a form of social governance is sometimes referred to as neoliberalism. Will the voracious appetite to make everything—even the heart—into a sellable asset stop at nothing? Is emotional labor the sign of neoliberalism gone amok?

This kind of critique raises important questions, but it misses key points, the first being that in modern memory, money and matters of the heart have always been intertwined. Not for nothing is Mrs. Bennet in Jane Austen's 1813 novel *Pride and Prejudice* obsessed with prospective sons-in-law making "10,000 a year." In her book *Marriage, a History,*[7] historian Stephanie Coontz explains the idea that one should marry for love only began to take hold in the nineteenth century when the private, "emotional" sphere started being defined as separate from the public, moneymaking sphere. Before this, marriage was long an economic arrangement, and in patriarchal systems—the norm for the last twelve thousand years[8]—women were treated as assets exchanged between two male-headed households.

The evil in this system is not that we dared think of love and women in relation to money or value; it is that in this system, women were first treated like a dehumanized good, and then—as they gained in partial humanity—the worth they created was totally obscured. The recent manufactured ideological separation between private and public, emotions and profits, in this more modern version of patriarchal postindustrial capitalism has only consolidated the obscuring of the worth women create.

The point of this book—in putting true value on the feminized work of women, in this case emotional labor—is not to entrench women as exchangeable goods in a global market. The point is to illuminate the worth they create through their work. And the point is then in turn to restore the self-governance women have long been denied.

It is important to state that love and economics are thoroughly intertwined so that we can better scrutinize the conditions of exchanges and where this real worth lies. With emotional labor in private, an accepted framing still goes that if you love your husband and children, truly, how could that constitute work? How could your concern for others, coming from a kind place, be compensated for, if it is real? Asking for money, acknowledgment, or status is seen as violating the sacredness of what is ethically seen as having to be "naturally" produced—from emotions of love to a happy environment.

As discussed in chapters 1 and 4, this kind of mentality—casting emotional labor as natural—holds women hostage. Of course, behind this fake discourse of nature is something else entirely. Social psychologist and sociologist Rebecca Erickson put it this way to me: "Family has never been outside of power. I mean, what's a dowry? Families were arranged because they're meetings of power. We cover that up with issues of love and choice and all these romantic notions, but that's just a story we like to tell ourselves so we can sleep well at night. But that's not really what's happening." Moments in which women claim the right to access the value of their labor are "extraordinarily threatening," she told me: not just to individuals but to society.

The real con with a supposedly principled stance decrying mixing love and money is that when you look closer emotions are already being recognized as profitable in the marketplace. This is often happening in ways we find totally normal and not morally objectionable at all. It's just that the emotional laborers are mostly not the ones making the profits.

As established in chapters 2 and 3, emotions for a fee are on display in the care, health, and service industries, which represent gigantic proportions of our economy today and tomorrow. This is due in part to how hard it is to convincingly automate human care, touch, connection, or intimacy. We are fine with paying for our elderly relatives to be cared for. Indeed, we expect and hope for them to be very well cared for when we pay for a service. We are fine with our toddlers going to day care or, if we can afford one, having a nanny, and expect the level of care to be top-notch. We berate overstretched doctors for their lack of bedside manners and expect restaurant staff to have friendly demeanors—precisely because our paying or tipping them empowers us to have expectations. Paying for this emotional labor doesn't taint these types of services.

Beyond these obvious emotional labor–heavy industries, titans of our economy, emotions have entered previously masculine corporate cultures, in ways celebrated as innovative and forward-looking. There, the lines previously drawn between private and public have been blurred with little commotion. Corporations increasingly encourage their employees to "bring their whole selves to work," expressing themselves as individuals, not simply as workers.[9] Corporations are now taking stances on issues relating to their employees' personal lives and well-being that affect them outside the workplace. This can be seen when they express support for the LGBTQ community, sponsoring floats at annual gay prides, or when corporations like Coca-Cola and Delta speak out against voter suppression, in support of Black Americans targeted by such measures.[10] New age work environments aim to evoke positive emotions in their employees to entice them into staying more hours and lengthening productivity. At Google, employees get catered free meals and free fitness classes and can bring their dogs to work.[11]

The idea that an upbeat, friendly work environment makes for a good work environment and helps execute the idea of a community-minded, inclusive space has spread way beyond tech. As workplaces morph, creating emotionally pleasing environments is becoming more of a priority, not less.

In Detroit, I became acquainted with a culture of coworking spaces, where people from dozens of different industries, in a wide variety of income brackets and at all career stages, could have access to endless coffee, printers, open desks, brainstorm rooms, and conference rooms. In one of them, Evelyn, a "community manager," held it all together. She was the glue giving the disparate workers the coworking space welcomed a sense of belonging and shared community. She had an ability to always be "on": remaining charming, attentive, and sweet to all people passing through the doors of these offices, knowing whose feathers needed to be smoothed, who looked like they needed perking up, who had a new haircut, and how to remain unfailingly polite in the face of the few people who acted haughty, abrupt, or plain rude.

Often, she came in with Tupperware filled with a delicacy she had made the night before. Lightly browned chocolate chip cookies, or pieces of freshly baked banana bread, each individually topped at the last minute with swirls of homemade frosting. She left the treats in the kitchen area and placed a sign indicating the name of the day's treat but never her own. Throughout the day, little piece by little piece disappeared, carrying with it an ounce of thoughtfulness, another of care, a sprinkling of human love and connection. Evelyn's knack at being relentlessly witty, alert, and welcoming all at once was uncanny. Most impressive was that her efforts came across as totally effortless, even if there were days she confided she was exhausted and depleted, and she slipped away a few minutes early to go and recharge.

Evelyn was central to the functioning of pretty much everything in the coworking space. In seen and unseen ways, as well as in paid and unpaid ways, Evelyn was the emotional laborer in chief. There's another term for this, of course. "I've always been the mother in a group," Evelyn told me when I interviewed her. Evelyn was a paid employee, but the value of her work was cheapened because of how concealed and disregarded precisely this kind of maternal emotional labor was across all spheres of society. Her income was a very modest one. Still, in this distinctly modern, forward-looking culture of work, it was her reassuring presence that made the environment one that people returned to, her work that kept memberships coming in.

Our acceptance of—and even insistence on—emotionality at work is mirrored by an embracing of work as part of our most intimate selves. Millennials came of age in a world that invited them to listen to their inner voices and transform their passion into a job to unlock money, fulfillment, and even liberation.[12] Find what you love, generations entering adulthood are now told, *and you will never work another day of your life*. And even if this promise is continuously exposed as hollow, the ideal that love and work should be one and the same has never been clearer.

Beyond the supposed romance of work, it is now seen as fair game for employers to scrutinize the private lives of job candidates. After the beginning of the COVID-19 epidemic, white-collar workers became accustomed to virtually letting their colleagues into their physical homes on a daily basis on video calls and meetings—featuring meandering pets and runaway babies. Across all industries, due to the all-reaching presence of social media, individuals are expected to pay attention to their "personal brand," including in their most private spheres. For those self-employed individuals—whether in the creative economy or beyond—branding yourself is now seen as an activity that is all-encompassing. Our whole self, both public and private, is expected to be minutely tailored, ready for packaging, distribution, and consumption. This has become most recognizable in the rise of reality television, where people have transformed details of their personal lives—from existing as a family to finding a partner—into a display that becomes work and that they can sell. Not all of us may feel we have the guts to do this, but millions of us participate in this new arrangement, as we pay our streaming subscriptions and watch on.

Philosopher Eva Illouz says we are now in an age of "emotional capitalism," where exchanges between people are often seen in terms of market logic, and economic activities are imbued with discourses of affect and emotions.[13]

But when have we not been in a state of emotional capitalism? Have our private selves really ever been separated out from the market-place? The present state of emotional capitalism may make the lack of actual boundaries abundantly clear, but it is hard to think of market exchanges as ever being separate from the personal, emotional self.

This question, as temporarily discombobulating as it may be, touches on something far deeper than whether or not we approve of paying for a hug or whether, given the chance, we would appear on *The Bachelor*. What it invites us to reckon with is what the relationship between emotional labor and currency exactly is.

In more ways than one in situations observed and described to me, it became obvious that emotional labor not only had value but it some-times ended up feeling like it was currency. Not just *a* currency—like an eighteen-year-old who gets into the club because he knows the owner—but on a much deeper level it felt like *the* currency. It was not only the glue that kept us all together, it was a form of exchange, of connec-tion, of energy distribution and redistribution that led us to act—and grounded us in being. Emotional labor at times began to feel like value itself—just not necessarily of the kind that could be divided into units.

These abstract musings narrowed into focus one winter day of 2020 when I heard an interview by Shankar Vedantam of anthropologist Bill Maurer, who heads the Institute for Money, Technology and Financial Inclusion at the University of California, Irvine.[14] Maurer explained that while our mainstream economics teachings tell us one very basic story about how money came about—as an evolution out of barter—widespread historical and anthropological research begs to differ.

To explain the origin of money, economics textbooks, quoting revered men like eighteenth-century Scottish economist and philos-opher Adam Smith, describe a fictitious town where humans have exited the hunter-gatherer phase and have started specializing in pro-duction activities. Maybe someone started just raising hens, another made bread, while someone else made doors. Under this theory—if David has a cow that he milks and Sylvia makes shoes, Sylvia and David can exchange a pair of shoes for milk when both have a need for each other's goods. But they can engage in this kind of barter only when what is called a double coincidence of wants occurs. When Sylvia the shoemaker still needs milk, but David the milkman no longer needs shoes, the two have a problem. How can Sylvia's needs be met? This is where mainstream economics tells us money is born: to resolve the problem of what happens when two individuals cannot satisfactorily engage in a perfect exchange of goods.

This is a pleasantly neat story harkening back to abstract ancient times we have become very familiar with. But the only problem with this tale is that it is as fictitious as it seems. The explanation makes sense in terms of why money is useful, but anthropologists, historians, and comparative economists have pointed out that there is simply no evidence to support it.[15] Barter has been noted historically, but it has only been observed in instances when people who are already used to money are suddenly extensively deprived of it—like during wartime or in situations of incarceration.

The evidence of what came before money is far more detached from individual possessions, goods, or measurement units than we have come to believe today. What historians and anthropologists have instead found to predate money are systems of symbolic gift giving tying complex webs of exchange and reciprocity between individuals and groups. What predates money are markers of relationships.[16]

Maurer uses an example in the highlands of New Guinea of a large shell as an object of high value that may be given by one individual to another as a symbol of a bond between the two. The shell doesn't garner any fixed value—the shell doesn't buy you a pig, say—but because it acts as a symbol of an active bond, it is the reminder that if I need a pig and you have one, because of our relationship symbolized when I gave you that shell, you may give me one. Objects exchanged between people become the marker of relationships, symbolizing ties and ongoing, enduring relations of mutuality and indebtedness.

In this situation, if Sylvia the shoemaker needs milk, which David the milkman has, she does not need to give David a pair of her shoes for his milk. She needs to have a relationship with him, which will be marked by an object. When David married five years ago, maybe Sylvia gave him and his new wife a precious box of beads her father had once made. In so doing, Sylvia marked an enduring bond between her household and David's, meaning David will simply gift her milk when she needs it. Sylvia may, down the line, in turn, give David shoes when he needs those, but also show up to help David's spouse harvest their sweet potatoes—and so on and so forth. The box of beads marks their relationship, which ties them into a bond of open-ended indebtedness. These beads are a symbol of their relationship and a symbol that ties their relationship in an enduring, mutual IOU. That is the precursor to money: symbols of relational bonds.

This symbolic form of gift exchange has survived in our society to this day. You may show up with a box of tea when visiting someone's house or bake some cookies on their birthday. They may then give you a ride to the airport when you need to leave town, last minute. Around holiday season, you may exchange gifts with loved ones that are not about enhancing the value of each other's households but more about expressing an ongoing relationship, and an ongoing love or bond expressed through mutual obligations that both feel reciprocal and open-ended.

In primitive societies, exchange was not about wealth accumulation, or extraction, but about reproducing society by constantly strengthening the ties of reciprocity and redistribution.[17] The precursor to money then was the exchange marking and re-marking human ties and relationships. I cannot think of a better way of describing what emotional labor is, and how emotional labor was described to me time and time again by women.

But if, once upon a time, in a very different world, emotional labor was currency itself, what happened for it to be buried so deep that it rarely garners a name, let alone value, visibility, or status? Is it possible that emotional labor is the expression of this system, persisting but pushed to the shadows as far more hierarchical systems of power have taken hold?

Connecting to the knowledge that emotional labor once wasn't just valued and acknowledged but was value itself is invigorating to be sure, but it takes us only so far in the realm that we are in today. In turn, the notion that we are living in an age of emotional capitalism is validating in that it acknowledges that emotional labor is not only real but ubiquitous, but it doesn't alleviate frustrations over inequities.

The key difference between a bygone era and today is not that emotional labor ceased to be valuable; it is that emotional labor ceased to be treated as valuable, even as it was extracted. And because we cannot realistically go back to a world pre-money, we are left dealing with a world as it is.

For some, the marketplace has become a place for a redressing of injustices. Women and all people performing emotional labor do deserve to get paid for their work, especially when it generates profits, among other benefits. It seems only fair that the value workers are creating should be recognized. If we don't want to pay women and other workers for their emotional labor, then we should stop expecting it or even coercively requiring them to perform it.

There is some change to this effect afoot. Since the financial domination community launched #GiveYourMoneyToWomen in 2015, it has become entirely acceptable for people on a variety of platforms to share their Venmo, Cash App, Patreon, or PayPal details, and expect pay for emotional labor, attention work, and the creation of content. The sex work industry has offered us all a way to refuse to do time-consuming labor other people enjoy and benefit from for free.

But these models rest on individual instances and are far from systemic. We are still a long distance away from women getting their due pay being mainstream. It is likely in part only because it is mostly men who have embraced the practice of asking for money on venues like YouTube and Substack that the shame of selling one's labor so explicitly has lifted. Shaming of women asking pay for work is still a part of the culture.

So, what's the takeaway here? Is emotional capitalism bad, or is it a useful understanding that can help connect women to their value? Is it demeaning, or is it liberating?

Neither. Or rather, both. We need to stop seeing the marketplace either as a solution or as a source of tarnish. All it is is a reflector of subjective value systems—hierarchies and morals—in place. It is a reflector of social structures, even as it is more often seen as the shaper of social structures. To be sure, we need to move past being horrified at love and money interacting. Once we have done that, we need to go one step further and look closely at the ways in which they do. We need to reckon with what they reveal about our different treatment of different groups of people.

It is only then that we can have a frank conversation about the subjective value system we are operating under, and whether we think it is one that needs redrawing. When we deny that emotional labor is a performance that requires time, effort, skill, or even training, we deny emotional laborers their due profit. But we see that the marketplace actually acknowledges emotional labor as a form of work that generates value, and that we live in a state of emotional capitalism. Women's labor—feminine labor—has always been a part of our society and economy, now more than ever.

This immediately dispels the myth that love and money interacting is a rarity we should decry as shocking or even wrong. Such a myth is only useful because it stops emotional laborers from claiming the true value of their work.

Right now, real benefits like profits generated, experiences enjoyed, or even time and health gained are mostly going not to the workers but to other individuals or companies. This extractive state of emotional capitalism that gaslights women into believing their work is not work and holds no measurable value all the while generating profits for others off their backs leads to persistent gender inequality.

It is a form of inequality that feels both overwhelmingly ancient and urgently unjust.

This is where the marketplace falls short, and it becomes clear that we must go deeper and tackle women's dehumanization that in this patriarchal economy has long gone hand in hand with women's labor exploitation to maintain dominance. Our lower view of femininity is what prepares women to be marketable or market adjacent through their physicality and heavily discounted emotional and feminine labors, but little else. Our lower view of femininity protects men's freedom at the cost of women's through the concomitant exploitation and denial of women's labor.

Look closely, and you will see that it is not so much that women are denied access to the marketplace but rather it is that being a vehicle for others' profits at the center of the marketplace is where women have been placed all along. Putting a price on our labor is a real step in upsetting that paradigm, but it will not free us as women so long as we are not treated as full subjects outside the narrow behavior requirements of a subservient gender. Without that, we will always be primed to be pimped under capitalism.

Objecting to this starts with requiring a total acceptance that our existence—and therefore experience—as women is worth the same as the existence of men. That all people's existences are worth the same. That femininity does not sit below masculinity. That feminine labor generates power and value. That if serving is a core, needed part of humanity, we should all be serving one another.

Emotional labor as a co-opted way of enforcing artificial hierarchies is everywhere and we do not see it. To move forward, and restore its objective value, we must first insist on full visibility.

EIGHT

Abolishing Imbalance

VISIBILITY

Erica ended our coffee shop interview in a very similar way to how she started it. "I think it's fine if you use my name," she ventured. "I don't think I said anything that would upset my husband? I think this was fine."

I had just asked her a second time whether she would like to be on the record. She had previously insisted she did, but with this caveat—that she didn't think her husband, James, would react negatively to anything she had said.

I wondered silently whether she saw the irony in preemptively adapting to a husband's opinion and feelings—catering to his emotions—after an interview on emotional labor, which centered around their relationship. Even her transgression carried modulation.

Regardless, her remark was enough for me to anonymize her immediately. I once interviewed a brilliant woman on the record about the seemingly innocuous dynamics within her relationship. The ensuing article, which explicitly centered overlooked women, made her partner so furious he took the time to write me a long email rewriting it from his own, male perspective. A couple of months later, he also had her write a letter he made public through his own professional platform about how great a partner he was, how egalitarian their relationship was, and how grateful she was for him.

The incident appeared absurd in one way—such an extreme reaction to simple household debates involving tea towels and scheduling—but in another it showed the underlying emotional danger women still faced if they spoke up about these.[1] Power, threatened, has a way of asserting itself. Emotional labor may seem laughable as a topic to some—"Oh, women, talking about emotions, what do they want now?!"—but gendered inequality in emotional labor without a doubt rattles the foundations of ongoing, still-enduring patriarchy. Addressing this inequality is far more earth-shattering than it may first seem.

What does it mean to step toward more equality when it comes to unremunerated emotional labor in a relationship or a group? What are ways for moving forward, large and small? There are a few very clear individual solutions.

The first step is insisting that emotional labor, together with other private, unremunerated feminized forms of work, be rendered visible. Instead of people treating emotional labor as an extension of being sexed or gendered as female, emotional labor should be seen as a form of work demanding time, effort, and skill. Nor should emotional labor, in the same vein, be seen as a passive expression of an innate trait, say, an expression of possessing emotional intelligence. What we see as the expression of emotional intelligence is emotional labor in action, and we should acknowledge it and reward it as such.

The next step is marking the emotional labor provided and relied on as valuable, and sometimes even vital. Such a marking needn't necessarily be rewarded with money. Marking a performance as valuable can involve nonmonetary rewards like affording the doer of the task real status, expressing gratitude, and marking the performance as deserving of reciprocity or even an IOU for another type of performance.

For couples seeking to make their relationship more egalitarian, emotional labor sweat equity can start being attained with timekeeping as one way of measuring output, as long as emotional labor is seen as its own category on top of other activities and chores. Whose feelings are being put first? Whose experience is being protected? Who is filtering their emotions for the benefit of the group? Who is taking up space? Negotiating different responsibilities, including sharing the overall responsibility of the well-being of a family unit or a group, or deciding in a way that feels fair who can carry the burden of that responsibility, is an obvious part of it too.

Licensed psychotherapist Shirley Johnson said that she often reminds people who have been in relationships for decades that it is never too late to renegotiate labor divisions or dynamics. Communication lines need to be open. Johnson, who works with individuals and couples, explained in an interview that emotional labor came up especially as an issue in "hetero cis" couples. She agreed with studies and interviews that this was mostly an unequal burden carried by women even if they worked, or by those playing traditional feminine roles in non-breadwinner situations.

But Johnson warned that better dynamics when it came to emotional labor also involved women letting go of what she called "compulsive caretaking at one's own expense." This was something the psychotherapist had observed in all people who at one point had been socialized as women, regardless of age, race, ethnicity, or religion. "I see this so prominently in my practice that women are very much in this compulsive caretaking role. And often they don't know it, and it is so entrenched as the norm in our society. Even the idea that they should keep someone happy. It becomes very toxic."

Erica, my coffee shop interviewee, was particularly reflective on the amount of personal responsibility she carried in performing an inordinate amount of emotional labor and household duties, on top of working and being the primary parent. "The men say, 'I didn't ask you to do it, nobody cares if our kid's sandwich is cut into little stars.' That's always a balance. My husband, when I get frustrated, I come home and I am going to have to do the dishes, and he says, '*I will do them, I will do them!*' And I say, 'I know, but I want to start dinner,' and he says, 'Why don't we just order something,' and I say, 'I know we can just order something but I have this nice really healthy meal planned for all of us. So that we can stay healthy and not die.'"

Erica's emotional labor lies in the details of the tasks she performs—injecting thoughtfulness into pretty sandwich cutting and doing what needs to be done to get her husband to be healthy and avoid hereditary heart disease. Some of it she sees as superfluous, and some of it is necessary, even if she ends up caring more for her adult loved one than they are caring for themselves. "The world wouldn't stop if I didn't do it," she told me. "So part of this is that whole balance of how much of this is because we choose to do it, because this is what we think we are expected to do."

Johnson explained that "often the person doing that labor is scared of handing over that labor because their identity is baked into that labor." This was something I also encountered in some interviews with parents, particularly a few mothers of toddlers, who were desperate for more hands-on help but were also unwilling to give up much of their role. Erica despaired at the amount of labor, including unpaid emotional labor, she did, but also took some of the blame.

"Part of it is me. I like keeping everyone around me happy. I want to be a good hostess, I want to be a good mom, I want to be a good wife, I want everyone to be happy and healthy. I want to keep our son's teachers happy. I want to make sure he has all his extra clothes, and he doesn't run out of diapers."

Johnson suggested a two-pronged approach to address compulsive caretaking. First, women, or people socialized in feminine roles, needed to learn "to tolerate a bigger array of emotions" and accept that not everyone was going to be happy all the time. Accepting this would lead to the withholding of the labor to other members of the family or the group, who—through the absence of the labor—would be forced into acknowledging it was there. The second component involved each person taking responsibility for their needs, identifying what they were, and seeking to fulfill them, including through communicating them to their partner. "The more each person is caring for their needs, self-caring, the stronger the relationship is," Johnson said.

Doing an inventory of needs and sharing that with a partner was key not only because it helped fulfill that need but also because it decreased a key component of emotional labor: constant preemptive thoughtfulness. "We are supporting decreasing anticipating one another's behavior," Johnson said, as constant projection into the future causes anxiety. This exercise disrupts the notion that one person or group should have their needs seamlessly anticipated and catered to, and another person should be in a constant, anxious state of multidimensional projection.

Harvard researcher Allison Daminger looked into this weight of constantly anticipating the needs of others. In her 2019 article in the *American Sociological Review*,[2] she sought to unpack the gender distribution of nonphysical components of household labor by doing in-depth interviews with thirty-five couples. Her article used the term "cognitive labor" to describe what is often in nonacademic terms described as the mental load or emotional labor. Daminger divides the four components of this kind of labor as entailing: anticipating needs, identifying options for filling them, making decisions, and monitoring progress.

Both men and women were equally as good at filling needs and making decisions, the two elements of cognitive labor most associated with decision-making and therefore power and influence. But women were disproportionately the ones who took on the two activities least associated with decision-making—the more painstaking, less tangible tasks of anticipating needs and monitoring progress.

Johnson's suggested interventions—inviting women to abstain from the nonreciprocal forms of emotional labor, insisting on everyone taking charge of their own needs—work in a situation where both parties are willing to have a self-reflective conversation on emotional sweat equity. If they are not, and a beneficiary refuses to do the work, let alone acknowledge it, abstinence will at least serve as a form of protest.

But for Erica, abstaining from caregiving wasn't that easy. Instead, she was choosing whether to actually bring things up or to surrender.

"I bottle stuff up a lot, though. I don't want to cause problems or upset him," she told me. "He is very sensitive. I am frustrated but I prefer being frustrated quietly and have a nice evening rather than bring something up. I have held a lot back, because I am extra nervous about wounding his pride. Nine times out of ten I just don't bring up things that are bothering me."

Her nervousness at home and during the interview was a reminder that, for some, speaking up to change emotional labor dynamics still feels dangerous. There is a widespread mafia-like omertà, or vow of silence, around this kind of deeply intimate disparity, especially when it comes to talking about a loved one—because it is seen as a betrayal of private life but also because of the power dynamics at play.

Individual efforts to create more emotional sweat equity are futile if a few key points are not also confronted. These include: Should groups lacking power always be the ones to create the experiences, and groups in power always get to enjoy experiences? Should we accept this hierarchy of experience? We need to bring these questions to light so that there can be a reckoning with experiential privilege. Correcting experiential privilege would correct a large part of the overall privilege, of course. Which brings us to the next, more thorny question.

We cannot be naïve and believe that many beneficiaries of emotional labor are not already abundantly aware of their privilege and would therefore not be reluctant to forgo it. Infantilizing men as being blissfully ignorant of what they are gaining under the current emotional labor distribution is not only disingenuous but harmful to progress.

Erica's answers suggest there is a concern of retaliation for seeking to change the dynamic. Part of her omertà may not be about compulsive caregiving but rather about fear of a temper, fear of emotional or physical violence from her partner—reactions that often happen after a loss of sense of control. Not rocking the boat would seem prudent in such an instance, especially if leaving did not feel like an option—if children or financial dependency are involved, say. In such a case, assuming the responsibility for avoiding conversations around inequality in her relationship would be an avenue toward gaining a feeling of agency.

We are still far too comfortable living in a world totally geared toward men, and many structures, including romantic heterosexual relationships, are built on this principle. For some, changing this paradigm—as an insistence on a forfeiture of power—will likely take more than a simple conversation.

Part of what hinders change is a dearth of social scripts actually describing the reality of exchanges taking places.

In 2016, Canada-based public speaking coach Erin Rodgers captured the sentiment of giving emotional labor rightful worth and visibility in relationships when she tweeted, "I want the term 'gold digger' to include dudes who look for a woman who will do tons of emotional labour for them."

I loved the tweet, not just because it resonated with so many of the frustrated accounts people had entrusted me with—of coaching male partners through feelings, tempers, deciphering their sadnesses and joys. I loved the tweet because it clearly pointed to the emotional labor plundering that men often did in relationships with no accountability. People talk very openly about women putting "work" into their male partners, often in relation to their emotional development: helping them mature, figuring out internal struggles or childhood traumas, or giving them the tools to identify and communicate their feelings. It's an entirely accepted, widespread social phenomenon. Why the reluctance to give it a name? Not naming it keeps the value and the exchange hidden.

The framing in the tweet—so simple, and yet quite profound—also shifted the old-fashioned economic paradigm of the conniving, "gold-digging" woman who has everything to materially gain from a relationship with a man: a stereotype that serves to strip women of the value of what they bring to the table when they enter a straight relationship, hiding the particularity of their contributions and worth. As things stand, the gold-digging trope casting women as scheming manipulators seeking a kept-wife life also consolidates and justifies a social hatred—a true despising—of women who are economically more dependent on their partners in relationships. This misogyny feeds back into the loop of yet again blurring the vision of women's work and value and the exchange actually taking place. It's hard to see clearly when you are blinded by hate.

There are other ways beyond tweets—however clever those may be—of shining a light on what is being emotionally as well as materially gained by men in nonreciprocal emotional labor relationships.

An extraordinarily grim academic article[3] from 2009 looked at the marital outcome of 515 patients diagnosed with life-threatening diseases, observing groups battling malignant primary brain tumors, other forms of cancer, and multiple sclerosis. The study, which monitored male and female patients who were in heterosexual marriages over the course of five years, found there was a significant difference in the rate of "abandonment" depending on the gender of the patient. When the patient was male, and the supporting spouse female, divorce happened in 2.9 percent of cases. When the patient was female and the supporting spouse was male, divorce happened in 20.8 percent of cases—it was seven times more likely to happen. Abandonment affected quality, degree, and consistency of care when it came to these life-threatening diseases, having a tangible effect on quality of life as well as health outcomes of patients.

Coauthor Marc Chamberlain, a practicing neurological surgeon and professor of neurology at the University of Washington, told *Science Daily* that the study was initiated because doctors practicing neuro-oncology had noticed the increased risk female patients faced of losing their immediate source of support after diagnosis.[4] The upside is that this study, however depressing, does show that a majority of people stick through it when their spouses are faced with life-altering illness—male or female. But the disparity is too big to brush under the carpet. It shows a severe gender gap in terms of who steps up to provide care and emotional labor in the most essential times, and an incredible gender gap in terms of who benefits.

The emotional weight women do carry in relationships has measurable health and well-being impacts even in less extreme situations.

Surface acting, the kind of emotional labor that involves changing the appearance of emotions rather than the actual emotions internally felt, is consistently found to cause burnout, increased stress, and even insomnia.[5] But unequal distribution of emotional labor among other forms of domestic work also enhances burnout. A 2004 study[6] in Australia surveying 102 parents of young children found that women's psychological well-being was negatively affected because they were constantly expected to meet people's needs, improve well-being, and maintain harmony.

The American Psychological Association has consistently reported a gender stress gap, weighing more significantly on women than men. Its recent studies[7] have shown that women were 40 percent more likely to report having a great deal of stress. Married women were, in turn, far more likely to report high levels of stress than single women—with 54 percent of married women reporting they had felt compelled to cry due to stress in the past month before being surveyed, compared to 33 percent of single women. Single women had a much better handle on managing the stress they did have. Six times as many women as men said that increased help with household chores would help them feel able to care for their own stress. Once more—emotional labor may not encompass all domestic tasks, but their execution is so often part of caring for the whole family and protecting other people's experiences that, for many, they thoroughly overlap.

Johnson, the psychotherapist, said such inequalities could affect the broader quality of a relationship, including intimacy. "One thing I am noticing is the ways that emotional labor impedes the libido, impedes continued sexual connection between partners," she warned. "When it's a couple and they are both breadwinners, I find it becomes very taxing on them. When there is that imbalance, one person starts to get resentful. Whether they realize it or not, they start to withhold sex, or their libido drops."

Studies from the first couple of decades of the twenty-first century have started showing that egalitarian couples have marginally more active and more satisfying sex lives than couples in more conventional gender dynamics, where women perform the majority of domestic work.[8] Interestingly, previous research using older data from the 1980s and 1992 showed that married couples back then in more traditional gender arrangements were the ones who had the most active sex life.[9]

This reversal may hint at a couple of different social factors: changing norms around desirable private dynamics in straight couples that are matching social progress, but also changing norms around how sex happens in relationships, and what a fulfilling sex life actually is. Husbands forcing themselves on their wives had largely not been prosecutable during the time twentieth century data was collected. This is not to accuse a generation of husbands of being rapists. Rather, this is to point out that the notion that a husband had the right to access his wife's body when he pleased by virtue of their union, as a convention, may have contributed to previous higher sexual frequency—especially in traditional couples.

It is hopefully easy to agree that society moving away from this automatic right to access another person's body is a positive, needed change. But beyond no longer legally tolerating nonconsensual violent intimacy between partners, sexual scripts in straight dynamics—portraying sex mainly as penetrative intercourse and an act a man does and a woman receives—have been remarkably slow to change. Emotional labor plays a big, often overlooked role here.

Training women to be emotional laborers—catering to the experiences of others—helps prop up straight sex as something that, yet again, is an experience performed or enhanced by women for the benefit of men.

Emily, a woman in her thirties who grew up in a Christian

environment, told me that when she first started having sex as a teenager, her own pleasure barely factored into encounters in part because of a total lack of knowledge. "We didn't have the vocabulary for it.

"Men's bodies had orgasms. So, it was like, 'Okay, well, I guess it's like just we are done when you're done and then we are done.' If someone said, 'Did you enjoy yourself?' yes would be the answer, but I didn't have a reference point. I was never clear that something more was supposed to happen until people started talking of orgasms."

Female pleasure has remained out of sight of much of mainstream culture. The sexual liberation of the 1970s combined with the proliferation of widely available contraception loosened values around people having sex generally, but the same work was not done around uncovering the kind of sex men and women wanted to have more specifically.

A sexist Freudian theory that supposedly mature women enjoy orgasms through penetration has survived—in spite of clear and consistent discrediting over decades. In recent years, the explosion, with the internet, of male-gaze-centric porn has only entrenched nineteenth-century belief systems. This, combined with a lack of comprehensive, centralized sex education, has produced a culture of opaqueness around female sexuality, maintaining a patriarchal belief that the main goal of hetero sex is men's pleasure.

One man I interviewed, Felix, a doctor also in his thirties, explained that when he first started having sex with women as a teenager and young man, he was "confused that women weren't coming through penetration like in porn." Lacking proper sex ed, porn had effectively been his education, he said, but it didn't match up with reality.

Thankfully, we are finally having better conversations about female pleasure, in part because of increasing reports of pleasure inequality. One article that came out in 2017 surveying the sexual experience of 52,588 adults across America showed significant orgasm differences between different groups based on gender and sexual orientation.[10] Heterosexual men surveyed were the most likely to report usually experiencing orgasm when they were sexually intimate, with 95 percent of those surveyed declaring they always expected it to happen. Meanwhile, heterosexual women were the least likely group to report an orgasm as the norm during sexual intimacy, with only 65 percent declaring the same. Lesbian women experienced an orgasm far more routinely than their straight sisters, with 86 percent of them sharing that orgasm was the norm during sex.

These findings dispel any theories about a lack of orgasm having to do with the mysteriousness of the female anatomy or a woman's lack of maturity. Instead, they confirm that the unequal hierarchy of experience in mixed-gender situations is alive and well in the bedroom too.

Sara McClelland, a psychology professor at the University of Michigan, coined the term "intimate justice" in 2009, arguing that sex should be treated as a part of larger political and social inequalities. In a study surveying students of different genders and sexualities, she found that men tended to be more likely to measure sex as satisfying through the lens of their own pleasure, whereas women were more likely to measure sex as satisfying through the lens of the pleasure of the person they were having sex with.[11] LGBT and queer-identified men also measured satisfying sex based on how pleasured their partner was, linking sex to duty or even work, especially when they identified with more feminine roles. McClelland's study's findings suggest that the only group to fully measure sexual satisfaction through the lens of their own pleasure and not their partners' was straight cis men.

Ingrained entitlement to pleasure and experience meant that while Felix, as a young man, professed confusion about women not screaming ecstasy the way they did in porn videos, he also didn't give it too much thought. "I didn't really give a shit," he said. Just like in the study, his main concern was his own gratification.

Emily, a straight woman, told me the orgasm and experiential disparity came as no surprise. Talking about the reality of her orgasm made lovers defensive. "They always happened to have a girlfriend, their last girlfriend, who would come four or five times in a session. I was like, 'So why did you break up with her? If that was your main measure of how good you are as a lover, or how you value yourself, why did you end that?'"

Up until her late twenties, she faked orgasm a lot, to keep men off her back. "I would put on a good show and just hoped that they never asked," she confided. If she was honest with the men she was sleeping with, it didn't result in curiosity or closeness. It usually backfired. "They take it so personally." It barely seemed worth it.

From an emotional labor standpoint, it seems clear that part of what is going on in these dynamics of intimacy is men expecting to be catered to, and women performing emotional labor in the bedroom for men—even in casual encounters. Not only are women more often centering partners' pleasure over their own, they are prepared to perform extra emotional labor under the form of faking it to protect men's egos and not ruffle their psychological feathers.

Psychologists Gayle Brewer and Colin Hendrie sought to find out how often—and why—women were faking it. For their study published in 2011,[12] they collected data from seventy-one sexually active heterosexual women, forty-nine of whom were in committed relationships, and all of whom reported having previously experienced orgasm. It found that women reported most often reaching orgasm through self-manipulation of the clitoris, manipulation by a partner, or oral sex, and least often through penetrative sex. But it found that 79 percent of them faked orgasm during penetrative sex over 50 percent of the time, and 25 percent of surveyed women faked 90 percent of the time.

The reasons the respondents gave for these "copulatory vocalizations" during penetration in spite of the absence of orgasm? Speeding up the male partner's orgasm was reported as a reason in 66 percent of cases, which was done "to relieve discomfort, pain, boredom and fatigue in equal proportion as well as because of time limitations."

But most poignantly, 92 percent of the surveyed women reported they very strongly felt the vocalizing-in-spite-of-no-orgasm technique boosted their partner's self-esteem, which 87 percent of them listed as the main reason for doing it. Similar to what Emily professed to have been doing, reluctantly, for years, women were faking it to cater to the emotions of the men they were in bed with. The findings also confirmed women's lower self-prioritization: 68 percent of them reported that having their own orgasm was secondary during sex with a partner.

Felix, the doctor, admitted that as he got older, when female sexual partners told him they had not experienced an orgasm with him, he became defensive and raised questions about the women in question having physical problems. He felt insecure and compelled to make the women feel it was an issue they had, not one he had. "I did it to defend my honor. In my mindset back then, if that didn't happen, I was somehow inferior."

Emotional labor by women in bed in these moments isn't just about prioritizing the other's needs; it also can be a form of emotional self-preservation to avoid a lashing out. The problem with this kind of dynamic, aside from the fact that it reveals subtle forms of intimate danger, is that the culture doesn't move forward. Men, taught only to center their pleasure, remain misled by cultural and interpersonal messaging around women.

Felix said he evolved, and in his thirties became more educated about women—by asking and listening, and not putting pressure on women either way—by doing some emotional labor. Pleasing his current female sexual partner took work, he said, but it was worth it, even if it was just to show that he had some form of concern for her needs. "Frankly, as long as I am making the effort honestly, then she seems to be very content about that."

Of course, emotional labor and thinking about the other person in this context needn't be an actual problem, especially if both parties can take ownership of their needs and show up for the other person. Once more, the problem is not emotional labor on its own but our current patriarchal system, prizing men's experiences and needs over women's. A balancing out of emotional labor, in the form of either men finally matching women's work with their own efforts or women asserting their own rules for engagement based on their needs as well as the needs of others, can do a lot toward redressing unfairness.

Nowadays, Emily practices polyamory and has a primary romantic partner who centers and respects her, including in the bedroom. When she takes on new lovers, she is giving but uncompromising when it comes to expecting pleasure to go both ways. She is also no longer interested in the kind of emotional labor she felt pressured, or even forced, into providing when she was younger—whether to flatter a man's ego or break the news as to women's actual anatomy.

"I am not interested in doing more training, I am interested in benefiting from the previous training. So, a man needs to have dated a lot of women and have actually been interested or have inquired about feedback. Or you need to have dated a couple of women for multiple years that actually knew themselves and were not highly religious. Otherwise, you can't make the cut because that means I am going to have to do the work and I just don't have the time, particularly if it is just going to be a weekend adventure."

In intimate situations, she will no longer let men get away with primarily taking for themselves and disregarding her pleasure. "If I didn't have an orgasm, if they didn't, if they can't get hard, I am no longer going to fret about it. If I am still up for it, I might say, 'I am ready to roll still. I am still here, so my expectation is that you are still going to participate.' I am not going to give someone an out any longer, where I totally would [have] when I was younger.

"If someone was at this point going to suggest they were going to be out of it, I would make enough of a fuss that it's like, I am not going to emotionally hold this, you will have to [. . .] If you want out, okay, but you are going to have to actually say it to my face. But you don't actually get a pass any longer. Whereas now, now it's like 'No, no, ball is in your court: GO!'"

Rectifying the balance is a sensitive topic for men, whether because they are reluctant to give up their experiential privilege or because they simply hate the idea of being cast as the bad guy and see constructive, honest feedback as a loss of honor. This may not be true for all of them, but the problem remains: How do you move toward justice if one group has been largely absolved from any meaningful accountability or effort? Are individual acts of correction and courage enough to achieve accountability, or must a larger social shift be achieved so that those in power not only receive but also value and perform emotional labor? Should it be something they come to voluntarily, or is this a shift that should be demanded?

Rory Carroll, an editor and publisher of a major national car magazine at the time of our interviews, told me that he had been working on redressing emotional labor injustice ever since the topic started to surface on social media. "Part of the reason it was so impactful was that it was jarring," he said of seeing the Twitter campaign demanding pay.

Reflecting on what emotional labor meant politically, professionally, and personally, he grew to understand it as "trying to avoid introducing suffering in the world or causing people hardship." Suddenly, he became more aware of his posture, more aware of the importance of how he made other people feel, how he spoke to them. In many situations, he changed the way he carried himself. With women and people who worked under him, he tried to be less imposing, to avoid raising his voice or standing too close to people, even as he switched to standing straight and remembering a firm handshake with men who held more authority.

Married to a woman, and the father of two daughters, he said he was trying to take steps to share responsibility at home and shed any entitlement he witnessed his father enjoy as the "fun," less implicated parent. He also acknowledged the immense invisible labor women did, and where he could not make up in chores or thoughtfulness, he sought to make up in money. This included supporting women's online work through Patreon and other fundraising campaigns. "I am trying to unravel for myself what my blind spots are. Once you've seen the world in a different way, all that stuff is up for examination," he said.

This was no small feat for someone of his background. "When you grow up as a privileged white male of middle-class status, it's hard to understand suffering, it's hard to understand empathy," he shared. Rory grew up in northern Michigan and said he had long been oblivious to the invisible labor enabling his life, let alone the injustices surrounding it. He may very well have come across the term "emotional labor" on Twitter and been wholly unmoved by it had it not been for three factors he identified as key to his ability to empathize.

The first, and most important, catalyzing factor for Rory's empathy building was that his brother became very sick. Over the course of months, he visited his beloved sibling in the hospital and watched him slowly die. He says witnessing the suffering of his brother and other hospital patients opened his heart.

Second, Rory moved to Detroit, a city where people, through the lottery of birth, were born to far less privileged circumstances and opportunities. That seemed unjustifiably unfair.

Third, Rory felt that, as a man who had attained economic stability and professional status, it was far easier for him to challenge other traditional ideals of masculinity. "Throughout my twenties, there was this sense of I had to be someone. I was highly motivated by a sense of economic insecurity. As a young man, there were a lot of impulses toward trying to dominate situations, trying to dominate male colleagues, trying to have a greater sense of control over the people around me that relaxed.

"As my status and economic situation changed, that coincidentally or maybe not coincidentally changed," he told me. Rory was able to do emotional labor, a traditionally feminine performance, once he felt he had proven himself as a man. Once he had ascended socially and economically, performing emotional labor was no longer threatening to his masculinity. He got a pass. Maybe even talking about emotional labor as a man, and no longer needing to assert himself with peers, was a very advanced form of status signifying.

Rory's story is heartening in that he shows what the research confirms: that empathy can be acquired with practice, motivation, and unflinching exposure. Empathy in action becomes emotional labor. But Rory's third identified reason for growth—one that I am grateful he so honestly shared—points to the difficulties in relinquishing traditional masculinity for those who are not as privileged as he is. And in a world where emotional labor is not valued, relinquishing power for even more work is a hard sell.

Still, Rory made a case for his pivot to providing more emotional labor as a decision that had paid off dividends to him internally, as a human being. "I always think, *What am I doing today that in five or ten years will embarrass me?* That experience of trying to work on this stuff has made me a happier and a more fulfilled person. Trying to be more empathetic, and trying to be more aware, I guess I feel better. I feel more of a person, surer of my place and my impact. I used to take apart every single social interaction and think of how I fucked it up or how I could have been better. I still do that. I now think I hurt people less."

Some of Rory's emotional labor may have been impressive, and sometimes even enchanting, but it was hard to think he constituted a model to reproduce because of the degree of power he possessed. And yet, on the flip side, so many men in his position take few steps to consciously, positively affect other people's feelings, let alone care to scrutinize their own emotional labor output.

For our second interview, he turned up with two fistfuls of toy cars. "Here," he said to me cheekily, handing them all over, grinning from ear to ear. He had just come from Detroit's velodrome where he and his work team had hand-glued eighty-two hundred donated Hot Wheels to the floor to look like they were racing, en masse, around the bicycle track. The wacky display was set up to mark the half century of the toy company's existence and was organized by the media company Rory headed.

His eyes glistened from his day's work. The event had involved inviting public school kids to come and check out their wildly scaled miniature car spectacle. "We told them they could bring all the Hot Wheels they wanted home. They were so happy," Rory said. It all seemed like a slightly lower-key, *Charlie and the Chocolate Factory* version of that time Oprah donated actual cars to her whole audience with repeated cries of "YOU GET A CAR!" Many a kid's dream, and a delightful way of making them feel good. The emotional labor had paid off too, returning dividends to its instigator. Rory was buoyant.

But identifying, naming, and insisting on others seeing emotional labor is only one step for redress. Sometimes all visibility around emotional labor creates is a snapshot of privilege as it currently is—and individuals will not always see visibility as a lesson in independently stepping up and flattening the unequal distribution of emotional labor; quite the contrary.

Luis Alejandro Tapia, a social impact equity and transformative justice consultant in New York City who works with private, nonprofit, and public institutions, tells me he sees this on a regular basis in his work. It was while attending one of his workshops in 2019 for teachers in a public high school that I witnessed a man with far less social status than Rory, but also possessing white male privilege, cling to his right not to perform emotional labor.

That freezing January day, I had speed-walked my way through the streets of Midtown New York to join Luis and his colleague Sofia as they led an implicit bias training in one of the city's hundreds of public schools. The school was on the fifth floor of a building you might not know was a school, except for the small group of police officers present at the entrance, sitting and standing behind a desk, guns visible, metal detectors to each side. Inside, I headed to the library and joined twenty-five school staff and teachers. The school, I was told, was mostly made up of minority students, coming in from low-income areas. Our group was majority female and non-white.

On the board ahead of us, our day's trainers had written instructions to bear in mind as we moved through exercises. Among them: "Make space, take space, give space." Emotional labor wasn't mentioned explicitly that day, but it was everywhere. In conversations narrowing in on identities, power, and forced inauthenticity, the day's activities were clearly beseeching participants to become aware of the ways in which they were either performing emotional labor for others or perpetually expecting it to be performed for them.

Luis, who identifies as a Black, Afro-Latino, cisgendered, fat, gap-toothed, bearded Dominican New Yorker, led us in a series of interactive exercises inviting us to reflect on our multiple identities and the ways in which they affected our interaction with the world.

As a first exercise, we were asked to privately write on five separate Post-its our gender, sexual orientation, nationality, religion, and race, after which we were instructed to discard one at a time based on which one defined us the most, then the least. While we were doing the exercise in a circle, next to one another, nobody was called on to share what they were writing or discarding. It was a private activity performed in a group with no requirement or invitation for disclosure.

Barely an hour into our training, a hand shot up. "I see you," Luis affirmed, signaling that he would come back to it later and continuing with instructions. But still, the hand insisted, waving more and more vigorously, and the teacher it belonged to eventually started speaking without visible prompt. "I disagree with this exercise," he announced, having not yet finished it, or in fact had its intention explained. "I think these identities are less important than other things like individual experiences. I think individual experiences matter more."

Mike, our interlocutor, was a white man, one of three in the room that day. Maybe the exercise would be best discussed once it had been completed? the trainers told Mike. A couple of minutes later, we were left with just one Post-it with one random descriptor and were invited to ponder it. Participants shifted in their chairs. How did it feel to be holding this one Post-it identity—neither our most important one nor our least important one? Do some of you feel like you are able to always carry these five identities with you at all times, or do you need to leave some at home? How about your colleagues or students? Are they able to?

This conversation, which would continue throughout the day, started to inspire thoughtful, if hesitant, comments. One Black female teacher talked about code-switching, referring to the expectation that Black people should change their way of speaking in formal, professional, or whiter spaces to adapt to white norms. She did not feel it was right that she had to do it, even if she knew it was necessary. Another Black female teacher engaged in debate with her colleague, responding that she did not mind code-switching. "It sits well with me," she said.

Quickly, Mike's hand was back up again, and he burst into their conversation. As educators, he said, they had a responsibility of teaching children how to speak, including, if not especially, to code-switch, so that they could thrive in the system. Pleased with his point, Mike continued. He grew up in Long Island where he was bullied—one of a few Jewish children in a Christian community, he said. People might not know about his experiences by looking at him, he told the room, but his experiences meant he understood the experience of Black people and Black students. He also explained, gaining momentum, that he once experienced racism when, as a white man, he sought to rent an apartment in Chinatown, but his application was denied, based on the fact, he believed, that he was not Chinese.

Sofia nodded calmly, responding that religion definitely played a factor, which is why it was one of the Post-its, and that deciding how open or not to be about your religion, based on very tangible ramifications, was definitely a part of what we were addressing. But these experiences were often not equivalent, she said. Luis, taking advantage of a brief moment of silence to guide the conversation back to the matter at hand, asked the rest of the circle to contribute thoughts on how people were often reduced to a single identity. But by then, the room had gone back to being tentative, and Luis and Sofia swiftly moved us all on to our next exercise.

As the day wore on, Mike's unabashed efforts to center himself continued, his interventions seeking to point out injustices he felt he, too, faced. Every time he did this, Sofia and Luis acted in tandem to redirect the attention to the rest of the room, insisting on centering people who were not normally centered in wider society: people of color, women. Two other white men in attendance, however, did not act in this way, and so I wondered whether Mike's astounding lack of emotional labor that day came down to personality.

I later asked Luis whether Mike's inability to center any feelings but his own had been an exception. Nope, the answer came back. White people, especially white men, but sometimes women, too, were unfailingly the loudest voices in the room. There was always one person. Luis's job was in part to insist on a reversal of usual patterns of emotional labor: for people normally centered to hold space, give the stage to those people who were not normally afforded such privileges, and listen. But such an exercise obviously felt like a threat to some rather than an opportunity to ponder what it felt like to walk in other people's shoes and reflect on the drastic experiential differences in a group of people otherwise occupying the same room and working in similar professions.

Toward the end of the day, as I slipped out for a bathroom break, I passed Mike in the corridor, being consoled by two of his female colleagues. "I am just done," he told the two women—two women of color. "I just want to leave. Today has been so hard for me."

"We know, Mike. We are sorry you had to go through this," one said. "We felt really awful for you."

I was shocked. Although why should I have been? Regardless of how his colleagues actually felt deep down (I did not get to ask them, and I was just a spectator for a day), Mike was still enjoying the privilege of having his feelings centered and catered to—the absolute opposite of the point of the day. At an event where he was invited to make space for others, he was unquestioningly grabbing space for himself. His experiential entitlement laid bare.

Later, when I debrief with Luis, he explains that for all the Mikes—and the Mikes are plentiful—there are always others, often not white men, who respond to his workshops and trainings with gratitude. Gratitude for feeling like they can breathe and their experiences are seen. And for the limits of empathy building that the workshop appeared to represent for Mike—although who knows what has happened since—the events of that day, coloring in emotional labor distribution and its predictable inequalities, did seem to present a rare, clear moment of truth.

For a short moment in that room on the fifth floor of a Midtown New York public school, it became clear that the emperor had no clothes. What would happen if we all stopped playing along with it? What would happen if we just told the emperor he was naked?

Truth through real and acknowledged visibility is crucial, but it's hard to push individual solutions forward without connecting them to larger emotional networks. Doing this forces the question of what it means to move toward emotional justice in a way that acknowledges that as individuals we are all, inevitably but also mercifully, interconnected. Doing this might even move us beyond justice and toward emotional freedom.

NINE

Radical Love
in a New World

EMPATHY

In his 1980 memoir, *Fearfully and Wonderfully Made*, the late British physician Paul Brand recalled attending a lecture by the great American anthropologist Margaret Mead.[1] Describing Mead's interaction with her audience, Brand, a medical pioneer in the field of leprosy, wrote: "[Margaret Mead] asked the question, 'What is the earliest sign of civilization?' A clay pot? Iron? Tools? Agriculture? No, she claimed. To her, evidence of the earliest true civilization was a healed femur, a leg bone, which she held up before us in the lecture hall. She explained that such healings were never found in the remains of competitive, savage societies. There, clues of violence abounded: temples pierced by arrows, skulls crushed by clubs. But the healed femur showed that someone must have cared for the injured person—hunted on his behalf, brought him food, and served him at personal sacrifice. Savage societies could not afford such pity."[2]

This story makes a case for care and emotional labor, or the willingness to vitally cater to the needs of someone beyond oneself, as not just a detail of our lives but the beginning and, in many ways, the center of our civilization. The recounting also forces an examination of the degree to which we still operate with this value system in mind.

If empathy and care were the beginning of civilization as we understand it, where does that leave us now? How central are these values still, really? Have we long ditched this idea of progress, trading it in with the idea that dominant masculine individualism is the highest form of value? Can we still proclaim in all honesty that prosperity is only to be found in our societies and economies by prioritizing egotistic, dominant actions and individuals? Can that belief even stand on its legs anymore when so much of our economy is now driven by humans performing emotional labor, by the creation of experiences tied to care, service, love, and connection? Are we still progressing? And if so, which direction are we heading in?

The United States is the wealthiest nation on earth.[3] It is also among the world's most unequal, tolerating extreme wealth even as it tolerates broad poverty.[4] The United States still does not possess a comprehensive universal health-care system. The effect of this factor alone on the lives of individuals well beyond health is chilling. Medical bills and hospital visits are still cited as catalyzing reasons in two-thirds of personal bankruptcy filings.[5] Which is not to say Americans do not care. In 2019, the CEO of GoFundMe, Rob Solomon, said that one-third of the donations on his fundraising sites were related to campaigns to cover medical bills.[6] According to its own website, GoFundMe claimed it hosted over 250,000 medical campaigns a year, raising more than $650 million.[7] Americans are prepared to give individually, but the United States lags behind in reflecting a general, systemic empathy for all its people. It is the only country among the world's twenty wealthiest to not provide affordable universal health care to its citizens.[8] Among forty-one developed nations, the United States is the only country to still not guarantee its citizens—mothers or fathers— any paid parental leave at all.[9]

In March 2021, after a year of economic crisis during which unemployment doubled because of the coronavirus pandemic that by then had killed half a million people in the United States, President Joe Biden signed into effect a $1.9 trillion COVID-19 relief package that was set to create the largest expansion to the social safety net in a generation. Among the policies introduced was an expanded child tax credit that would provide families up to $3,600 a year per child. This policy alone was projected to cut nationwide child poverty by 45 percent.[10]

But why did it take such extraordinary circumstances to push comprehensive social reform that would acknowledge that, in such a historically wealthy nation, it doesn't make sense for millions of people to face bankruptcy if they get sick, it doesn't make sense for people to be pushed to the brink of poverty or, worse even, to be born into it? How have we accepted the contours of such an unempathetic system?

The answer lies, in part, in how inured we have become to the intimate extraction and violence at the heart of our current emotional labor arrangements. It lies in the comfort we have in disparaging—and even mocking—what are seen to be feminine work and traits even as we constantly turn to them and rely on them.

Systemically, this simultaneous reliance and denigration means the emotional labor demands resulting from monumental, brutal policies go unnoticed, even if they define the lives of millions. The United States is both the biggest military spender in the world and the harshest incarcerator in the world. This means that in a nation that employs over 1.3 million active military personnel, 84 percent of whom are men, more than a million families are coping with, supporting, and absorbing the effects of an armed global superpower in very real emotional ways, at home.[11] It also means that in a nation with an incarcerated population of 1.9 million people, there are millions of families and loved ones invisibly coping with, supporting, and absorbing the ripple effects of a punishing system on individuals, families, and communities.[12]

Gina Clayton-Johnson, the founder of Essie Justice Group, told me that when the United States invested in four decades of mass incarceration, it effectively invested in social isolation and the rupturing of communities. Incarceration rates have exploded in the last four decades in large part because of harsh drug laws especially targeting Black communities and communities of color.[13] While nine out of ten incarcerated people are men, those bearing the brunt of such aggressive policies are often entire communities held together by women. One in four women in the United States, and every other Black woman, has a loved one who is incarcerated.

The harm that comes as a result of incarceration is something women have to take on as their own responsibility, Clayton-Johnson said—with a myriad of extra forms of emotional labor added on. Her organization, based out of Oakland, California, serves women who have loved ones on the inside. "For women with incarcerated loved ones, the cognitive load is more than figuring out kids' preschool. For them, it is also getting that look from a loved one in a court or inside, saying, *What should I do? Should I take the plea?*"

That half a million people sit in American jails every day without a conviction because of not being able to make bail means women on the outside are forced into making impossible choices.[14] Paying rent or paying for a loved one's bail was just one of many agonizing decisions women had to face, said Clayton-Johnson, whose organization is among those advocating an end to the cash bail system. "These decisions are more than just cold calculations of plusses and minuses. They are hugely emotional decisions women are expected to take on," she said.

These burdens take a toll. A report[15] published by her organization to document what was happening to women as a result of mass incarceration found that 70 percent of women with incarcerated loved ones were the primary wage earners in their family. It further found that 86 percent of them said the impact of having a loved one incarcerated had a severe or extreme effect on their emotional and mental health, and 63 percent said that their physical health had been significantly or extremely affected. A third of the women surveyed faced homelessness, eviction, or an inability to pay their rents or mortgages on time.

A system that throws millions of men behind bars relies, once more, on the free labor of women to act as buffers and absorbers of pain. Not only that; it entrenches gender inequality by forcing them to bear the brunt of an unending list of negative consequences. On this subject, the report reads:

> During the period of a loved one's incarceration, many women are forced to deviate from personal plans that might have led to longer term stability

in order to address the immediate needs of their loved one's incarceration and the needs of other family members. Women bear the costs of phone calls, prison visits, and commissary bills. Most commonly, women with incarcerated loved ones work more hours, change jobs, miss out on job opportunities, and cannot pursue their own education.

Clayton-Johnson's brother is a musician, she shared, which led her to become acquainted with the Piedmont blues style of music. People think this style is happy and fun, she said, but her brother shared that there were early-twentieth-century teachings inside these songs. One of them instructs women to smile in the face of trauma or they will face more harm. "The consequences of looking how you feel can be deadly. Even through song in Black communities, we have been taught to reorient and manipulate our feelings to avoid death, trauma, and brutality," Clayton-Johnson reflected.

Emotional labor, taken on by marginalized groups, is hidden, and as it remains in the shadows, so does the force it contains within. The healing aspects, the ability to empathize, to create connection, meaning, and belonging. As the work is taken for granted, as we demean the work and the people doing it, we do not just forgo an appreciation for real value, we lose our ability to engage in it as a practice.

Jamil Zaki, a professor of psychology at Stanford University and the director of the Stanford Social Neuroscience Laboratory, illuminates in his book *The War for Kindness* that we are experiencing a decline in empathy. Empathy is described as one of three capabilities—feeling vicariously what someone is going through (emotional empathy), thinking about their experiences (cognitive empathy), and wanting that person to feel better (empathic concern). In 2009, the average American declared himself to be less empathic, or caring, than 75 percent of Americans thirty years before.[16]

Reasons for this abound. There are external, tangible factors to point to. More people live alone and in cities, our lives are increasingly online, and politics continue to drive a larger and larger wedge between people. In anonymous settings, both kindness and empathy decline. But there are theoretical problems too. As a society, misconceptions based in conjectures have mistakenly become absorbed as fact, one of the biggest and most damaging of which is the idea, driven by mainstream economics, that people are naturally, inherently selfish, and that selfish people get ahead. The "invisible hand" theory in economics posits that left to their own devices, and fueled by the self-interested, competitive nature of man, financial markets will regulate themselves and create great prosperity.[17] Such a philosophy justified, over the last forty years, government divestment from public goods and social safety nets, and has led to ever increasing income and wealth inequality.[18]

The problem? Aside from other limitations, there's a simple, logical fallacy in this line of argument. Humans aren't inherently selfish. We are actually the most empathic animals on the planet. We thrive in community. This is part of where emotional labor as a form of empathy in action comes in, and the good news is our empathy losses can be regained. We can all *do* emotional labor, and connect back to where we thrive the most. As I went over in the opening chapter of this book, empathy is not a fixed trait you have or you don't have. Empathy can be learned. You can practice it and gradually get better at it. Empathy is a skill.

It also isn't a zero-sum game where one person giving will automatically lose. Empathic people reap benefits for themselves and for those around them—having more friends, higher-quality romantic relationships, being happier across the board, and succeeding more in professional contexts, Zaki writes. This means there's an incentive for people to engage in emotional labor across the board. It's a win-win.

Where there needs to be a rewrite is around our social organization, our social hierarchies, and our fundamental value systems. It is entirely possible, based on literature surrounding "motivational empathy," that if empathy, care, and love in action—or emotional labor—signified power or status, far more people would do it routinely. Maybe even, lo and behold, everyone would do it.

But building such a world is complicated. Emotional labor has been so baked into our rigidly hierarchical world that is not only patriarchal, but white supremacist, economically exploitative and extractive, homophobic, and transphobic, that the entire system effectively relies on it. Our entire system relies on a hierarchy of experiences and feelings that puts white men at the top. Not just economically, politically, and socially—but experientially. The most ludicrous aspect of this is that those with the most power are told that their acting in a self-interested way is not only allowed of them; it is, they are reassured, *good* for society. Never mind the good silently being extracted from the armies of emotional laborers they are standing on.

It may not be at the top of the pyramid now, but there is no doubt that emotional labor—empathy, love, care, and human connectedness as actions—is powerful. Emotional labor, and putting another person's needs above our own, sets us apart as a human race. How do we get to a world that catches up to this reality? How do we build a world with empathy and love as its beating heart, at its center, not on its margins?

One rainy, winter evening, I headed down from northern Manhattan's Dominican neighborhood Washington Heights to the Guggenheim Museum, situated right next to Central Park on the Upper East Side. There, in the museum's bunker-like restaurant space, as tourists looked at million-dollar art pieces, I was set to attend a panel on corporate culture and sexual harassment featuring some of the world's leading organizational psychologists.

The panel was staid at first—and aside from the futuristic spaceship aesthetic of its setting, possibly even a total waste of time. *Changes in company policies!* one person said. *Training employees so that they alter behavior! Opportunity to set and lead the culture!* another exclaimed. It was a small gathering, and I began to ponder a discreet exit, until one speaker, a man, veered thoroughly off the common script.

The panelist in question, Tomas Chamorro-Premuzic, an organizational psychologist and professor at Columbia University and University College London who specializes in psychometrics, had been asked to weigh in on what "respect" at work might now mean, "post–'Me Too.'" "I am going to say something that may seem controversial. In a world where presenting as your authentic self is seen as a priority, there is fundamental incompatibility between respect and authenticity." My eyes shifted from the blur of the room and focused.

I waited to hear more. "Respect requires inauthenticity. A lot of the times you have to pick between one and the other," Chamorro-Premuzic continued pushing. In case anyone in the audience was unsure where he fell, he made it abundantly clear he felt corporations should prize respect. The psychologist added that respectful workplaces were far more effective than ones where people felt they could express themselves, unfiltered.

The conversation was heavily coded, I now realize looking back, and could be misinterpreted. This was effectively a point about free speech, a topic that has been inflaming and dividing political and academic arenas in recent years. Respect here was being used to describe an intolerance of expressions of prejudice, while authenticity was being used to describe a lack of emotion and thought filtering, as a lack of emotional labor. If your unfiltered self is prejudiced, being authentic is harmful to the work environment. It's better—and more productive—to be respectful, Chamorro-Premuzic's point was. Basically, your freedom of speech to be an asshole at work should be limited. In emotional labor language, and with a power lens, the point becomes: do the emotional labor and think about how your words and actions impact those around you as a priority, including—or especially—if you are in a position of power.

But this is not just a question of ethics; it is a question of being honest about efficiency in the workplace and not having our views blinded by prejudice that prizes masculine traits over feminine ones. Chamorro-Premuzic's public-facing research and writing in the last decade have challenged a collective understanding around what makes for the best kind of leadership. Great leaders are not those unrestrained, charismatic, competitive people we have tended to associate with dominant roles, he advances; great leaders are actually other-oriented people who are able to unite a team with a common vision, while displaying high levels of competence and integrity. Great leaders are not those who perform what we see as masculinity at the highest-octane levels but those who expertly perform traits associated with femininity—and emotional labor.[19]

These assertions are heavily backed by research. Filtering one's authentic expression and becoming a good "impression manager," or doing emotional labor, is consistently shown to create higher levels of interpersonal effectiveness, career success, and psychological well-being in people.[20] Meanwhile, studies find that lacking a filter, or having "low self-control" and a disregard for future consequences, is associated with psychopathy rather than good governance.[21]

While we have become accustomed to, and have indeed enforced, essential emotional labor being the work of subordinate groups, it turns out it should be the work of leaders. Ironically, this makes subordinate groups arguably far better trained—at the onset—for positions of leadership.

This is part of what Chamorro-Premuzic advances in his book *Why Do So Many Incompetent Men Become Leaders?* Instead of focusing on what is wrong with women to understand why they are not rising to positions of leadership more, we need to look at what is wrong with the system's way of interacting with men, he argues. The problem is not in individuals but in the traits we mistakenly treat as valuable. We are over-rewarding selfishness and narcissism, disproportionately found in men. While supreme confidence is useful to inspire followers, it fails to deliver on the goods when it comes to making complicated and thoughtful decisions during moments of crisis. If feminine traits, like humility, sensitivity to others, and the ability to be considerate—traits disproportionately exhibited in women—were recognized for their objective power, more women would be getting to the top. Such a system would also incentivize all people, regardless of gender, to develop better prosocial skills.

Instead, because we insist on remaining blind to the real value of emotional labor, the change that we are seeing is going in the complete opposite direction. Clinical narcissism remains almost 40 percent more prevalent in men, a gender contrast that is the highest among any other psychological trait, but this gap is narrowing—not because men are becoming less narcissistic but because women are becoming more so. Women, encouraged to lean in and emulate men to get ahead, are shedding the very traits we disparage and that should be rewarded.

So is it time to shed authenticity and make place for emotional labor? Are the two directly opposed to each other? Not necessarily. But we need to spell out what authenticity really means, how it interacts with privilege and gender, and how emotional labor modulates this.

Authenticity as the consistent expression of one's true self, personality, and sets of values, uninfluenced by outside pressures or expectations, holds undeniable value. It's a valuing of genuineness that opposes itself to the dictatorship of conformity, to an over-curated world of traps and scams—where online, retouched appearances are oceans away from off-line ones. Dare I say, it is even the valuing of a trait my parents' generation of boomers would shudder at: earnestness.

I live in a city that prizes authenticity quite vocally, above many other attributes—something I love about it. Here, authenticity means being real: not fake, not having an alternative agenda, not pretending to be something you are not, not having a sweet, seemingly generous front while you are in fact out to profit from or get people. In a city that recent history has economically devastated, authenticity is currency—access, credibility, trust, respect—that no money can buy.

Authenticity is not just an attribute of the interpersonal; it holds value in business settings too. Marketers, advertisers,[22] and business leaders,[23] seeking to make themselves relevant and keen to capture the attention of millennials and Gen Zs, have argued that authenticity is the way to our hearts, minds,[24] and wallets. Gen Z superstar singer Billie Eilish's stratospheric popularity is in part rooted in a purported authenticity.[25]

But for all the cries to bring your full, authentic self to your every day, the degree to which you can realistically do this heavily depends on what group you either belong to or are perceived as belonging to, and where that group sits in the social hierarchy.

In corporate America, just being yourself might be all very well if your name is Brad, you attended a top-ranking school, and you are white, straight, cis, and male. But it might not get you very far if you switch up just one of those categories. A woman with all the same characteristics as Brad named Brenda will likely face backlash if she brings her full self to work, including if this full self is entirely professional, but if this full self doesn't correspond to what it sounds and looks like to be a competent, confident worker as well as a *demure, altruistic,* and *thoughtful* woman. If your name is Bri and you veer from yet another category as Brad, bringing your whole self to work gets worse still.

In 2010, Chastity Jones, a Black woman in Alabama, was offered a job as a customer service representative for Catastrophe Management Solutions, with the caveat that she should cut her hair. Jones, who attended her job interview in a blue suit, wore her hair in short locs. When she refused to forfeit a style of hair that was authentic to herself and a very common style for Black Americans, her offer of employment was rescinded.[26] Her employer's decision was upheld in the courts, although the case fell shy of being heard and ruled on by the Supreme Court. In other words, Jones brought her authentic and professional self to work and was denied employment based on her culturally specific hairstyle.

The tides are very slowly turning on this kind of matter, in some places. In February 2019, the New York City Commission on Human Rights issued a legal enforcement guidance on race discrimination on the basis of hair, to be included within our understanding of what racial discrimination consists of.[27] The commission declared protection of "the rights of New Yorkers to maintain natural hair or hairstyles that are closely associated with their racial, ethnic, or cultural identities," including in employment situations, highlighting the racist legacy of referring to non-European hairstyles as unkempt. California followed suit.

But for now, there is no federal policy protecting American women of African descent from wearing their hair in non-European-centric ways, meaning women sporting non-European hairstyles are often forced to choose between their identities and their economic advancement. Who gets to be authentic and who doesn't often ends up being about privilege, and for those who lack privilege, authenticity can still happen, but it might come at a high price. This makes authenticity, at least in some circumstances, an entitlement afforded to some groups and not others.

Emotional labor and its dispensation interact with almost all aspects of this kind of negotiation. Not only are some groups not allowed to be authentic for fear of severe penalty—here in a work environment—but, because of the social kudos now given to authenticity, when they do alter their behavior for the benefit of their surroundings, they have to make it believable too. They have to do very convincing emotional labor so that their surroundings do not perceive them as being inauthentic or phony. If they are found to be fake, a second kind of backlash awaits.

Be feminine and caring, but don't forget to tell me that you love doing it. Straighten your hair, but don't forget to mention that that is your preferred choice. Be a good girl and tell me you want to be. In a deeply hierarchical world, part of the emotional labor you have your arm twisted into doing is simply performing a supposed authenticity. People, forced into performing genuineness, become complicit by necessity. If their mask is exposed, a society that proclaims it loves authenticity but is in fact quite hateful has the choice to express intolerance toward what is behind the mask or decry the manipulation of the person who chose to wear it. Either way, the marginalized individual is set up to lose once the charade they were cornered into participating in is revealed.

This plays out all too predictably with people who veer from cisgender, heterosexual scripts. Here, a collective requirement for authenticity combines with continued intolerance to punishing effect.

In her twenties, LaSaia Wade was on track to fulfilling her dream. Growing up on the south side of Chicago, she wanted to be a rich woman with no problems and "wear all the fine things in life." After graduating from college, she worked for a Fortune 500 company, where she became the director of communications, making six figures. All of this came to a halt, she told me, when "reality came down, and said: *You wish*."

One night, slowly coming into herself, she headed to a gay club. When a man came up to her and asked her whether she was trans, she said yes. She didn't think she had anything to hide after work hours. "I should be able to live my life the way I want to live it," she told me of what she believed to be her uncontroversial thoughts at the time. The next day, during a director's luncheon at the office, the man reappeared. He worked for the same company. He walked up to her and said, "Oh, you're that beautiful trans woman that I saw at the gay club."

By the next day, she was fired for being "deceptive on the application to the job," as if her assigned sex at birth had anything to do with her ability to do her job. LaSaia sought to do good work and live authentically, but she was punished for it.

In 2020, just a few years after LaSaia was fired from her job, the US Supreme Court ruled that employees could no longer be fired for their sexual orientation or gender identity, explicitly including transgender people. But by then, she had moved on to entirely new horizons. After taking time to travel, learn, and organize, LaSaia returned to her hometown and founded her own trans-centered LGBT community center in Chicago in 2017, the Brave Space Alliance, providing residents and community members access to services around employment and health, and resources like food. Authenticity was the right personal choice for LaSaia as a human, but she was still punished for it economically, in our system. And even if her rights were now theoretically protected in the workplace, she still continued to face considerable discrimination.

When rights move forward to protect a broader array of people, the burden of emotional labor shifts from people deemed subordinate having to perform the emotional labor to people deemed dominant having to perform it. That is the crux of a lot of the debates that have been raging across campuses and beyond over the last few years around freedom of speech.

In the fall of 2015, Erika Christakis, a Yale lecturer who also served as a house master in one of its colleges, resigned following an email to students advising them to ignore directives to be culturally sensitive around Halloween costumes. The email she had reacted to, from the university's Intercultural Affairs Committee, encouraged students to avoid offending minority students with culturally insensitive or unaware costumes, specifically advising against anything that may include turbans, feathered headdresses, or blackface.[28]

In response to this, in an email to the students in her college care, Christakis decried that young people were no longer able to be "obnoxious," "inappropriate," "provocative," or "offensive." "American universities were once a safe space not only for maturation but also for a certain regressive, or even transgressive, experience; increasingly, it seems, they have become places of censure and prohibition," the *Yale Daily News* reported her lamenting.[29]

Her point earned her some fans. Free speech sounds great on its own. But the problem with free speech that you refuse to contextualize is that sometimes, when you protect the free speech of some, you muzzle the rights, freedoms, and dignity of others—including their free speech. What was being defended here was the long-protected free speech of a majority-white student body at the expense of non-white students. Minority students told to suck it up and deal with racist costumes worn by white students are being given a lesson in whose feelings are being protected and whose feelings are being ignored. If theirs are being ignored for the benefit of white fun, then that is a powerful lesson in who a space is made for, whether it is advisable to take up space—and, yes, speak.

The human rights agenda relies on an idea of complementarity in which rights are in conversation with one another. Rights may be limited in an individual to allow for the rights of others to exist. The first article of the Universal Declaration of Human Rights states: "All human beings are born free and equal in dignity and rights. They are endowed with reason and conscience and should act towards one another in a spirit of brotherhood."[30]

The free speech debate is a false one, really. Pure free speech doesn't exist in a world where some forms of speech act to silence, marginalize, and therefore impede the free speech of others. Such debates are really about clasping on to a power hierarchy we are used to versus loosening up its seams.

As it stands, authenticity, or lack of filter, is an entitled expression of privilege, and emotional labor is the work expected of anyone falling by its wayside. We need to create a world where the ability to express one's true authenticity is evened out not just on the surface, as is the tandem requirement of doing emotional labor.

Such a world would not just be philosophically fairer, such a world would be higher functioning. For those proponents of evolutionary thinking, this also makes the most sense.

Back at the Guggenheim, Tomas Chamorro-Premuzic's comments had pivoted to a solutions-based approach in societies beyond the workplace, priming respect and emotional labor over alleged authenticity. "In the future, altruistic societies will outperform more rational societies. Altruistic societies will be able to adapt and accommodate diversity, whereas so-called rational ones will be more selfish and ill-adapting."

And this is where the light really turned on. Emotional labor may have been at the beginning of what we think of as civilization, but it also must be in our future, as we live more and more globally, collectively, as our planet feels smaller and smaller, as we as humans seek to survive.

In a follow-up conversation, Chamorro-Premuzic confirmed that he was not using the phrase "rational society" to describe societies that believed that 2+2=4, in opposition to societies that believed 2+2=5. Rather, he was using the term in a behavioral economics context, where rational agents are described as those who maximize individual gains and profits regardless of collective impact. In a so-called rational society, if too many people act only out of self-interest, say if no individual or corporation recycles, the planet collapses—for everyone. The critique of rational societies is that they do not scale up well for the collective, while in collective societies, the benefit of the group is optimized but individual joys can feel suppressed. That is what we are told.

The truth is that in this society that primes individualism and allows for men, especially white men, to center themselves, their experiences, their fun, only a select few are able to act as so-called rational agents. The rest must do the collective community work, the emotional labor, to compensate and buffer for these actions. We do not live in an entirely rational society at all. It is a society of groups of selfish free riders propped up by many, many emotional laborers.

But neither should an altruistic society necessarily kill all individual joy. A society in which emotional labor was centered and valued would simply even out the spread of who could lay claim to individual joy. In a truly altruistic society, emotional labor would be spread out and treated as a valuable act all should be performing and aspiring to be good at. The sharing of emotional labor across society may initially limit the authenticity of a few people who were not used to having it limited, but it would also have the effect of enhancing the ability of marginalized groups to exist authentically. Eventually, in an altruistic society emotional labor would spread, and so would the ability to live authentically.

"Emotional labor is in essence a vehicle for the collective good . . . or at least it could be. Societies benefit from prosocial etiquette, effort, and civility. But if only women or minorities have to do it, then authenticity becomes the entitled privilege of the few," Chamorro-Premuzic wrote to me in an email as I was finishing this book.

Modern gender debates in recent years have obsessively focused on marking the line in inherent differences between the sexes. But to me, this moment in history, rather than being a moment for debating what is inherently masculine versus inherently feminine, is an incredible opportunity to reexamine our value system and the evidence behind it.

Shifting our reward system is not only the key to creating more equity in the burden of emotional labor but also the key to building a happier, fairer, more functional, truthful, and transparent world for all.

LaSaia Wade, the Black trans woman founder of the Brave Space Alliance, did not dream of being a community leader. She dreamed of a form of economic liberation she assumed would come through a successful career in corporate America. But when she was fired from that Fortune 500 job in her twenties, she had to look for new ways, and when she found them, it became clear that liberation—economic and otherwise—had to be done through community.

In 2020, when the COVID-19 pandemic hit, her focus went from worrying about her own family's safety to feeding her community. Through her organization, she built a pantry, organized food drop-offs, and established and consolidated mutual aid networks. Her efforts were responsible for feeding two thousand people a week. Her organization may have been an LGBT center that explicitly centered trans and gender nonconforming people, but it provided resources to the whole community, including cis and heterosexual people—so long as they adapted and respected the culture and order installed.

This pecking order, the opposite that is currently in place in broader society, is not a way to force-feed straight and cis people a dose of their own oppressive medicine. It is a way to require emotional labor be done by everyone. LaSaia didn't believe in a world void of emotional labor; she believed in a world filled with it but emptied of the entitlements and judgments she associated with transphobia and patriarchy. A world in which care, community, and trans people were centered meant freedom for everyone. If trans people were free, everyone would be free, she told me. "Because we don't fit the narrative of society, if we are free, you are free—automatically.

"It's always been emotional labor with trans women. We are not just mama bears but mothers to a community of children that are displaced. Mothers to children that sometimes care, sometimes don't care. Mothers to a community that disregards their womanhood, or even humanhood. But still mothers at the end of the day."

LaSaia, in her midthirties at the time of her interview, said she had buried five hundred community members in her lifetime—too many of them to murder. When we spoke, she was mourning the loss of a trans woman, Jahaira DeAlto, who in May 2021 had been stabbed to death by a man in her home. Just a year before, on Mother's Day, DeAlto had written on Facebook: "I am the mother who raised the children whose rainbow sparkled too brightly and blinded their birth moms. I cherished what they discarded. I took on earthly assignments for moms who earned their Heavenly reward. For their babies who still needed raising. I did that. And I'm still doing that. And I'll keep doing that. Because I will never know what seeing my DNA reflected in another's eyes could look like, but I know what gratitude in the eyes of a young person who finally feels seen looks like. And for me, that's enough."[31]

Jahaira DeAlto, who became an advocate for survivors of domestic violence as one herself, was described by those who knew her as "unapologetic." In the ball culture she was known for her "realness."

What does love, and emotional labor as solution, look like? Is it not worth fighting for a world with emotional labor at its heart, rather than on its margins—so that a future Jahaira can survive this time, even thrive?

A radical shift in our view of the value of feminine, prosocial, community-driven, and communal skills would lift up health, life outcomes, and peaceful living on the local, national, and international levels. A world where emotional labor is acknowledged and then valued is a revolutionary concept that would address some of the clearest, deepest causes for gender inequality and inequality of all types. But even further to the point, it is the key to a better, more fruitful, peaceful world for all.

CONCLUSION

In this book, I sought to engage with the world as it is with brutal honesty, even as I dared to dream of change that could start coming individually and systemically as fast as next year, or even as fast as next week, as tomorrow.

Recognizing emotional labor with real honesty has massive consequences on individual people as well as social functioning. This may seem incredibly threatening to entities or people who have been beneficiaries of emotional labor's unequal distribution, but there is healing, and a healthier, happier, more viable society, on the other end.

Searching for this system is a project that has already been started by some.

Over decades, Esther Armah, a Ghanaian British journalist and playwright, developed a theory of "emotional justice" after connecting the dots between her personal family journey and the national and international events she had become intertwined in.

For years, the former BBC reporter had nightmares in which she heard the vivid sounds of boots stomping the ground and guns going off. She would wake up screaming but could never trace the terrors back to a tangible memory. Eventually, as an adult, she turned to her mother for an answer, who shared that when Armah was a very young girl, during Ghana's first military coup after independence from the British in 1966, soldiers and tanks came to their family home in Accra. Her mother, the wife of a prominent Ghanaian political figure who was out of the country at the time, faced the soldiers alone with her children behind her. It was a terrifying moment of life or death. For years, the family lived under house arrest until they eventually fled to London, where they lived in exile.

The awareness of what she contained within her, once her mother broke the silence of her own experience, led Armah to a cathartic realization. She began to contend with not only the legacy of trauma, but the legacy of emotions and emotionality, and the power they held within familial and larger histories. She became fascinated with the question of what happens when a silence is broken, and the silence we have to break is a gendered one. "Since all the initial stories are by men, the breaking of silence by women completely reimagines how you think about this history."

Armah's thinking around the overlooked centrality of emotions and the stories of women continued to take form when, in 1997, she headed to South Africa for work. There, she was set to cover the Truth and Reconciliation Commission, organized under Nelson Mandela's government, which aimed to bring the country forward after the end of the half-century-long apartheid regime. The unprecedented national restorative justice effort set up to move the country forward peacefully gave space to white perpetrators of atrocities and encouraged them to acknowledge crimes in exchange for possible amnesty alongside the testimonies of their Black victims of abuse.

After a meeting with Winnie Mandela, the then president's ex-wife, who urged Armah "to go into the townships and go and ask the women about forgiveness and what they think of it," the journalist started to see a less idyllic side to the process in course. One testimonial, that of Ntsiki Biko, the widow of the celebrated anti-apartheid activist and Black Consciousness movement leader Steve Biko, stood out to her in particular. In 1977, Steve Biko had been arrested by the apartheid regime, and two years into his prison stay he was beaten to death. Twenty years after his killing, five white former apartheid police officers tied to Steve Biko's killing appeared before the Truth and Reconciliation Commission, revealing some details from the fatal incident and seeking formal forgiveness.

Armah recalled observing the moment, watching white men "being given all of this media and this space and this whole stage to talk about how bad they felt and why this is a problem for them, and what happened from their lens." But when the cameras turned to Ntsiki Biko, the widow refused to follow expectations.

"Who are you to tell me to privilege the feelings of murderers—of white men—over those of me and my child?" Armah remembered Biko, a Black woman, challenging her audience, rather than expressing any forced forgiveness.

"There is a lot of talk about reconciliation, but I don't know who is supposed to be reconciled with whom. Is it the families of the victims who are supposed to be reconciled with the perpetrators of these crimes, or is it the government which is supposed to be reconciled with the perpetrators? What I want is for the proper course of justice to be done," *Independent* reported Biko's words as being.[1]

"That is when I came up with idea of ritualized emotionality. Black women were being asked to privilege the feelings of white men to guide the process of what was considered a reconciliation," Armah said of the experience. The gendered element of this "ritualized emotionality" was consolidated in a follow-up interview with Ntsiki Biko when Armah asked her why she always brought her son to the hearings. "He must not learn that his feelings matter more than mine when it comes to how we think of this reconciliation and forgiveness process," was the answer she received.

Ultimately, Steve Biko's killers were not tried in court, but neither were they granted amnesty, and Ntsiki Biko's criticism shed light on one of the weak points of the commission's mission. In seeking resolution, they had continued to put the emotional weight on those already emotionally harmed.

These experiences—over years—led to Esther Armah creating the Armah Institute of Emotional Justice and developing an emotional justice framework. The framework consists of confronting four well-defined pillars: racialized emotionality, emotional patriarchy, emotional currency, and the emotional economy. Racialized emotionality acknowledges the different ways in which humans' emotions are treated according to what racial group they are seen to belong to. Emotional patriarchy refers to a society that caters to, privileges, and prioritizes the feelings of men. Emotional currency treats women as currency whose value increases or diminishes according to their degree of service to whiteness and men. An emotional economy describes a social organization in which the feelings of men are centered no matter the consequences to the nation.[2]

Emotional justice and racial healing, Armah told me, comes about once you start diligently dismantling all of these.

Is this the answer? Armah's four pillars certainly align with the findings in this book, even if Armah's context is more explicitly global and more explicitly concerned with the remnants of European colonialism—which, to be sure, is a part of the background here, but almost exclusively in an American-specific iteration.

During our interview, Armah expressed a frustration with the ways in which emotional labor had become equated with the struggles of white, middle-class women in relation to their families and to their men, without connection to wider systems of inequity. This lack of contextualization enabled emotions and emotionality to be trivialized, reduced, and their connection to larger structures of power cut off, she explained.

This book is an investigation into the roots of gender inequality, but it is also an answer to this concern. Once you understand the webs of connection and hierarchies forged by emotions and emotional labor, you understand that everyone is implicated and no one gets a pass. Groups of women may be experiencing very real injustices at home when it comes to emotional labor, its current devaluing, and its unequal distribution, but that does not absolve those same women from actively situating their responsibility as part of larger structures beyond the familial one. On the flip side, it is important to note that women who are not white, women who are not socioeconomically privileged, also struggle with emotional labor disparities—not only in public, but in private, within their familial networks too.

I am a white woman. This fact neither makes me an endless victim, nor does it make me an infinite perpetrator. It places different burdens and responsibilities on my shoulders. Emotional labor being extracted from me in ways that are unfair and need to be addressed does not free me of responsibility in the broader emotional network.

It may seem complicated to some—fraught even. But the fact that it's complicated does not mean that any of us should run away from confronting it. Just as men must be a part of the solution, so must white women. Not at the center, but as part of. Not as the only story, but as one of the stories. This time around, I got to be the narrator, but next time it should be you, and your fresh insight, your inclusion of new perspectives, and your narration will bring us closer to truth.

The stories at the margin must be told hand in hand with the stories at the center for reparation to happen, for loving growth to happen, and for obscene, unjustifiable hierarchies to cease. It is precisely because of how inevitably interconnected it reveals us to be that emotional labor offers such compelling insight and such a promising path forward for change.

Through the stories in this book, I came to see the true connection between **love and power**. Many of us doing the work of love and empathy in action—those doing the emotional labor—are women and members of subjugated groups. Our emotional labor is rendered invisible and devalued. In performing a kind of work seen as lowly and demeaning, we reinforce our place as the powerless appeasing the powerful.

But there is something else that we must also hold true. Emotional labor is a vital force. It is the backbone of humanity, the secret to longevity. It not only shapes the world's present, it crafts its future. This is too great a load for women and people of subjugated groups to carry alone. In shaping our future, we must spread this vital labor out across groups, not only as a way to heal from past grievances but as a way to correct artificial, exploitative hierarchies.

We must question **the way we have been taught to think of value**. Emotional labor has to be seen to be shared. Only when it is marked as real can we unburden ourselves. When we bring it into the light it becomes easy to see it as an essential form of work supporting communities large and small and supporting our economy. We are currently taught that dollars are the only way to confirm that a performance is valued, but rendering emotional labor visible only reveals that every dollar created exists in part because of emotional labor. If emotional labor is the ultimate enabler of work and dollar creation, it is hard to deny it as a source of value.

Truly understanding emotional labor in this way calls into question how we think of worth, provoking a conversation around the importance of time, connection, belonging, and meaning instead of simply the dollar. It is here that instead of asking whether emotional labor has value that the conversation pivots toward it *being* value. It is arguably not *a* source of value, but *the* source of value.

Beyond seeing the value of emotional labor, understanding the ways in which emotional labor is currently extracted for free or at a discount forces a reckoning that must go to the very **roots of our social organization**. Valuing emotional labor goes hand in hand with truly valuing those who have been doing this essential work. Valuing emotional labor means valuing women as human beings who are as fully human as men, and whose experiences are to be as fully respected and protected as those of men. Valuing emotional labor means valuing ourselves; it means valuing each other.

If we really mean that all humans are equal, we cannot in good faith expect one group to serve another and one group to be made accountable for the feelings of another. This goes for women, as it goes for other subjugated groups, including racialized groups. No one is born with the inherent obligation—through their status as a gender or their status as part of a minority group—to serve the feelings of another group. No one is born with the inherent right to have their feelings served. The only way forward, if we want to redress inequalities, and if we want to enact an ethos in which all humans are equal, is to fight for a system of visible and open-ended reciprocity and abolish status obligations.

We need a new and humane way to value emotional labor that is honest and transparent. We need our workplaces to acknowledge and contend with the significance emotional labor plays in the bottom line and the well-being of those contributing to that bottom line. We must recognize, accurately compensate, and elevate emotional labor, expecting it at all levels of hierarchy. Outside of formal workplaces, we need our reliance on the emotional labor of women and people in feminized and racialized groups to be recognized—and more systems of support, including cash support, need to be devised. This is especially pressing within the context of increased automation, which will eliminate jobs, even as our population continues to grow. It is here that emotional labor as a framework is so promising. In forcing us to think of actions we have never in the mainstream considered work, it pushes us to rethink our very attitude toward work and compensation, casting people we have never thought of in such a manner as workers. Emotional labor blurs the line between private and public, exposing it as artificial to begin with, and that is a good thing. It is a rethinking we desperately need.

We live in the wealthiest nation in the history of nations. Whether the answer is a universal basic income combined with stronger worker rights, whether it involves significantly strengthening Social Security combined with stronger worker rights to include parents and caregivers outside of the formal workplace, or another combination entirely does not matter. Finding a solution is entirely possible and within grasp.

The hardest part is shifting our mentality. That means no longer demeaning and concealing tasks and work deemed feminine, no longer cutting off women and minority workers from the rightful profit they

have produced. That means no longer believing that women by virtue of being women owe anything to society—including something as
seemingly innocuous as a smile. Believing women owe society smiles is
not only wrong, it is oppressive, it is economically exploitative, and it
has proven deadly. That means no longer blindly uplifting aggression,
domination, and self-interest above all else. That means evening out
hierarchies.

Doing so offers an exciting vision for a future in which all of us can
play a part, and in which all of us can seize opportunities to thrive.
**This is a world in which power and love are far from polar oppo-
sites, but are instead recognized as one and the same.**

This book, in being critical of capitalism as it currently works, is
not rejecting it wholesale; it is calling for consequential reform. It is
not saying private businesses and profits are bad; it is arguing for the
real value of emotional laborers to be recognized, so that fair profits
can go to them too. It is arguing for an end to exploitative practices;
it is arguing for bias-sensitive regulation, oversight, and nondiscrimi-
natory worker rights. It is arguing for an end to abusive belief systems
around women and minorities and their work. It is arguing for an
expansion of our notion of public good but also for an expansion of
what we openly admit are marketable goods. It is arguing for an end to
bad-faith arguments and moral hypocrisy.

Nor is this book an embracing of capitalism as solution. If the push-
back on emotional labor from some is a rejection of the importance
of community, to others it has been a moralizing stance that the heart
should not be monetized, that this is neoliberalism gone amok. Progressives and conservatives may find common ground on this one—at
least initially. But here lies the problem with that: hearts have already
been monetized, and not recognizing this only allows for further invisibility, an obscuring of exchanges, and therefore more fruitful exploitation. Admitting emotional labor's transformative, earth-shaping
role in remunerated settings will only help recognize its role in unremunerated ones, and vice versa. It needn't be either-or. As things

stand, the marketplace has benefited from emotional labor's devaluing in private. Both need to be rectified. A normative change needs to happen across the board—it doesn't matter if it starts at home or in the workplace.

Maybe it will start in both. Maybe it will start with you. Because the incredible realization within emotional labor is that we all hold the keys to connection, healing, and humanity past, present, and future. We are all linked to this greater force that grounds us in our individual abilities even as it helps us transcend our individual selves to form timeless community. This power is within each of us, within each of you. It's time for us to reverse its misuse for domination, extraction, and dehumanization. It's time to bring emotional labor into the light and to plant the seeds for reckoning and transformation, for a new kind of understanding of what it means to live together, in society. Our joint humanity depends on it. This is the magnitude of what is at stake.

ACKNOWLEDGMENTS

I am immensely grateful to the many people who played a role in helping this book come to life.

First, I want to thank the hundreds of people who believed in this issue enough to talk to me, write to me, and trust me with parts of themselves and their stories. While only a fraction could fit into these pages, each of your shared truths and pieces of insight are the foundation, the cement, and the bricks of this book.

Second, I am grateful to those people who played a pivotal role in this book's formal creation. Jessica Reed, my features editor at *The Guardian*, who assigned me an article on emotional labor in 2015 and, in so doing, set me on the most enriching of paths. Sarah Murphy, whose idea this book was, who never stopped fighting for it, and who changed my life one summer day in 2017 by messaging me on Twitter. My agent, and what now feels like fellow combatant, Mackenzie Brady Watson, whose steely, unrelenting support shepherded me through more than one unforeseen obstacle. My editor, Bryn Clark, who did not ask for me or for this book, but who treated both of us like her own. Your sharp brain and editing pen helped me sleep at night. Ruben Reyes and the rest of the team at Flatiron, as well as the team at SKLA, whose help in the background I suspect was far greater than I understand.

Third, I am grateful to my family. My mother, Judith Faulks Hackman, whose willingness to act as a sounding board and call out poorly constructed thoughts and sentences helped move this book forward one slow paragraph at a time. My sister Alice Hackman, an incredible journalist and editor, who sacrificed days off from her apartment in Beirut to read drafts of chapters and who gave me the confidence to let go. My sister May Hackman—the general—whose patience, presence, sponsored meals, and pep talks have kept me writing through it all. The three of you are my blueprint for female solidarity. I am also grateful to my father, Robin Hackman, who left this earth too early, but not before teaching me essential lessons in equality and the necessity to question everything.

Fourth, I am grateful to my village. I am grateful to Detroit, my adopted city, and the many people and places within it that played small and large roles in my journey toward finishing this book. I am grateful to my army of friends and loved ones—near and far—whose fierce brains and hearts continuously move, challenge, and lift me up, and who helped me formulate the spirit of this book. Alice Elliot, Charlotte Sunnen, Laura Sunnen, Elmira Raeifar, Sara Thompson, Katie Hackman, Jigar Bhatt, Jenny Fauci, Diala Shamas, Amanda Alexander, Imani Day, Sara Maria Glanowski, Burton Williams, Mylene Spence, Martina Guzman, Joe Pace, Sarah McFadden, Jennifer Lena, Crissaris Sarnelli, and many more still. A life in conversation with you is a life of constant change and transformation—a life in full color. A special thank you to Sarah Rice, not only a dear friend, but also a stunning documentary photographer who took the author photo for this book.

Finally, I am grateful to my partner, Andrew Colom, whose love and support have been nothing short of miraculous these last few years. Your undaunted truth seeking in life, in written word, and in debate and your radical respect for your fellow human beings inspire me to step up firmer, taller, and louder. Immense gratitude also goes to your family: Judge Dorothy Winston Colom and Wilbur Colom, heroes to so many; Scott Colom and Nadia Dale Colom; Xris Omotesa and Niani Colom Omotesa, who I know is with us; and Zion, Aliyah, Gwendolyn Lucille, and Brooklyn Madison—the future.

NOTES

INTRODUCTION

1. Arlie Russell Hochschild, *The Managed Heart: Commercialization of Human Feeling*, 3rd ed., updated with a new preface (Berkeley: University of California Press, 2012).
2. Arlie Russell Hochschild, "Emotion Work, Feeling Rules, and Social Structure," *American Journal of Sociology* 85, no. 3 (1979): 551–75.
3. Hochschild, *The Managed Heart*, 163.

   Today, as the concept has started to permeate the mainstream, nonacademics have ceased to distinguish between "emotional labor" at work and "emotion work" in private—both are just known as "emotional labor." This amalgamation has been a point of contention in academic circles, but this is the lexicon I will use—not only because it is less confusing but because a separation of the exact same effort in private versus public only serves to legitimize its hushed extraction. The very point of this book is for this extraction to be identified and to cease.

4. Mitra Toossi and Teresa L Morisi, "Women in the Workforce Before, During, and After the Great Recession," US Bureau of Labor Statistics, July 2017, 21.
5. Brian Kreiswirth and Anna-Marie Tabor, "What You Need to Know About the Equal Credit Opportunity Act and How It Can Help You: Why It Was Passed and What It Is," Consumer Financial Protection Bureau, October 31, 2016, accessed June 19, 2020, https://www.consumerfinance.gov/about-us/blog/what-you-need-know-about-equal-credit-opportunity-act-and-how-it-can-help-you-why-it-was-passed-and-what-it/.
6. Luke Rosiak, "Fathers Disappear from Households Across America," *The Washington Times*, December 25, 2012, accessed July 6, 2020, https://www.washingtontimes.com/news/2012/dec/25/fathers-disappear-from-households-across-america/.
7. "Name Keeping, on the Rise," *The New York Times*, June 26, 2015, https://www.nytimes.com/interactive/2020/admin/100000003765839.embedded.html?
8. Jillian Berman, "Why So Many Women Still Take Their Husband's Last Name," MarketWatch, December 27, 2017, accessed June 16, 2020, https://www.marketwatch.com/story/why-so-many-women-still-take-their-husbands-last-name-2017-11-30.

9. *Women in Congress: Statistics and Brief Overview*, Congressional Research Service, updated January 31, 2022, accessed February 7, 2022, https://sgp.fas.org/crs/misc/R43244.pdf.

10. "Women CEOs of the S&P 500 (List)," Catalyst, March 25, 2022, https://www.catalyst.org/research/women-ceos-of-the-sp-500/.

11. Karry A. Dolan (ed.), Chase Peterson-Withorn (deputy ed.), and Jennifer Wang (deputy ed.), "The Forbes 400 2021," *Forbes*, accessed February 7, 2022, https://www.forbes.com/forbes-400/.

12. "A Profile of the Working Poor, 2016," *BLS Reports*, US Bureau of Labor Statistics, July 2018, accessed June 16, 2020, https://www.bls.gov/opub/reports/working-poor/2016/home.htm.

13. "The Great Resignation: Why People Are Leaving Their Jobs in Growing Numbers," NPR.org, October 22, 2021, accessed February 12, 2022, https://www.npr.org/2021/10/22/1048332481/the-great-resignation-why-people-are-leaving-their-jobs-in-growing-numbers.

14. "Men Have Now Recouped Their Pandemic-Related Labor Force Losses While Women Lag Behind," National Women's Law Center, February 4, 2022, accessed February 12, 2022, https://nwlc.org/resource/men-recouped-losses-women-lag-behind/.

15. "Low-Paid Women Workers on the Front Lines of COVID-19 Are at High Risk of Living in Poverty, Even When Working Full-Time," National Women's Law Center, April 2, 2022, accessed February 13, 2022, https://nwlc.org/press-release/low-paid-women-workers-on-the-front-lines-of-covid-19-are-at-high-risk-of-living-in-poverty-even-when-working-full-time/.

16. Gus Wezerek and Kristen R. Ghodsee, "Women's Unpaid Labor Is Worth $10,900,000,000,000," *The New York Times*, March 5, 2020, https://www.nytimes.com/interactive/2020/03/04/opinion/women-unpaid-labor.html.

17. Clare Coffey et al., "Time to Care: Unpaid and Underpaid Care Work and the Global Inequality Crisis," Oxfam, January 20, 2020, https://doi.org/10.21201/2020.5419.

18. Heidi I. Hartmann, "The Unhappy Marriage of Marxism and Feminism Towards a More Progressive Union," *Capital & Class* 3, no. 2 (July 1, 1979): 33.

19. A curious trend appeared in pseudonym choosing. I noticed women tended to choose names that made them sound less ethnically or racially distinguishable and more white. I respected their choice, but it is worth noting that not all women who have names that sound white are, in fact, white.

ONE: WHAT IS EMOTIONAL LABOR, EXACTLY?

1. Tattwamasi Paltasingh and Lakshmi Lingam, "'Production' and 'Reproduction' in Feminism: Ideas, Perspectives and Concepts," *IIM Kozhikode Society & Management Review* 3, no. 1 (June 17, 2014): 45–53, https://doi.org/10.1177/2277975214523665.

2. Marianne A. Ferber, "A Feminist Critique of the Neoclassical Theory

of the Family," in *Women, Family, and Work*, ed. Karine S. Moe (Oxford: John Wiley & Sons, 2007), 9–24, https://doi.org/10.1002/9780470755648.ch2.

3. Gail D. Heyman and Jessica W. Giles, "Gender and Psychological Essentialism," *Enfance; Psychologie, Pedagogie, Neuropsychiatrie, Sociologie* 58, no. 3 (July 2006): 293–310.

4. Gina Rippon, *The Gendered Brain: The New Neuroscience That Shatters the Myth of the Female Brain* (London: The Bodley Head, 2019).

5. Gina Rippon, "The Trouble with Girls? Gina Rippon Asks Why Plastic Brains Aren't Breaking Through Glass Ceilings," *The Psychologist* 29 (December 2016): 918–23, https://thepsychologist.bps.org.uk/volume-29/december-2016/trouble-girls.

6. Smaller-scale academic studies have sought to measure emotional labor as a stand-alone category and have found that emotional labor is done more by women, as an explicit expression of their gender.

    In a 2005 seminal academic article on the subject, which defines emotional labor as "socioemotional behavior" or the "activity that maintains the relations among family members," using data on 355 heterosexual married parents who were both employed, sociologist Rebecca Erickson found that the brunt of emotion-related work taken on at home, on top of childcare and housework, was done by women.

    While she did find that men who identified as more expressive in terms of their personalities—more emotionally astute, more attuned to others, and gentler—did more emotional labor than their traditionally more masculine male counterparts—who identified as more assertive, confident, and driven—she found that all women, regardless of their personality traits and including those women who did not identify as expressive, were assertive and less other-oriented. What's more, Erickson found that the men doing more emotional labor than their male counterparts perceived doing it as an expression of their personalities, whereas women with all types of personality traits understood the emotional labor they all disproportionately provided as part of their "family work role."

    See Rebecca J. Erickson, "Why Emotion Work Matters: Sex, Gender, and the Division of Household Labor," *Journal of Marriage and Family* 67, no. 2 (May 2005): 337–51, https://doi.org/10.1111/j.0022-2445.2005.00120.x.

7. Laurie A. Rudman and Kimberly Fairchild, "Reactions to Counterstereotypic Behavior: The Role of Backlash in Cultural Stereotype Maintenance," *Journal of Personality and Social Psychology* 87, no. 2 (2004): 157–76, https://doi.org/10.1037/0022-3514.87.2.157.

8. This policing mechanism threatening a member of a perceived gender if they veer from expected traits is called "counterstereotypic backlash." Jordan Peterson, "Weak Men Can't Be Virtuous," Interview, GeenStijl, January 23, 2018, https://www.youtube.com/watch?v=bWYrAU5mmXE; Nicole Lyn Pesce, "Donny Deutsch: Elizabeth Warren's Problem in the Polls Is That She's

Strident and Unlikable," MarketWatch, February 7, 2020, accessed July 6, 2020, https://www.marketwatch.com/story/donny-deutsch-elizabeth-warrens -problem-in-the-polls-is-that-shes-strident-and-unlikable-2020-02-07.

9. This, in spite of the dominance of essentialist ideas in the media landscape, such as the empathizing-systemizing theory, coined by psychiatrist Simon Baron-Cohen, which argues that there is a "biological foundation" to stronger systemizing traits in males and empathizing traits in females, which have largely remained highly contested and controversial. Simon Baron-Cohen, Rebecca C. Knickmeyer, and Matthew K. Belmonte, "Sex Differences in the Brain: Implications for Explaining Autism," *Science* 310, no. 5749 (November 4, 2005): 819–23, https://doi.org/10.1126/science.1115455. For an exploration of the controversy, see Angela Saini, *Inferior: How Science Got Women Wrong—and the New Research That's Rewriting the Story* (Boston: Beacon Press, 2017), https://www.penguinrandomhouse.com/books/553867 /inferior-by-angela-saini/9780807010037.

10. Kristi J. K. Klein and Sara D. Hodges, "Gender Differences, Motivation, and Empathic Accuracy: When It Pays to Understand," *Personality and Social Psychology Bulletin* 27, no. 6 (June 1, 2001): 720–30, https://journals.sagepub .com/doi/10.1177/0146167201276007.

11. William Ickes, Paul R. Gesn, and Tiffany Graham, "Gender Differences in Empathic Accuracy: Differential Ability or Differential Motivation?," *Personal Relationships* 7 (2000): 95–109, accessed June 27, 2019, https:// www.academia.edu/22072178/Gender_differences_in_empathic_accuracy _Differential_ability_or_differential_motivation.

12. Sara E. Snodgrass, "Women's Intuition: The Effect of Subordinate Role on Interpersonal Sensitivity," *Journal of Personality and Social Psychology* 49, no. 1 (1985): 146–55, https://doi.org/10.1037/0022-3514.49.1.146.

13. Tiffany Graham and William Ickes, "When Women's Intuition Isn't Greater Than Men's," in *Empathic Accuracy*, ed. William Ickes (New York: Guilford Press, 1997), 117–43.

14. Even as this book mostly focuses on a wide variety of female experiences, it is worth noting that emotional labor as a taxing performance imposed because of being on the losing end of a power differential need not be just a female experience.

15. *Knowledge at Wharton* Staff, "Managing Emotions in the Workplace: Do Positive and Negative Attitudes Drive Performance?," *Knowledge at Wharton*, April 18, 2007, accessed April 2, 2019, http://knowledge.wharton.upenn .edu/article/managing-emotions-in-the-workplace-do-positive-and-negative -attitudes-drive-performance/.

16. Sigal G. Barsade, "The Ripple Effect: Emotional Contagion and Its Influence on Group Behavior," *Administrative Science Quarterly* 47, no. 4 (December 2002): 644–75, https://doi.org/10.2307/3094912.

17. Jacques Charmes, "Time Use Across the World: Findings of a World Compilation of Time Use Surveys," UNDP Human Development Report Office, 2015, updated February 2016, 97; National Film Board of Canada,

Who's Counting? Marilyn Waring on Sex, Lies and Global Economics, dir. Terre Nash, 1995 documentary film, https://www.nfb.ca/film/whos_counting/.

18. Marilyn Waring, *Counting for Nothing: What Men Value and What Women Are Worth*, 2nd ed. (Toronto; Buffalo, N.Y.: University of Toronto Press, 1999).

19. Cynthia Hess, Tanima Ahmed, and Jeff Hayes, "Providing Unpaid Household and Care Work in the United States: Uncovering Inequality," Institute for Women's Policy Research, January 2020, 26, https://iwpr.org/wp-content /uploads/2020/01/IWPR-Providing-Unpaid-Household-and-Care-Work-in -the-United-States-Uncovering-Inequality.pdf.

20. In the case of households where both parties worked full-time, women still provided just over one entire extra hour of unpaid work a day.

21. The slight differences shouldn't be diminished, and clues and solutions toward more equality might be found, say, with more research into household chore divisions of those relatively more equal multiracial couples who might very likely be freed of some of the in-group expectations they were brought up with, feeling compelled into more explicit negotiations, the same way that the most egalitarian of couples across the board, same-sex couples, negotiate chore division explicitly and cannot rely on gender constructs in the same way.

22. Feminist economists and social scientists use the term "reproductive labor"— in opposition to "productive labor"—to describe the extensive kinds of work that serve to rear and maintain current and future generations of formal, paid workers. Without reproductive labor, there is no productive labor—because there are no functional workers, there is no social fabric.

    "The unpaid work by which labor is reproduced is the root of the exploitation of women in the capitalist society; for this labor is the main social function expected from us, and the pillar upon which every other form of work and the accumulation of wealth depend," wrote Silvia Federici, one of the thinkers behind the 1970s Wages for Housework campaign.

    Of course, "reproductive labor"—including the emotional labor of constant care, sustenance, and support—is not just happening in unpaid circumstances, even if within our imaginings it has come to encapsulate the idea of "home." When it hits the marketplace, emotional labor, impaired by how feminized, invisible, and spurned it is in nonmarket settings, tends to also be undervalued. The academic reproductive labor and nonacademic emotional labor are not strictly the same, but their overlap in understanding and consequence is significant.

    Silvia Federici, "Women, Reproduction and Globalization," in *Économie mondialisée et identités de genre* (Geneva: Graduate Institute Publications, 2002), 57–78.

23. "Graduation Rates by Race," Annie E. Casey Foundation, KIDS COUNT Data Center, accessed August 24, 2021, https://datacenter.kidscount.org/data /tables/6120-graduation-rates-by-race; "2021 Accountability," Mississippi Department of Education, accessed August 24, 2021, https://www.mdek12 .org/OPR/Reporting/Accountability/2021.

24. "Indigo Williams, et al. v. Phil Bryant, et al.," Southern Poverty Law Center, accessed August 24, 2021, https://www.splcenter.org/seeking-justice/case -docket/indigo-williams-et-al-v-phil-bryant-et-al.

25. Nina Banks, an economist and head of the National Economic Association, has argued that unpaid work as an uncounted, overlooked contribution to society doesn't happen just within domestic dynamics. It also happens within less valued communities, where individuals—often racialized or Black women—find themselves having to organize and provide for the collective in a way that individuals in more privileged communities need not. Nina Banks, "Black Women in the United States and Unpaid Collective Work: Theorizing the Community as a Site of Production," *The Review of Black Political Economy* 47, no. 4 (December 1, 2020): 343–62, https://doi.org/10 .1177/0034644620962811.

TWO: DOMESTICITY AT WORK

1. Ryan Nunn, Jana Parsons, and Jay Shambaugh, *A Dozen Facts About the Economics of the US Health-Care System*, Brookings, March 10, 2020, https:// www.brookings.edu/research/a-dozen-facts-about-the-economics-of-the-u-s -health-care-system/.

2. Derek Thompson, "Health Care Just Became the U.S.'s Largest Employer: In the American Labor Market, Services Are the New Steel," *The Atlantic*, January 9, 2018, https://www.theatlantic.com/business/archive/2018/01 /health-care-america-jobs/550079/.

3. Pamela Loprest and Nathan Sick, *Career Prospects for Certified Nursing Assistants: Insights for Training Programs and Policymakers from the Health Profession Opportunity Grants (HPOG) Program*, OPRE Report 2018– 92 (Washington, DC: Office of Planning, Research, and Evaluation, Administration for Children and Families, US Department of Health and Human Services, August 2018), 1–48, https://www.urban.org/sites/default /files/publication/99279/career_prospects_for_certified_nursing_assistants _0.pdf; "National Nursing Workforce Study," NCSBN, accessed August 3, 2020, https://www.ncsbn.org/workforce.htm.

4. "Occupations with the Most Job Growth," US Bureau of Labor Statistics, accessed August 3, 2020, https://www.bls.gov/emp/tables/occupations-most -job-growth.htm.

5. Elise Gould, *State of Working America Wages 2019: A Story of Slow, Uneven, and Unequal Wage Growth over the Last 40 Years*, Economic Policy Institute, February 20, 2020, accessed August 3, 2020, https://www.epi.org/publication /swa-wages-2019/.

6. "Living Wage Calculator," accessed November 24, 2020, https://livingwage .mit.edu/articles/61-new-living-wage-data-for-now-available-on-the-tool.

7. Olivia Marks, "The Train Driver, the Midwife and the Supermarket Assistant: Meet the 3 Front-Line Workers on the Cover of British *Vogue*'s July Issue," *British Vogue*, June 1, 2020, accessed August 1, 2020, https://www.vogue.co .uk/news/article/keyworkers-july-2020-issue-british-vogue.

8. Molly Kinder, Laura Stateler, and Julia Du, *The COVID-19 Hazard Continues, but the Hazard Pay Does Not: Why America's Essential Workers Need a Raise*, Brookings, October 29, 2020, accessed November 21, 2020, https://www.brookings.edu/research/the-covid-19-hazard-continues-but-the-hazard-pay-does-not-why-americas-frontline-workers-need-a-raise/.

9. Roy F. Baumeister and Mark R. Leary, "The Need to Belong: Desire for Interpersonal Attachments as a Fundamental Human Motivation," *Psychological Bulletin* 117, no. 3 (June 1, 1995): 497–529, https://doi.org/10.1037/0033-2909.117.3.497. Psychologists find that people who are housing insecure and have mental health needs that continue to be unmet will find it far harder to hang on to housing once they find it than people who are housing insecure but have their mental health needs met. Michael Price, "More Than Shelter," *Monitor on Psychology* 40, no. 11 (December 2009): 58, accessed February 25, 2022, https://www.apa.org/monitor/2009/12/shelter.

10. Julianne Holt-Lunstad, Timothy B. Smith, and J. Bradley Layton, "Social Relationships and Mortality Risk: A Meta-Analytic Review," *PLOS Medicine* 7, no. 7 (July 27, 2010): e1000316, https://doi.org/10.1371/journal.pmed.1000316; J. S. House, K. R. Landis, and D. Umberson, "Social Relationships and Health," *Science* 241, no. 4865 (July 29, 1988): 540–45, https://doi.org/10.1126/science.3399889.

11. Steven W. Cole, "Social Regulation of Human Gene Expression: Mechanisms and Implications for Public Health," *American Journal of Public Health* 103, no. Suppl 1 (October 2013): S84–92, https://doi.org/10.2105/AJPH.2012.301183.

12. Evelyn Nakano Glenn, *Forced to Care: Coercion and Caregiving in America* (Cambridge, Mass.: Harvard University Press, 2010).

13. Sylvia A. Allegretto and David Cooper, *Twenty-Three Years and Still Waiting for Change: Why It's Time to Give Tipped Workers the Regular Minimum Wage*, Economic Policy Institute, July 10, 2014, accessed December 8, 2020, https://www.epi.org/publication/waiting-for-change-tipped-minimum-wage/.

14. The living wage stood at $16.54/hour in 2020, according to researchers at MIT. Carey Ann Nadeau, "New Living Wage Data for Now Available on the Tool," Living Wage Calculator, May 17, 2020, accessed December 8, 2020, https://livingwage.mit.edu/articles/61-new-living-wage-data-for-now-available-on-the-tool.

15. Allegretto and Cooper, *Twenty-Three Years and Still Waiting for Change*, 27.

16. Kalindi Vora, "Labor," in *Matter: Macmillan Handbooks: Gender*, ed. Stacy Alaimo (London: Routledge, 2017), 205–21, accessed April 20, 2019, https://www.academia.edu/38094297/_Labor._Chapter_14_in_MATTER_Macmillan_Handbooks_Gender._London_Routledge._Stacy_Alaimo_ed._2017.

17. Kerry Segrave, *Tipping: An American Social History of Gratuities* (Jefferson, N.C.: McFarland, 2009).

18. Mike Rodriguez, Teofilo Reyes, Minsu Longiaru, and Kalpana Krishnamurthy, "The Glass Floor: Sexual Harassment in the Restaurant Industry," Restaurant

Opportunities Centers United, 2014, https://nature.berkeley.edu
/agroecologylab/wp-content/uploads/2020/06/The-Glass-Floor-Sexual
-Harassment-in-the-Restaurant-Industry.pdf.

19. *Take Off Your Mask So I Know How Much to Tip You: Service Workers'
Experience of Health & Harassment During COVID-19*, One Fair Wage in
partnership with UC Berkeley's Food Labor Research Center, November
2020, https://onefairwage.site/wp-content/uploads/2020/11/OFW_
COVID_WorkerExp_Emb-1.pdf.

20. Caroline Criado-Perez, *Invisible Women: Data Bias in a World Designed for
Men* (New York: Abrams Press, 2019).

21. "Droit du Seigneur," *Encyclopedia Britannica*, accessed December 17, 2020,
https://www.britannica.com/topic/droit-du-seigneur.

22. "White-Collar," *Cambridge English Dictionary*, accessed July 28, 2020, https://
dictionary.cambridge.org/us/dictionary/english/white-collar.

23. Sheryl Sandberg, *Lean In: Women, Work, and the Will to Lead* (New York:
Alfred A. Knopf, 2013), accessed January 20, 2021, https://leanin.org
/book.

24. According to the nonprofit organization that was created in the book's name;
"About," Lean In, accessed July 29, 2020, https://leanin.org/about.

25. "How Millennials Get News: Inside the Habits of America's First Digital
Generation," American Press Institute, March 16, 2015, https://www
.americanpressinstitute.org/publications/reports/survey-research/millennials
-news/.

26. Laura Guillén, Margarita Mayo, and Natalia Karelaia, "Appearing Self-
Confident and Getting Credit for It: Why It May Be Easier for Men Than
Women to Gain Influence at Work," *Human Resource Management* 57, no. 4
(2018): 839–54, https://doi.org/10.1002/hrm.21857.

27. Laurie A. Rudman and Kimberly Fairchild, "Reactions to Counterstereotypic
Behavior: The Role of Backlash in Cultural Stereotype Maintenance," *Journal
of Personality and Social Psychology* 87, no. 2 (2004): 157–76, https://doi.org
/10.1037/0022-3514.87.2.157.

28. Daniel Goleman, *Emotional Intelligence*, 10th anniversary ed. (New York:
Bantam Books, 2005).

THREE: THE HISTORY OF EXTRACTION

1. Magali Figueroa-Sánchez, "Building Emotional Literacy: Groundwork to
Early Learning," *Childhood Education* 84, no. 5 (August 1, 2008): 301–4,
https://doi.org/10.1080/00094056.2008.10523030.

2. This is a general observation but was not the case with all academics I
encountered by any means, many of whom, especially in the early stages
of my research, were very generous and patient in interviews with their
knowledge sharing and their time. #NotAllAcademics

3. Stephanie E. Jones-Rogers, *They Were Her Property: White Women as Slave Owners
in the American South* (New Haven, Conn.: Yale University Press, 2019).

4. Nell Irvin Painter, "How We Think About the Term 'Enslaved' Matters," *The*

Guardian, August 14, 2019, https://www.theguardian.com/us-news/2019
/aug/14/slavery-in-america-1619-first-ships-jamestown.
5. Patricia A. Turner, *Ceramic Uncles and Celluloid Mammies: Black Images and Their Influence on Culture*, 1st University of Virginia Press ed. (Charlottesville: University of Virginia Press, 2002).
6. David Pilgrim, "The Mammy Caricature," Jim Crow Museum, Ferris State University, October 2000, updated 2012, accessed August 14, 2019, https://www.ferris.edu/jimcrow/mammies/.
7. Evelyn Nakano Glenn, "From Servitude to Service Work: Historical Continuities in the Racial Division of Paid Reproductive Labor," *Signs* 18, no. 1 (1992): 1–43.
8. A Negro Nurse, "More Slavery at the South," *Independent*, January 25, 1912 (New York: The Independent, 1848–1921), vol. 72, pp. 196–200, accessed August 14, 2019, https://docsouth.unc.edu/fpn/negnurse/negnurse.html.
9. Kellie Carter Jackson, "'She Was a Member of the Family': Ethel Phillips, Domestic Labor, and Employer Perceptions," *WSQ: Women's Studies Quarterly* 45, no. 3–4 (October 26, 2017): 160–73, https://doi.org/10.1353/wsq.2017.0053.
10. She expands on this in her article: "Scholars have argued that the New Deal created a hierarchy based on two tiers: Social Security, where men received pension and unemployment, and welfare, where [B]lack women, in particular, were relegated to ranks of social dependency. Scholar Bridgette Baldwin contends that the policies of welfare discriminated among households based on *how* they became headed by single women: 'whether by death, divorce, abandonment, or single motherhood' (Bridgette Baldwin, "Stratification of the Welfare Poor: Intersections of Gender, Race, and 'Worthiness' in Poverty Discourse and Policy," *The Modern American*, Spring 2010, 4–14). Images of women within the [B]lack family became the focus of public scrutiny. Baldwin argues that New Deal programs ultimately failed to protect [B]lack women in two ways: 'as capable mothers and as capable workers' (Baldwin, "Stratification of the Welfare Poor")."
11. This is true of domestic workers more generally. See Linda Burnham and Nik Theodore, *Home Economics: The Invisible and Unregulated World of Domestic Work*, National Domestic Workers Alliance, New York, 2012, accessed August 6, 2019, https://www.domesticworkers.org/reports-and-publications/home-economics-the-invisible-and-unregulated-world-of-domestic-work/.
12. *Unfair Advantage: Workers' Freedom of Association in the United States Under International Human Rights Standards*, Human Rights Watch Report, 2000, accessed March 28, 2019, https://www.hrw.org/reports/2000/uslabor/index.htm#TopOfPage.
13. Point 4 under Article 23, which in full includes other rights applicable/violated here: "(1) Everyone has the right to work, to free choice of employment, to just and favourable conditions of work and to protection against unemployment.

"(2) Everyone, without any discrimination, has the right to equal pay for equal work.

"(3) Everyone who works has the right to just and favourable remuneration ensuring for himself and his family an existence worthy of human dignity, and supplemented, if necessary, by other means of social protection.

"(4) Everyone has the right to form and to join trade unions for the protection of his interests."

"Universal Declaration of Human Rights," https://www.un.org/en/universal-declaration-human-rights/.

14. "Are You Covered?," National Labor Relations Board, accessed March 29, 2019, https://www.nlrb.gov/about-nlrb/rights-we-protect/the-law/employees/are-you-covered.

15. Ariane Hegewisch and Heidi Hartmann, *The Gender Wage Gap: 2018 Earnings Differences by Race and Ethnicity*, Institute for Women's Policy Research, March 7, 2019, accessed August 6, 2019, https://iwpr.org/iwpr-general/the-gender-wage-gap-2018-earnings-differences-by-race-and-ethnicity/#:~:text=Men's%20real%20median%20weekly%20earnings,1.9%20percent%20for%20Hispanic%20men).

16. Burnham and Theodore, *Home Economics*.

FOUR: DISCIPLINED INTO OBEDIENCE

1. See Lisa Feldman Barrett, *How Emotions Are Made: The Secret Life of the Brain* (Boston: Houghton Mifflin Harcourt, 2017).

2. Paul Ekman, E. Richard Sorenson, and Wallace V. Friesen, "Pan-Cultural Elements in Facial Displays of Emotion," *Science* 164, no. 3875 (April 4, 1969): 86–88, https://doi.org/10.1126/science.164.3875.86.

3. Amy S. Wharton, "The Sociology of Emotional Labor," *Annual Review of Sociology* 35, no. 1 (2009): 147–65, accessed June 28, 2019, https://www.researchgate.net/publication/228173721_The_Sociology_of_Emotional_Labor.

4. Arlie Russell Hochschild, "Emotion Work, Feeling Rules, and Social Structure," *American Journal of Sociology* 85, no. 3 (1979): 551–75.

5. Alvin Chang, "Every Time Ford and Kavanaugh Dodged a Question, in One Chart," *Vox*, September 28, 2018, https://www.vox.com/policy-and-politics/2018/9/28/17914308/kavanaugh-ford-question-dodge-hearing-chart.

6. David Crary, "Kavanaugh-Ford Hearing: A Dramatic Lesson on Gender Roles," AP News, September 28, 2018, https://apnews.com/c3bd7b16ffdd4320a781d2edd5f52dea.

7. Kamala Harris, "Christine Blasey Ford," *Time*, n.d., accessed June 30, 2019, https://time.com/collection/100-most-influential-people-2019/5567675/christine-blasey-ford/.

8. Emotion-related socialization serves to maintain firmly split gender roles, which in turn maintains power and status differences between the genders. Agneta Fischer, ed., *Gender and Emotion: Social Psychological Perspectives* (New York: Cambridge University Press, 2000).

9. Patricia Mazzei, Tariro Mzezewa, and Jill Cowan, "How Black Women Saw Ketanji Brown Jackson's Confirmation Hearing," *The New York Times*, March 25, 2022, https://www.nytimes.com/2022/03/25/us/ketanji-brown-jackson-black-women.html.

10. *Hillary*, Hulu, documentary, accessed March 14, 2022, https://www.hulu.com/series/hillary-793891ec-5bb7-4200-ba93-e3629532d670.

11. In "Language and Woman's Place," Robin Lakoff, a UC Berkeley linguistics professor, pointed out that language rules—which encourage upspeak in women—serve to reinforce female second-class status. Robin Lakoff, "Language and Woman's Place," *Language in Society* 2, no. 1 (1973): 45–80. Studies have consistently shown since that at best people are indifferent to upspeak, and at worst they associate it with the expression of a position of inferiority. "What's Up with Upspeak?," UC Berkeley Social Science Matrix, September 22, 2015, https://matrix.berkeley.edu/research/whats-upspeak.

12. In her seminal 1990 book *The Beauty Myth*, feminist writer Naomi Wolf describes the introduction of beauty as a frame of scrutiny and tool for discrimination against women as a way of keeping women out of power at the same time as gender equality rhetoric was on the rise. Her commentary and frame of analysis only ring truer thirty years on.

13. Beauty standards are famously time- and culture-specific, holding high rewards and penalties under patriarchy. In the United States, beauty standards have been marked by classism and white supremacy. The institution of Miss America, once a whites-only contest, welcomed its first Black contestant only in 1970—half a century after its creation in 1921. It was dogged for years with accusations of racism through its Eurocentric beauty standards.

    Recent years have seen long-standing racial beauty hierarchies upended from within. In a historic moment, at the end of 2019, five of the industry's most major titleholders—Miss Universe, Miss World, Miss USA, Miss America, and Miss Teen USA—were all Black women.

14. Peter Glick and Susan T. Fiske, "The Ambivalent Sexism Inventory: Differentiating Hostile and Benevolent Sexism," *Journal of Personality and Social Psychology* 70, no. 3 (1996): 491–512, https://doi.org/10.1037/0022-3514.70.3.491.

15. Chris Brown, "Chris Brown—Loyal (Official Video) ft. Lil Wayne, Tyga," directed by Chris Brown, March 24, 2014, music video, 4:31, https://www.youtube.com/watch?v=JXRN_LkCa_o.

16. The opening lines are particularly explicit: "I'd rather see you dead, little girl / Than to be with another man." The Beatles, "Run for Your Life (Remastered 2009)," YouTube video, 2:21, 2018, https://www.youtube.com/watch?v=yzHXtxcIkg4.

17. Andrea Dworkin, *Intercourse*, 20th anniversary ed. (New York: Basic Books, 2006), 18–20.

18. I ended up doing a feminist profile and interview of Amber Rose in *The Guardian*, one of my favorite pieces to date. The answer is always solidarity, never division.

19. Ann-Derrick Gaillot, "Some NFL Cheerleaders Make Less Than Minimum Wage," *The Outline*, August 3, 2017, accessed July 1, 2019, https://theoutline.com/post/2053/nfl-cheerleaders-are-horribly-underpaid.

20. Dina ElBoghdady, "'Clean' Beauty Has Taken Over the Cosmetics Industry, but That's About All Anyone Agrees On," *The Washington Post*, March 11, 2020, accessed March 5, 2021, https://www.washingtonpost.com/lifestyle/wellness/clean-beauty-has-taken-over-the-cosmetics-industry-but-thats-about-all-anyone-agrees-on/2020/03/09/2ecfe10e-59b3-11ea-ab68-101ecfec2532_story.html.

21. Amanda Walker, "Inside $5bn Industry of Child Beauty Pageants," Sky News, December 30, 2015, accessed March 16, 2022, https://news.sky.com/story/inside-5bn-industry-of-child-beauty-pageants-10334507; Emily Regitz, "Beauty Pageants Can Lower Girls' Self-Esteem | Local Voices," Lancasteronline.com, January 12, 2020, accessed March 16, 2022, https://lancasteronline.com/opinion/columnists/beauty-pageants-can-lower-girls-self-esteem/article_66bf9bb8-32f3-11ea-851c-0f8bcb8f15b2.html.

22. Brandon Champion, "Miss Michigan Reads Nasty Comments People Make, and She's 'Thankful' for Them," Mlive.com, Muskegon, Michigan, August 23, 2016, accessed June 30, 2019, https://www.mlive.com/news/muskegon/2016/08/miss_michigan_responds_to_crit.html.

FIVE: THE CONSTANT THREAT OF VIOLENCE

1. "Female Homicide Victimization by Males," Violence Policy Center, https://vpc.org/revealing-the-impacts-of-gun-violence/female-homicide-victimization-by-males/.

2. Liana Y. Zanette and Michael Clinchy, "Ecology of Fear," *Current Biology* 29, no. 9 (May 6, 2019): R309–13, https://doi.org/10.1016/j.cub.2019.02.042.

3. C. J. Chivers, "Fear on Cape Cod as Sharks Hunt Again," *The New York Times Magazine*, October 20, 2021, https://www.nytimes.com/interactive/2021/10/20/magazine/sharks-cape-cod.html.

4. According to a 2016 study by the National Institute of Justice, Indigenous American women were 2.5 times more likely to be raped over the course of their lifetime than white women, and more than half of them had faced a sexual assault. See André B. Rosay, "Violence Against American Indian and Alaska Native Women and Men," National Institute of Justice, June 1, 2016, accessed March 8, 2021, https://nij.ojp.gov/topics/articles/violence-against-american-indian-and-alaska-native-women-and-men.

    Black female descendants of enslaved people also carry inherited trauma from historical sexual violence. In June 2020, writer Caroline Randall Williams wrote in *The New York Times* that she had "rape-colored skin." As a Black woman with light-brown skin whose ancestors within living memory were all Black, she wrote that family history relayed to her something DNA testing then confirmed: she was the descendant of white men who raped their Black workers. Caroline Randall Williams, "You Want a Confederate

Monument? My Body Is a Confederate Monument," *The New York Times*, June 26, 2020, https://www.nytimes.com/2020/06/26/opinion/confederate -monuments-racism.html.

Research confirms this type of anecdote. A paper in the *American Journal of Human Genetics* published in July 2020 revealed that enslaved women contributed to the gene pools of Black descendants of slaves in the United States at almost twice the rate of enslaved men. A majority of the people deported to America from Africa during the transatlantic slave trade were men. The study, in which fifty thousand people took part, lays bare the genetic impact of white male rape on enslaved Black women. Steven J. Micheletti et al., "Genetic Consequences of the Transatlantic Slave Trade in the Americas," *American Journal of Human Genetics* 107, no. 2 (August 6, 2020): 265–77, https://doi.org/10.1016/j.ajhg.2020.06.012.

5. In 2020, the Human Rights Campaign called the rates of violence against transgender people to be at "epidemic proportions," especially for trans women of color. Of the 180 murders of trans people the organization had managed to track over seven years, four out of five of them were Black and Brown trans women. For trans women, especially trans women of color, the burden of this heightened threat and misogyny, also referred to as transmisogyny, can make emotional labor a form of subsistence work in the realest of terms. Wyatt Ronan, "Pledge to End Violence Against Black and Brown Transgender Women," Human Rights Campaign, October 28, 2020, accessed March 8, 2021, https://www.hrc.org/press-releases/pledge-to-end -violence-against-black-and-brown-transgender-women.

6. Rose Hackman, "Femicides in the US: The Silent Epidemic Few Dare to Name," *The Guardian*, September 26, 2021, accessed March 29, 2022, https:// www.theguardian.com/us-news/2021/sep/26/femicide-us-silent-epidemic.

7. Numbers are likely worse, as much of this is using FBI data that is still quite incomplete. Perpetrators in killings of women are not always identified, some local police departments do not share their data with the federal agency, and FBI data does not capture ex-boyfriends as a category of killer to be included alongside current partners and ex-husbands. Still, and allowing for this number as an underestimate, the rate of gendered intimate killings of women in America year after year is staggeringly high. "Female Homicide Victimization by Males."

8. "Leading Causes of Death—Females—All Races and Origins—United States, 2017," Centers for Disease Control and Prevention, accessed June 21, 2021, https://www.cdc.gov/women/lcod/2017/all-races-origins/index.htm.

9. Emiko Petrosky et al., "Racial and Ethnic Differences in Homicides of Adult Women and the Role of Intimate Partner Violence—United States, 2003– 2014," *Morbidity and Mortality Weekly Report* 66, no. 28 (2017): 741–46, https://doi.org/10.15585/mmwr.mm6628a1.

Note: equivalent studies put causes of male homicide at 2 to 5 percent IPV (intimate partner violence) related.

10. Chris Harris, "Miss. Optometrist Killed by Ex While Working at Walmart

Clinic, Murderer Gets Life in Prison," *People*, August 3, 2021, accessed October 14, 2021, https://people.com/crime/mississippi-optometrist-killed -working-walmart-clinic-ex-gets-life-prison/.

11. Mattie Brice, "A Perspective on Unpaid Emotional Labor of Queer Acceptance—An Arse Elektronika Talk," *Mattie Brice* (blog), October 6, 2015, http://www.mattiebrice.com/a-perspective-on-unpaid-emotional-labor -of-queer-acceptance-an-arse-elektronika-talk/.

12. theorizingtheweb, "TtW18 #A3 QUEER RELATIONSHIPS," YouTube video, 1:11:05, 2018, https://www.youtube.com/watch?v=krEtr8YUcp8&t=1446s.

13. bell hooks, *All About Love: New Visions* (New York: William Morrow, 2000), 13, https://www.barnesandnoble.com/w/all-about-love-bell-hooks /1111738180.

SIX: WHAT ABOUT THE MEN?

1. Hari Kondabolu, "Boys Will Be Boys," track 4 on *Mainstream American Comic*, Kill Rock Stars, 2016.

2. David A. Fahrenthold, "Trump Recorded Having Extremely Lewd Conversation About Women in 2005," *The Washington Post*, October 8, 2016, https://www.washingtonpost.com/politics/trump-recorded-having-extremely -lewd-conversation-about-women-in-2005/2016/10/07/3b9ce776-8cb4-11e6 -bf8a-3d26847eeed4_story.html.

3. Juliet Macur and Nate Schweber, "Rape Case Unfolds on Web and Splits City," *The New York Times*, December 16, 2012, https://www.nytimes.com /2012/12/17/sports/high-school-football-rape-case-unfolds-online-and -divides-steubenville-ohio.html.

4. Associated Press, "Steubenville: Four Adults Charged in Ohio Rape Case," *The Guardian*, November 25, 2013, https://www.theguardian.com/world /2013/nov/25/steubenville-ohio-four-charged.

5. *Roll Red Roll*, directed by Nancy Schwartzman (Together Films: 2019), 80 min., https://rollredrollfilm.com/.

6. This has happened to me personally dozens of times off-line and on, with men I know and many more I do not—as a woman who writes about feminism-related issues.

7. Brian Heilman, Gary Barker, and Alexander Harrison, *The Man Box: A Study on Being a Young Man in the US, UK, and Mexico* (Washington, DC: Promundo-US and Unilever, 2017): 1–68, accessed September 28, 2020, https://promundoglobal.org/resources/man-box-study-young-man-us-uk -mexico/.

8. Lisa Feldman Barrett, *How Emotions Are Made: The Secret Life of the Brain* (Boston: Houghton Mifflin Harcourt, 2017).

9. Barrett, *How Emotions Are Made*, 106.

10. Barrett, *How Emotions Are Made*, 82.

11. Barrett, *How Emotions Are Made*, 95.

12. Charles Darwin, *The Descent of Man* (London: John Murray, 1874), 326–27.

13. A couple of pages later (*The Descent of Man*, 328–29), Darwin talks of men's

traits acquired and honed during "maturity" being passed down "more fully" to male as opposed to female offspring. "Thus man has ultimately become superior to woman," he concludes, seeking to apply erroneous evolutionary thinking to justify the difference in gender status.

14. Nellie Bowles, "Jordan Peterson, Custodian of the Patriarchy," *The New York Times*, May 18, 2018, https://www.nytimes.com/2018/05/18/style/jordan -peterson-12-rules-for-life.html.

15. Jordan B. Peterson, *12 Rules for Life: An Antidote to Chaos* (Toronto: Random House Canada, 2018).

16. "Elephant," Encyclopedia.com, https://www.encyclopedia.com/plants-and -animals/animals/vertebrate-zoology/elephant#J.

17. Suzanne W. Simard et al., "Mycorrhizal Networks: Mechanisms, Ecology and Modelling," *Fungal Biology Reviews* 26, no. 1 (April 2012): 39–60, https://doi .org/10.1016/j.fbr.2012.01.001.

18. Jordan B Peterson, "Chimpanzees and Dominance Hierarchies," YouTube video, 6:25, 2017, https://www.youtube.com/watch?v=Kyu0ip4RAn0.

19. Angela Saini, *Inferior: How Science Got Women Wrong—and the New Research That's Rewriting the Story* (Boston: Beacon Press, 2017), accessed April 24, 2019.

20. Janet S. Hyde and Janet E. Mertz, "Gender, Culture, and Mathematics Performance," *Proceedings of the National Academy of Sciences* 106, no. 22 (June 2, 2009): 8801–7, https://doi.org/10.1073/pnas.0901265106.

21. Michael Devitt, "CDC Data Show U.S. Life Expectancy Continues to Decline," American Academy of Family Physicians, December 10, 2018, accessed March 22, 2022, https://www.aafp.org/news/health-of-the-public /20181210lifeexpectdrop.html.

22. Kenneth D. Kochanek, Robert N. Anderson, and Elizabeth Arias, "Changes in Life Expectancy at Birth, 2010–2018," National Center for Health Statistics, January 28, 2020, https://www.cdc.gov/nchs/data/hestat/life -expectancy/life-expectancy-2018.htm.

23. "Unintended injuries," which includes drug overdoses, was the leading cause of death for people aged one to forty-four, and suicide was the second leading cause of death for people of the same group. "Injuries and Violence Are Leading Causes of Death," Centers for Disease Control and Prevention, Injury Prevention & Control, February 28, 2022, https://www.cdc.gov/injury /wisqars/animated-leading-causes.html.

24. Andrea E. Abele, "The Dynamics of Masculine-Agentic and Feminine-Communal Traits: Findings from a Prospective Study," *Journal of Personality and Social Psychology* 85, no. 4 (November 1, 2003): 768–76, https://doi.org /10.1037/0022-3514.85.4.768; Paula England, "The Gender Revolution: Uneven and Stalled," *Gender & Society* 24, no. 2 (April 2010): 149–66, https:// doi.org/10.1177/0891243210361475.

25. Heilman, Barker, and Harrison, *The Man Box*.

26. Robert Waldinger, "What Makes a Good Life? Lessons from the Longest Study on Happiness," TED Talk, 2016, https://www.youtube.com/watch?v =8KkKuTCFvzI.

27. Liz Mineo, "Good Genes Are Nice, but Joy Is Better: Harvard Study, Almost 80 Years Old, Has Proved That Embracing Community Helps Us Live Longer, and Be Happier," *The Harvard Gazette*, April 11, 2017, https://news .harvard.edu/gazette/story/2017/04/over-nearly-80-years-harvard-study-has -been-showing-how-to-live-a-healthy-and-happy-life/.

28. Ken R. Smith and Cathleen D. Zick, "Risk of Mortality Following Widowhood: Age and Sex Differences by Mode of Death," *Social Biology* 43, no. 1–2 (March 1996): 59–71, https://doi.org/10.1080/19485565.1996 .9988913.

29. Allison R. Sullivan and Andrew Fenelon, "Patterns of Widowhood Mortality," *The Journals of Gerontology: Series B* 69B, no. 1 (January 2014): 53–62, https:// doi.org/10.1093/geronb/gbt079.

SEVEN: THE REALITY OF EMOTIONAL CAPITALISM

1. "Cash Slaves," *Vice News*, October 22, 2015, https://www.vice.com/en/article /7bde84/cash-slaves-817.

2. Lauren Chief Elk, Yeoshi Lourdes, and Bardot Smith, "Give Your Money to Women: The End Game of Capitalism," *Model View Culture*, April 10, 2015, accessed May 15, 2019, https://modelviewculture.com/pieces /giveyourmoneytowomen-the-end-game-of-capitalism.

3. Jess Zimmerman, "'Where's My Cut?': On Unpaid Emotional Labor," *The Toast*, July 13, 2015, http://the-toast.net/2015/07/13/emotional-labor/.

4. "Where's My Cut?: On Unpaid Emotional Labor," MetaFilter.com, July 15, 2015, accessed July 8, 2019, http://www.metafilter.com/151267/Wheres-My -Cut-On-Unpaid-Emotional-Labor.

5. Wednesday Martin, "Poor Little Rich Women," *The New York Times*, May 16, 2015, https://www.nytimes.com/2015/05/17/opinion/sunday/poor-little-rich -women.html.

6. Silvia Federici, "Women, Reproduction and Globalization," in *Économie mondialisée et identités de genre* (Geneva: Graduate Institute Publications, 2002), 57–78.

7. Stephanie Coontz, *Marriage, a History: How Love Conquered Marriage* (New York: Penguin Books, 2006), https://www.penguinrandomhouse.com/books /291184/marriage-a-history-by-stephanie-coontz/.

8. Anil Ananthaswamy and Kate Douglas, "The Origins of Sexism: How Men Came to Rule 12,000 Years Ago," *New Scientist*, April 18, 2018, accessed April 16, 2021, https://www.newscientist.com/article/mg23831740-400-the -origins-of-sexism-how-men-came-to-rule-12000-years-ago/.

9. Henna Inam, "Bring Your Whole Self to Work," *Forbes*, May 10, 2018, https://www.forbes.com/sites/hennainam/2018/05/10/bring-your-whole-self -to-work/.

10. Drew Goins and Alyssa Rosenberg, eds., "As More Companies Wade in, It's Time to Ask: Is Pride for Sale?," *The Washington Post*, June 20, 2019, accessed April 6, 2021, https://www.washingtonpost.com/graphics/2019 /opinions/pride-for-sale/; Natasha Dailey, "Coca-Cola, Delta, United, and 7

Other Companies Blast Georgia's New Voting Law in a Wave of Corporate Backlash," April 5, 2021, accessed April 6, 2021, https://www.businessinsider.com/apple-united-delta-coke-companies-against-georgia-voting-law-elections-2021-4.

11. Jillian D'Onfro and Lucy England, "An Inside Look at Google's Best Employee Perks," Inc.com, September 21, 2015, https://www.inc.com/business-insider/best-google-benefits.html.

12. Marsha Sinetar, *Do What You Love, the Money Will Follow: Discovering Your Right Livelihood* (New York: Dell, 1989).

13. Eva Illouz, *Cold Intimacies: The Making of Emotional Capitalism* (Malden, Mass.: Polity Press, 2007).

14. Shankar Vedantam et al., "Emotional Currency: How Money Shapes Human Relationships," NPR, January 13, 2020, https://www.npr.org/2020/01/10/795246685/emotional-currency-how-money-shapes-human-relationships.

15. David Graeber, *Debt: The First 5,000 Years*, updated and expanded ed. (Brooklyn, N.Y.: Melville House, 2014); L. Randall Wray, "Introduction to an Alternative History of Money," *SSRN Electronic Journal*, 2012, https://doi.org/10.2139/ssrn.2050427; Bill Maurer, "How Would You Like to Pay?: How Technology Is Changing the Future of Money," October 14, 2015, https://doi.org/10.1215/9780822375173.

16. C. J. Fuller, "Review of *The Gift: The Form and Reason for Exchange in Archaic Societies*, by Marcel Mauss, trans. W. D. Halls," *Man* 27, no. 2 (June 1992): 431, https://doi.org/10.2307/2804090.

17. L. Randall Wray, "Introduction to an Alternative History of Money," *SSRN Electronic Journal*, Levy Economics Institute, Working Paper No. 717, May 2012, https://doi.org/10.2139/ssrn.2050427.

EIGHT: ABOLISHING IMBALANCE

1. The withholding of a real name in journalism, a field that has been under mounting attack in recent years as being so easily "fake," makes it easier for a piece to be accused as invented or a distortion. As a result, most news organizations that pride themselves as reputable avoid anonymization as much as possible, except for extreme cases where, for instance, information cannot otherwise be attained. At the time I wrote the article I am referring to in *The Guardian*, a story on gender equity involving tea towels and schedules would not have made a strong enough case for names to be withheld, but it has become clear to me since that women speaking up brings to the surface more underlying danger than we may be comfortable with acknowledging. For more on journalistic practices, see "Anonymous Sources," Associated Press, accessed April 26, 2021, https://www.ap.org/about/news-values-and-principles/telling-the-story/anonymous-sources.

2. Allison Daminger, "The Cognitive Dimension of Household Labor," *American Sociological Review* 84, no. 4 (August 1, 2019): 609–33, https://doi.org/10.1177/0003122419859007.

3. Michael J. Glantz et al., "Gender Disparity in the Rate of Partner

Abandonment in Patients with Serious Medical Illness," *Cancer* 115, no. 22 (November 15, 2009): 5237–42, https://doi.org/10.1002/cncr.24577.

4. Fred Hutchinson Cancer Research Center, "Men Leave: Separation and Divorce Far More Common When the Wife Is the Patient," *ScienceDaily*, November 10, 2009, accessed April 27, 2021, https://www.sciencedaily.com /releases/2009/11/091110105401.htm.

5. David T. Wagner, Christopher M. Barnes, and Brent A. Scott, "Driving It Home: How Workplace Emotional Labor Harms Employee Home Life," *Personnel Psychology* 67, no. 2 (June 2014): 487–516, https://doi.org/10.1111 /peps.12044.

6. Lyndall Strazdins and Dorothy H. Broom, "Acts of Love (and Work): Gender Imbalance in Emotional Work and Women's Psychological Distress," *Journal of Family Issues* 25, no. 3 (April 1, 2004): 356–78, https://doi.org/10.1177 /0192513X03257413.

7. "2010 Stress in America: Gender and Stress," American Psychological Association, 2012, accessed April 29, 2021, https://www.apa.org/news/press /releases/stress/2010/gender-stress.

8. Daniel L. Carlson et al., "The Gendered Division of Housework and Couples' Sexual Relationships: A Reexamination," *Journal of Marriage and Family* 78, no. 4 (2016): 975–95, https://doi.org/10.1111/jomf.12313.

9. Sabino Kornrich, Julie Brines, and Katrina Leupp, "Egalitarianism, Housework, and Sexual Frequency in Marriage," *American Sociological Review* 78, no. 1 (February 2013): 26–50, https://doi.org/10.1177 /0003122412472340.

10. David A. Frederick et al., "Differences in Orgasm Frequency Among Gay, Lesbian, Bisexual, and Heterosexual Men and Women in a U.S. National Sample," *Archives of Sexual Behavior* 47, no. 1 (January 2018): 273–88, https: //doi.org/10.1007/s10508-017-0939-z.

11. Sara I. McClelland, "Who Is the 'Self' in Self Reports of Sexual Satisfaction? Research and Policy Implications," *Sexuality Research and Social Policy* 8, no. 4 (December 2011): 304–20, https://doi.org/10.1007 /s13178-011-0067-9.

12. Gayle Brewer and Colin A. Hendrie, "Evidence to Suggest That Copulatory Vocalizations in Women Are Not a Reflexive Consequence of Orgasm," *Archives of Sexual Behavior* 40, no. 3 (June 2011): 559–64, https://doi.org/10 .1007/s10508-010-9632-1.

NINE: RADICAL LOVE IN A NEW WORLD

1. Paul Brand and Philip Yancey, *Fearfully and Wonderfully Made* (Grand Rapids, Mich.: Zondervan, 1997; orig. 1980), 68.

2. It is worth noting that this story is absent from Mead's own writings, and aside from Brand's own recollection, which presents him as being present at her lecture but was written two years after Mead died, this story has mostly and widely been stated as fact, without any original source.

3. "GDP (Current US$)," World Bank, accessed March 27, 2022, https://data

.worldbank.org/indicator/NY.GDP.MKTP.CD; https://databank.worldbank
.org/data/download/GDP.pdf.

4. Anshu Siripurapu, "The U.S. Inequality Debate," Council on Foreign
Relations, last updated April 20, 2022, accessed March 27, 2022, https://
www.cfr.org/backgrounder/us-inequality-debate.

5. David U. Himmelstein et al., "Medical Bankruptcy: Still Common Despite
the Affordable Care Act," *American Journal of Public Health* 109, no. 3
(March 1, 2019): 431–33, https://doi.org/10.2105/AJPH.2018.304901.

6. Gina Martinez, "GoFundMe CEO: One-Third of Fundraisers Are for
Medical Costs," *Time*, updated January 30, 2019, accessed May 11, 2021,
https://time.com/5516037/gofundme-medical-bills-one-third-ceo/.

7. "Get Help with Medical Fundraising," GoFundMe.com, accessed May 11,
2021, https://www.gofundme.com/start/medical-fundraising.

8. Singapore may be a possible, arguable exception, but average health-care cost
is still half of what it is in the United States, and citizens live four years longer.

9. Gretchen Livingston and Deja Thomas, "Among 41 Countries, Only U.S.
Lacks Paid Parental Leave," Pew Research Center, December 16, 2019,
accessed May 11, 2021, https://www.pewresearch.org/fact-tank/2019/12/16
/u-s-lacks-mandated-paid-parental-leave/.

10. Ashraf Khalil and Alan Fram, "COVID Relief Bill Could Permanently Alter
Social Safety Net," AP News, March 12, 2021, accessed May 11, 2021,
https://apnews.com/article/covid-19-relief-bill-social-safety-net-3bff45f1be9
d5f7eb8cd7c14a51c6732.

11. "Demographics of the U.S. Military," Council on Foreign Relations, updated
July 13, 2020, accessed March 27, 2022, https://www.cfr.org/backgrounder
/demographics-us-military.

12. Wendy Sawyer and Peter Wagner, *Mass Incarceration: The Whole Pie 2022*,
Prison Policy Initiative, press release, March 14, 2022, accessed March 27,
2022, https://www.prisonpolicy.org/reports/pie2022.html.

13. Sawyer and Wagner, *Mass Incarceration*.

14. National Partnership for Pretrial Justice (website), accessed May 17, 2021,
https://www.pretrialpartnership.org/.

15. Gina Clayton et al., *Because She's Powerful: The Political Isolation and
Resistance of Women with Incarcerated Loved Ones* (Los Angeles and Oakland,
Calif.: Essie Justice Group, 2018), 95.

16. Jamil Zaki, *The War for Kindness: Building Empathy in a Fractured World*
(New York: Crown, 2019).

17. F. Eugene Heath, "Invisible Hand," *Britannica*, accessed March 27, 2022,
https://www.britannica.com/topic/invisible-hand.

18. Juliana Menasce Horowitz, Ruth Igielnik, and Rakesh Kochhar, *1. Trends
in Income and Wealth Inequality*, Pew Research Center, January 9, 2020,
https://www.pewresearch.org/social-trends/2020/01/09/trends-in-income
-and-wealth-inequality/.

19. Tomas Chamorro-Premuzic, *Why Do So Many Incompetent Men Become
Leaders? (and How to Fix It)* (Boston: Harvard Business Review Press, 2019).

20. Dimitri van der Linden et al., "Overlap Between the General Factor of Personality and Emotional Intelligence: A Meta-Analysis," *Psychological Bulletin* 143, no. 1 (2017): 36–52, https://doi.org/10.1037/bul0000078.

21. Peter K. Jonason and Jeremy Tost, "I Just Cannot Control Myself: The Dark Triad and Self-Control," *Personality and Individual Differences* 49, no. 6 (October 2010): 611–15, accessed May 12, 2021, https://www.sciencedirect.com/science/article/abs/pii/S0191886910002783.

22. Jill Byron, "Brand Authenticity: Is It for Real?," AdAge, March 23, 2016, https://adage.com/article/digitalnext/brand-authenticity-real/303191.

23. Henna Inam, *Wired for Authenticity: Seven Practices to Inspire, Adapt, & Lead* (Bloomington, Ind.: iUniverse, 2015), https://wiredforauthenticity.com/.

24. Karl Moore, "Authenticity: The Way to the Millennial's Heart," *Forbes*, August 14, 2014, https://www.forbes.com/sites/karlmoore/2014/08/14/authenticity-the-way-to-the-millennials-heart/.

25. Rob Haskell, "How Billie Eilish Is Reinventing Pop Stardom," *Vogue*, February 3, 2020, accessed May 11, 2021, https://www.vogue.com/article/billie-eilish-cover-march-2020.

26. Eeoc v. Catastrophe Management Solutions, 852 F. 3d 1018 (Court of Appeals, 11th Circuit 2016).

27. *NYC Commission on Human Rights Legal Enforcement Guidance on Race Discrimination on the Basis of Hair*, NYC Commission on Human Rights, February 2019, 10, https://www1.nyc.gov/assets/cchr/downloads/pdf/Hair-Guidance.pdf.

28. Liam Stack, "Yale's Halloween Advice Stokes a Racially Charged Debate," *The New York Times*, November 8, 2015, https://www.nytimes.com/2015/11/09/nyregion/yale-culturally-insensitive-halloween-costumes-free-speech.html.

29. Joey Ye, "Silliman Associate Master's Halloween Email Draws Ire," *Yale Daily News*, November 2, 2015, accessed May 17, 2021, https://yaledailynews.com/blog/2015/11/02/silicon-associate-masters-halloween-email-draws-ire/.

30. "Universal Declaration of Human Rights," United Nations, accessed March 28, 2022, https://www.un.org/en/about-us/universal-declaration-of-human-rights.

31. Jeff Truesdell, "Transgender Activist and Suspect's Wife Are Killed in Stabbing That Took Place in Front of Kids," People.com, May 4, 2021, accessed May 17, 2021, https://people.com/crime/transgender-activist-suspects-wife-killed-in-front-children/.

CONCLUSION

1. Robert Block, "Justice Before Forgiveness, Say Families of Apartheid Victims," *Independent*, March 31, 1996, accessed October 23, 2011, https://www.independent.co.uk/news/world/justice-before-forgiveness-say-families-of-apartheid-victims-1344975.html.

2. "Emotional Justice," Armah Institute of Emotional Justice, accessed May 17, 2021, https://www.theaiej.com/emotional-justice.

ABOUT THE AUTHOR

ROSE HACKMAN is a British journalist and writer based in Detroit. Her work on gender, race, labor, policing, housing, and the environment—published in *The Guardian*—has brought international attention to overlooked American policy issues, historically entrenched injustices, and complicated social mores.